19/45 .

£3

g

FAMILY WORLDS

FAMILY WORLDS

A PSYCHOSOCIAL APPROACH TO FAMILY LIFE

By Robert D. Hess and Gerald Handel

 THE UNIVERSITY OF CHICAGO PRESS

The Library of Congress Catalogue Card

⌐   ⌐

HESS, ROBERT D.

    Family worlds: a psychosocial approach to family life, by Robert D. Hess and Gerald Handel. [Chicago] University of Chicago Press [1959]

    305 p. illus. 23 cm.

    1. Family.   I. Handel, Gerald, joint author. II. Title

HQ728.H4   301.42   59–5773‡

Library of Congress

L   L

THE UNIVERSITY OF CHICAGO PRESS, CHICAGO 37
Cambridge University Press, London, N.W. 1, England
The University of Toronto Press, Toronto 5, Canada

© 1959 by The University of Chicago. Published 1959
Composed and printed by THE UNIVERSITY OF CHICAGO PRESS
Chicago, Illinois, U.S.A.

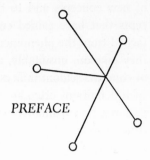

PREFACE

This volume attempts, by interpretive analysis of family psychological and psychosocial materials, to examine the complexities of family emotional organization and to indicate concepts that we believe may be useful for research on the internal processes of non-pathological family interaction and emotional structure.

In the belief that knowledge grows by instance and example as well as by generalization, we have chosen to illustrate our approach to family dynamics by describing five families selected from a research group. The detailed examination of cases suggests lines of thought, urges re-examination of contemporary theory, reveals areas of behavior in which our knowledge is sparse, and stimulates hypotheses that may be tested in other research formats. Case analysis serves another function, perhaps more important: it translates abstractions into the concrete components of actual lives. The social scientist loses touch with his subject matter if he confines his work to disembodied responses and acts grouped into categories. Learning in social science must have a sensory base; tables of data must have some connection with people who can be seen or heard in action. If tabulation of data advances our science, case study and analysis serve to remind us that our subject is human action and feeling.

Case studies have, perhaps, a particular usefulness when they deal with problems at the forward edge of an area of investigation. They make it possible to illustrate in detail the referents of new concepts and to think about their ramifications. Concepts that have gained currency sometimes become so far detached from the phenomena they are intended to represent that they take on, unsuitably, a life of their own. Formal definition of concepts seldom suffices to locate them appropriately; indeed, such definitions often are possible, not to say fruitful, only after prolonged acquaintance with the phenomena from which they issue. A group of cases serves to keep concepts closely related to the events we wish to understand.

Considerable illustrative material from the original raw data has been included in our case analyses. Presented in the context of interpretation, this material gives the reader an opportunity to see how we have reasoned from the data. At the same time, he also has a basis for working out interpretations of his own, whether in disagreement or along lines that we have not considered. It is our hope that case studies such as these will not only stimulate further research but will also prove particularly useful in the teaching of graduate courses on the family.

We believe that some new ways of looking at families are necessary. What these are we attempt to delineate in chapter i and to illustrate in the succeeding chapters. At this point we set down some assumptions we have taken for granted; they constitute the base line from which we have proceeded.

Certain features of family life and circumstance may be regarded as universal givens, or derivatives of the biological nature of the species. Overlying the biologically determined universals of family life are the cultural givens—the characteristics that emerge as a direct result of the family's membership in a social and cultural system of human beings. At this level, the features of the family are more complex and more diverse, varying not only from one culture to another but between subgroups within cultures. Cultural and social patterns impose expectations and limits of different kinds upon the sexual activity by which the species reproduces itself, regulating such behavior within the family as well as between family members and other individuals in the society. These patterns also are prescriptions for formal marital and parental ties as expressed in law and for informal definition of family obligation as expressed in custom.

Cultural expectations also regulate the basic elements of the socialization process and the features of roles that each family member must assume. Within rather broad limits the behavior of parent toward child is indicated by group norms; the child learns through experience those behaviors that are appropriate to the biosocial status of a child and gains a conception of the roles of adult family members.

The components of family roles common to members of a particular culture provide useful constructs for the study of the family as an institution and for cross-cultural comparisons of the family as a focal element of the social structure. However, the dynamics of family interaction are affected by powerful situational and idiosyncratic components, so that analysis of an individual family must push beyond the data provided by fitting the biological and cultural givens over family behavior. It is our purpose here to examine some of the variations in living that individual families have evolved, with a view to understanding their emotional and social consequences. This volume thus continues work which we have previously reported.[1]

Frames of reference and theories for comprehending family life are not lacking. Stimulated by diverse interests and concerns, social scientists have been led to consider what families are and what they should be. Within the social sciences, broadly considered, there are numerous approaches, elaborated in a great volume of writing. In proposing yet another perspective, we shall attempt to set forth what we conceive to be an area scantily attended. This task is perhaps most readily approached by considering briefly several of the professional approaches to the family.

The clinical practitioner—psychiatrist, clinical psychologist, psychiatric social worker—is concerned with assisting people in

[1] Robert D. Hess and Gerald Handel, "Patterns of Aggression in Parents and Their Children," *Journal of Genetic Psychology*, LXXXIX (1956), 199–212; Gerald Handel and Robert D. Hess, "The Family as an Emotional Organization," *Marriage and Family Living*, Vol. XVIII, No. 2 (May, 1956).

difficulty. An individual comes to him or is committed to his care for treatment so as to be able to resume adequate functioning. In most prevailing systems of psychotherapy the individual who needs the therapist's services is necessarily the focus of the therapist's interest. He explores his patient's family involvements to the extent necessary for achieving a therapeutic aim. This aim takes the form of one or another kind of personality alteration. Research on the family carried out by clinical investigators—stimulated by or incidental to their work with patients —has traditionally been directed to understanding the personality of the patient. The personality is disordered; the circumstances of the disorder must be understood; and this entails knowing how the patient's relationships with others contributed to his difficulty.

In the treatment of emotionally disturbed children, the concept of disturbance has often been relocated or extended so that —most often—the mother-child *relationship* rather than the *personality* of either one is regarded as the locus of disturbance. Treatment is seen to require a revision of the commitments they have to one another, the ways in which they take account of each other. Increasingly—though not yet extensively—this same conception has been extended to adult relationships. Work guided by this view finds expression in a recent collection of clinical papers.[2]

Also quite recently, some clinical workers have endeavored to move beyond the two-person relationship and to arrive at a diagnosis of the entire family unit—comprising parents and children —guided by the belief that a personality disturbance is essentially imbedded in, if not produced by, the entire matrix of intrafamilial relationships. The work of Dr. Nathan W. Ackerman is particularly noteworthy in this area, since he has called attention to the complexity of interpersonal involvements within the small family. Though he has pointed to the phenomena of the unit, his concepts remain those of the two-person or triangu-

[2] Victor W. Eisenstein (ed.), *Neurotic Interaction in Marriage* (New York: Basic Books, 1956).

lar relationship, so that, in effect, he studies the family by considering in turn each such relationship. As yet he has not developed any concepts for dealing with the entire group.

All of these clinical approaches derive from an interest in personality disturbances.

The study of the family as a group has traditionally been the province of the sociologist and anthropologist. The central concerns of their investigations have varied in different periods, though an underlying thread of continuity is woven through these disparate queries—the nature of the forces that link family members to one another and how these forces are related to the form of the larger society. The various conceptualizations of the problem of family cohesion have not typically included the idea that the particular personalities of the individuals who comprise a family are an essential element of its structure. Concerned as they are with understanding social aggregates, classifications, and groupings, the assessment of individual persons has not been part either of the method or of the thinking of sociologists and anthropologists. In a sense, then, it may be said that clinician and academician have each been working on the same problem from two essentially different perspectives. By reason of training, habits of thought, and professional responsibility, the clinician begins with the individual and moves toward extending the scope of his considerations step by step. For precisely the same reasons, the sociologist and anthropologist begin with the group.

Yet in certain respects the development of sociological interest in the family parallels and verges on the clinical. The similarity is most obvious in early origins: sociologists were also concerned with urgent problems—divorce, illegitimacy, delinquency. Some early American sociologists, at least, were clinicians in the formulation of their interests. But the more significant impetus toward convergence was provided by the interest in *social change*. Ogburn's memorable statement that the family was losing its functions necessitated reflection on what the family was doing, if it was no longer doing what it had been. The conclusion reached by some, such as Sorokin and Zimmerman, was that it wasn't doing much of anything except deteriorating. A larger phalanx concluded with near agreement that the family functions to develop personality. In their chapter on the American family, Parsons and Bales write: ". . . the functions of the family in a highly differentiated society are not to be interpreted as functions directly on behalf of the society, but on behalf of personality."[3]

The import of much of Burgess' work, as of the recent volume by Foote and Cottrell, is in this same direction. The same basic implication is pursued in different ways by Allison Davis, Waller, Hill, and many other notable investigators. While a detailed discussion of previous research and theory is not within our purpose in the present volume, we have rapidly sketched in this background to provide a context relating our work to what has already been accomplished.

Each of the five families presented in this volume was chosen because it represented in its interactional aspects a cluster of families of the total group. We passed over families whose personal circumstances and psychodynamics were more dramatic or unusual or deviant. These five families show no extremes of conflict or psychological crisis; their problems are typical. In each case we chose among two or three families that were highly similar in their interactional problems, style of life, and general sociological characteristics. Each of the families of our total research group has its problems. Our aim is not to dramatize a series of problem families but to describe families with typical stresses and internal relationships and to examine the ways families deal with the day-by-day tasks of family living.

To some extent we have found it necessary in the interests of furthering our understanding of family interaction to draw back the curtain of privacy that protects any family from the eyes of its neighbors. Out of consideration for the rights of the families

[3] Talcott Parsons and Robert F. Bales, *Family, Socialization and Interaction Process* (Glencoe, Ill.: Free Press, 1955), p. 16.

we have described, we necessarily disguised the five families of the book. We cannot, of course, indicate the kinds of disguise we have employed to conceal the identity of the families involved, other than to say that the names of the families and of their members are fictitious. We owe a tremendous and profound debt to these families who consented to participate in our study. We recognize the courage that they displayed in cooperating in an effort of this sort. Their only compensation is the gratification they may receive from the possibility that they have contributed to the understanding of family life and thus perhaps assisted other families whose troubles are greater than their own. They have our deepest thanks.

We have profited from the work of many people. Our greatest immediate debts are to Professors Allison Davis, Robert J. Havighurst, William E. Henry, and W. Lloyd Warner. Their thinking has been particularly influential, and the atmosphere they have created in the Committee on Human Development has been a most congenial one.

In writing this book, we have received helpful suggestions and criticisms from Drs. Henry Maas, Bernice Neugarten, and Sidney J. Levy. We wish especially to record our indebtedness to the late R. Richard Wohl, with whom we had many discussions concerning the problems of this volume. His comments were richly suggestive, and his enthusiasm greatly encouraging. His death, at the time this manuscript was nearing completion, deprived social science of a stimulating mind. We lost an esteemed colleague.

We express our thanks to Mrs. Fayette Loria, Mrs. Noreen Haygood, and Mrs. Florence Hamlish Levinsohn, who carried out all the interviewing and testing of family members. Their efforts were persevering and skilful.

Contributions to the analysis of portions of the data have been made by these former research assistants: Dr. Paul Baer, Mrs. Wendy Mesnikoff, and Mr. Leon Malan.

We acknowledge with thanks a grant from the Social Science Research Committee of the University of Chicago which enabled us to initiate the research of which this book is a product. Assistance from the Family Study Center of the University of Chicago, through the courtesy of Nelson Foote, helped maintain the study in its early stages. We are most appreciative of the substantial support provided by the National Institute of Mental Health of the United States Public Health Service through research grant M-543.

We also wish to thank Dr. John P. Spiegel, formerly of Michael Reese Hospital, Chicago, and now of Harvard University, for his interest and encouragement at the time our research was begun.

The office staff of the Committee on Human Development has been very helpful with the typing and the many details of preparing a manuscript. We thank them all, particularly Mrs. Mabel Frazier, Mrs. Alice Chandler, and Mrs. Dorothea Horton. We thank also Miss Dorothy Anderson, who helped type the final version.

Finally, we wish to acknowledge our debt to the graduate students who helped us—sometimes by criticism, sometimes by enthusiasm, and often by insightful comment.

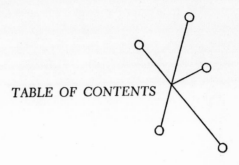

TABLE OF CONTENTS

CHAPTER ONE

THE FAMILY AS A

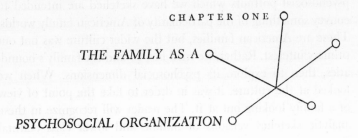

PSYCHOSOCIAL ORGANIZATION

However its life spreads into the wider community, there is a sense in which a family is a bounded universe. The members of a family—parents and their young children—inhabit a world of their own making, a community of feeling and fantasy, action and precept. Even before their infant's birth, the expectant couple make plans for his family membership, and they prepare not only a bassinet but a prospect of what he will be to them. He brings his own surprises, but in time there is acquaintance, then familiarity, as daily the family members compose their interconnection through the touch and tone by which they learn to know one another. Each one comes to have a private transcript of their common life, recorded through his own emotions and individual experiences.

In their mutual interaction, the family members develop more or less adequate understanding of one another, collaborating in the effort to establish consensus and to negotiate uncertainty. The family's life together is an endless process of movement in and around consensual understanding, from attachment to conflict to withdrawal—and over again. Separateness and connectedness are the underlying conditions of a family's life, and its common task is to give form to both.

This volume describes how five families have each, in distinctive ways, dealt with this and other tasks. The ways in which a family is a unit and the ways it provides for being a separate person are, in one sense, what every family's life is about. The psychosocial portraits which we have sketched are intended to convey something of the particularity of American family worlds. These are American families, but the wider culture was not our primary interest. Rather, we tried first to find the family's boundaries, then to explore its psychosocial dimensions. When we looked at the culture, it was in order to take the point of view of a family looking out at it. The reader will recognize in these analytic sketches versions of middle and lower class cultural themes; again, our aim has been to illustrate what this feels like to actual individuals who shape a life in an intimate group. The case study is the method of choice for this purpose, and its aim is to amplify the richness of perception of American family life.

Depiction is not our sole aim, however. We are concerned with developing a framework for understanding the nuclear family as a group. Within the family, events occur in far from random fashion; even uncertainty is given a customary place in a family's scheme of things. While illustrating distinctness, we work toward a systematic view of the family as a psychosocial organization. How may one describe a family, taking account of all its members? The multiplicity of household events takes place in a round robin of interaction which is a shapeless swirl only to the casual observer. There are nodes of connection, points at which feeling is concentrated and significance declared. There are tracks to which the interaction returns again and again. A family has discernible pattern and form.

We set ourselves the task of searching out the elements that give shape to a family's life. In so doing, we examined the personalities of the individual members, the relationships between pairs and in triangles, and the integration of these individual psychodynamic features and multiple relationships in the psychosocial structure of the group. We tried to comprehend in one view the supporting convergences and the intrinsic disruptions of a family, seen as a set of individual personalities, a system of interpersonal relations, and a local culture.

It is imperative to relate the nature of individuality to the form of the particular family group in which it occurs and to examine the participation of family psychological modes of interaction in the personalities of individual members. As a guiding principle we are proposing that the intrapsychic organization of each member is part of the psychosocial structure of his family; the structure of a family includes the intrapsychic organization of its individual members. For example, if separateness and connectedness constitute one of the most fundamental problems which a family must solve, then it is necessary first to adopt a standpoint from which one can see both tendencies as parts of the same solution and second to view this solution both as an extension of individual needs into the group interaction and as a significant determinant of individual personality.

An understanding of the relationship between individual dynamics and family interactional matrix may be furthered by a second principle: in his relationship in the family an individual member strives toward predictability of preferred experience, attempting to discover or create circumstances which fit his image of what the world around him should be—how it should respond to him and provide opportunity for expression of his own preferences. This principle indicates how one might examine the fashion in which individual uniqueness is transformed into family uniqueness as a result of his own and others' experience. It attends also to the impact upon the individual member of his success, or lack of it, in obtaining the emotional atmosphere he desires. Neither the ties that bind the members to one another nor the barriers that separate them are adequately indicated by overt social behavior alone. Connection to others is outward and inward in infinite variety. In the study of ordinary people, as in this book, the inner connections and the inner enclaves must command attention no less than the external encounters and the occasions for social privacy. Taking for granted, then, that the members of a nuclear family have personalities of their own, that each has a psychobiological individuality, and that each is guided by cultural role expectations, how shall we understand how they fashion a life together?

It is the purpose of this introductory chapter to indicate some concepts which are useful in understanding and describing in non-pathological terms the complexities of ordinary family interaction. The major processes described here give shape to the flux of family life, coherence to the extended array of events, perceptions, emotions, actions, learnings, and changes which the members experience or undertake. The essential processes discussed below are these:

1. Establishing a pattern of separateness and connectedness.
2. Establishing a satisfactory congruence of images through the exchange of suitable testimony.
3. Evolving modes of interaction into central family concerns or themes.
4. Establishing the boundaries of the family's world of experience.
5. Dealing with significant biosocial issues of family life, as in the family's disposition to evolve definitions of male and female and of older and younger.

THE EFFORT TO ACHIEVE A SATISFACTORY PATTERN OF
SEPARATENESS AND CONNECTEDNESS

Two conditions characterize the nuclear family. Its members are connected to one another, and they are also separate from one another. Every family gives shape to these conditions in its own way. Its life may show greater emphasis on the one or the other; yet both are constitutive of family life. The infant is born from the womb into the limits of his own skin, with individual properties of sensitivity and activity. He possesses an irreducible psychobiological individuality that no amount or kind of intense socialization can abolish. His parents, too, remain individual persons no matter how deep their love, how passionate their desire for one another or how diffuse their individual identities. Through the wishes and capacities of its members, the family defines and gives shape to separateness so that it looms large or small in family affairs, gives rise to pleasure or unhappiness. The range of possibilities is wide. The autistic child or the psychotic parent represents the pathological extreme of separateness. The benign extremes are more diverse—emotional richness, ego autonomy, individual creativity. Perhaps Erikson's concept of a clearly delineated ego identity best conveys the benign meaning of separateness.[1]

Yet connectedness of family members is equally basic. No human infant survives without ties. Connectedness can range from physical proximity and rudimentary child care to an intensity of mutual involvement which all but excludes all other interests. Separateness remains always, yet it can be transcended. Love and passion do unite family members and can make separateness seem infinitesimal—or comfortable. The signs of being connected to one another that the members of a family seek differ greatly even within the middle range. In one family intense emotional exchange is sought; the members need to relax defenses and public façade, and they respond freely. In other families such confrontation is threatening, though the wish to feel themselves together in binding ties may be great. A family of this kind may be able to approach its desire only through much formalized or ritualized action, such as giving gifts, celebrating birthdays and holidays, making joint excursions.

This fundamental duality of family life is of considerable significance, for the individual's efforts to take his own kind of interest in the world, to become his own kind of person, proceed apace with his efforts to find gratifying connection to the other members. At the same time, the other members are engaged in taking their kinds of interest in him, and in themselves. This is the matrix of interaction in which a family develops its life. The family tries to cast itself in a form that satisfies the ways in which its members want to be together and apart. The pattern it reaches is a resultant of these diverse contributions. This dual condition of inevitable individuality and inescapable psychosocial connection is a dynamic condition; it requires a family to make some kind of life together, lest the family dissolve. The family and its members must meet these two condi-

[1] Erik Erikson, *Childhood and Society* (New York: W. W. Norton, 1950).

tions in *some* way. The investigator's effort to understand family life is facilitated insofar as he asks constantly, In what way does this event or tendency or action bring the members together or keep them apart?

CONGRUENCE OF IMAGES

It is useful to regard life in a family as the family's effort to attain a satisfactory congruence of individual and family images through the exchange of suitable testimony. This view initially directs attention to the family as a group of members. Family research must somehow face up to this very obvious fact. All the members of the nuclear household must be taken into account if we are to understand the family's life. Data must be obtained from each member. We do not understand a family if we know the spouses' roles as mates and as parents but nothing of their children, nor is our foundation adequate if we have firsthand materials from a mother and child in therapy but see the father and other children only through their eyes. Thus, this first implication is methodological. It says something of the range of data to be collected.

Living together, the individuals in a family each develop an image of what the other members are like. This image comprises the emotional meaning and significance which the other has for the member holding it. The concept of image is a mediating concept. Its reference extends into the personality and out into the interpersonal relationship. Referring to one person's emotionalized conception of another, an image is shaped by the personality both of the holder and of the object. The image emerges from the holder's past and bears the imprint of his experience, delimiting what versions of others are possible for him. It says something about him as a person. But it is also a cast into the future, providing the holder with direction in relating to and interacting with the object. While it represents the holder's needs and wishes, it also represents the object as a source of fulfilment.

Each family member has some kind of image of every other member and of himself in relation to them. This image is compounded of realistic and idealized components in various proportions, and it may derive from the personalities of its holder and its object also in various proportions. It draws from cultural values, role expectations, and the residue of the parents' experiences in their families of origin. One's image of another is the product of one's direct experience with the other and of evaluations of the other by third parties. From this experience, from evaluations of it and elaborations on it in fantasy, a conception of another person is developed, a conception which serves to direct and shape one's action to the other and which becomes a defining element of the interpersonal relationship. *An image of a person is one's definition of him as an object of one's own action or potential action.*

In studying a family, then, it is necessary to investigate both the images which the members hold of one another and the ways in which these images are interrelated. It is necessary to understand how the interaction of the members derives from and contributes to this interrelation of images. The implication of this stance is that interaction cannot be fully understood in its own terms, that, instead, it must be viewed in the context of how the participants define one another as relevant objects.

From his experience with the other members of his family and from experiences outside the family, an individual comes to have another kind of image—an image of his family which expresses his mode of relationship to the unit and which defines the kind of impact the family has on him. A woman may gratifyingly conceive of her family as dependents who need and reward her, or she may see them primarily as the group that enslaves her and for whom she wears herself out. A man may feel proud of his family as a demonstration of his masculinity, or his image may be of a group of perplexing people with emotions and reactions he doesn't understand, or his family may mean to him primarily a welcome retreat from and contrast with his workaday world. For a child, too, the family may have diverse meanings. To one it is the group he is happy to belong to. For another it consists of those he lives with because he has no place else to go. A person's image of his family embodies what he expects from it and what he gives to it, how important it is and what kind of importance it has.

The images held of one member by the others diverge in varying ways from one another and from his image of himself. The intimate and constant exchange that characterizes the nuclear family makes such divergence far from a matter of indifference. The members of a family want to and have to deal with one another; from the beginning they are engaged in evolving and mutually adjusting their images of one another. This mutual adjustment takes place in interaction, and it is, in part, the aim of interaction. Since complete consensus is most improbable, life in a family—as elsewhere—is a process ongoing in a situation of actual or potential instability. Pattern is reached, but it can never be complete, since action is always unfolding and the status of the family members is undergoing change.[2]

If a family system of interpersonal relations is to have any continuity, the images which members have of the family and of one another must in some sense tend toward compatibility. This is only to say that they strive toward some sort of stability or predictability of preferred behavior. When a child is born, the parents entertain an image of the child—which will be altered and elaborated with time, to be sure—which the child cannot share. The concept of socialization refers to the parents' efforts to get the child to regard himself in substantially the same way they regard him. From birth, also, the child is engaged in acquiring conceptions of his parents, striving to form a view of them which accords with their self-images. In an absolute sense, neither goal can be attained, but the efforts to reach satisfactory

[2] George Herbert Mead gave theoretical significance to this uncertainty of future action in his concept of the "I." "It is because of the 'I' that we say that we are never fully aware of what we are, that we surprise ourselves by our own action. It is as we act that we are aware of ourselves. . . . I want to call attention to the fact that this response of the 'I' is something that is more or less uncertain. . . . The 'I' gives the sense of freedom, of initiative" (*Mind, Self, and Society* [Chicago: University of Chicago Press, 1934], pp. 174, 176, 177).

FAMILY WORLDS

approximations—or congruence—constitute one of the springs of interaction.

It seems useful to draw an analytic distinction between the actual image which a person holds of another and his desired image. Not only does an individual have an ideal for his own behavior, an ego ideal, but he also forms conceptions of what he wants others to be. In some families the greatest discrepancies may occur among these ideal versions of each other. Such a discrepancy may be described as the discrepancy between a person's ego ideal (his own image of what he strives toward in himself) and another's desired image of him (what the other strives to realize in him). This type of situation appears in fairly clear outline in our discussion of the Littleton family (chap. iv).

In other families there may be relatively little strain of this order. Such a family's inter-involvement may be characterized as its effort to live as a satisfactory example of what is accepted as desirable. The "problems" of living in systems of this type are more likely to arise from "falling short" of what is consensually desirable and from the difficulties of living up to all desirable claims simultaneously rather than from disagreement about what is desirable.

Families also differ in their tolerance of incongruence of images. In some there is pressure toward closeness of fit in minute particulars. In others a looser relationship is accepted as satisfactory, or the system can deal with incongruence strains short of disruption.

The issue involved here is not one of how similar the members must be to each other, that is, whether a neat housekeeper requires her husband and children to be equally neat, or whether a serious man requires the other members of his family to be likewise. Rather, the issue is whether the differences and similarities among the members are mutually acceptable. Child guidance clinics echo with parents complaining that the offending child does as they do rather than as they say. The personalities of the parent and the child may be quite similar; yet they may hold images of each other which are discrepant and unsatisfactorily so. But personality dissimilarity—at whatever level—may provide a firm basis for a satisfactory congruence of images. If a serious man finds himself responsible but his gay wife frivolous, and if she feels that he is dull but she is sparkling, an incongruent set of images characterizes their relationship. Where the serious husband relishes his wife's gaiety as lively and stimulating, where she welcomes his sobriety as a form of strength and stability, and where both concur in what each should be, the images they hold of each other are satisfactorily congruent.

The commonality of experience in a family will conduce to some congruence of family images among the family members. The intrinsic distinctions of age, sex, birth order, and role in society conduce to divergence of images. The overlap and the divergences are expressed and acted out in family life, each member participating in terms of the definition incorporated in his image.

Even when the congruence of images is satisfactory, interaction still has reference to it. If exploration and testing diminish in importance, affirmation and reiteration of what has been established become the content of interaction. The family members demonstrate their agreement with the group and strive toward validation of personal worth in family terms. The positive features of the family image provide the criteria for evaluating individual behavior. The audience toward which testimony is directed may be primarily composed of the family itself, or it may be extended to non-family persons. Whatever its audience, validation is pursued through those dimensions of behavior that the family regards as significant.

A stable human relationship is one in which the members have reached a high degree of consensus about one another; the terms in which personal worth may be demonstrated are clear and are shared. Their interaction is an exchange of testimony of what the members are to one another. The action of each person in his family testifies to his image of it, of himself, and of the others. The members realize or seek out in interpersonal encounters those kinds of experiences which seem meaningful to them and with which they are comfortable. Feelings and actions are responded to in terms of their felt suitability. *Responsive judgments and feelings are responsive first to the inward images of self, other, and family. They then become responses to and for others, so that family life is shaped within the participants as well as between them.*

We have tried to sum up in a general statement how a family's life may be understood in terms of the images family members have of one another and themselves; the inevitable divergences and fluctuations of these images; the psychosocial task of relating to others and attaining viable stability amid this potential fluctuation; the image members develop of the family as a unit —its meaning to family members, the character of its emotional and social exchange; and the utilization of the positive features of the family image in affirming to each member and to the group their personal worth and their right to emotional acceptance and participation.

THE FAMILY THEME

Individual images and responses are interrelated. In any particular family the kinds of action we have called testing, exploring, and affirming take place in terms of a particular content which may be termed a "family theme." A family theme is a pattern of feelings, motives, fantasies, and conventionalized understandings grouped about some locus of concern which has a particular form in the personalities of the individual members. The pattern comprises some fundamental view of reality and some way or ways for dealing with it. In the family themes are to be found the family's implicit direction, its notion of "who we are" and "what we do about it." In delineating a particular family theme, we may bring several criteria to bear.

First, the theme affects behavior in several important family areas and activities. It is a postulated mold which exerts a variable impress on the observable events and ascertainable consequences of a family life. Thus, a family's feelings about most of its activities can be construed as particular manifestations of a more inclusive organizing principle, which for one type of family might be stated in this way: The family feels itself to be essentially alone in the world. Individual members endeavor to communicate with one another. They strive to foster any symbol or semblance of communication. The process of communication itself is important to all family members, and attempts to achieve contact with one another must be pursued whenever possible. Failure or disruption in communication is a failure in meeting the family objective.

The theme is an implicit point of departure and point of orientation for this family's behavior. Father's return to the family at the end of the day stimulates a flurry of greeting and excitement; the family dinner becomes one of the most important events of the day. Chores around the home are seen as opportunities for conversation. Members are expected to be "considerate" of one another, avoiding the conflict and disharmony that might threaten communication. Independence or solitude is discouraged; the individual family member should keep himself ready and available for interaction; activities that take a member out of the group are discouraged.

This is a brief illustration of a theme. A fuller statement would take greater account of the forces that have to be contended with in holding to the direction of solution and integration actually followed.

Second, a theme is a significant issue in the life of the family, expressing basic forms of relating to the external world and of interpersonal involvement.

Third, all members of the family are involved in the psychosocial definitions and processes which enter into the theme, though each may be involved in a different way. Thus the theme arises from and has consequences for the personalities of all the members.

The theme, then, is a particularly useful unit for analysis of family life, for it provides a way of characterizing the family group in terms of broad and significant psychosocial and psychocultural dimensions. At the same time, it permits flexibility, since it is not an arbitrary unit and does not require that a family be understood in terms of a set of a priori categories. The investigator can assess the family in its own terms, responding to and following the saliences that center its life.[3]

The concept of the theme is advantageous in two other important ways. Since it is a characterization of the family in terms of a significant issue in its life, the concept provides a point of reference for understanding the individual members and particular interpersonal relationships as specific versions and expressions of the theme. The individual's place in the family—what he does and what happens to him there—can be understood as the way in which he participates in these broader currents which help to determine the quality of his family membership. If we understand a theme as consisting of some significant issue and the general direction of attempted solution or resolution of that issue, each member has some part to play in this larger configuration. His part is complexly determined, as is every role—in some measure assigned by others, in some measure self-created. By determining the salient themes in a family's life, we are able to see more clearly how any individual's fate is shaped, what opportunities he has for interlocking his life with others, and what pressures he must contend with.

The concept of the theme also makes it possible to compare one family with another. It provides a way of characterizing a whole group in a fashion that is relevant to the group's individual members; yet since it is a group-summary statement, it can be arrayed with other such characterizations.

ESTABLISHING BOUNDARIES OF THE FAMILY'S WORLD
OF EXPERIENCE

The concepts we have suggested are oriented toward revealing not only the family's internal functioning but its stance, the

---

[3] The concept of the theme has been introduced into social science by Henry Murray in psychology and by Morris Opler in anthropology. See Henry A. Murray et al., *Explorations in Personality* (New York: Oxford University Press, 1938), and Morris Opler, "Themes as Dynamic Forces in Culture," *American Journal of Sociology*, LI, 198–206. Though he does not use the word, Fritz Redl's approach to group structure makes use of similar logic. See his "Group Emotion and Leadership," *Psychiatry*, V (1942), 573–96.

position it has taken up vis-à-vis the outer, non-family world. The significant themes consequently not only subsume the psychic content of the family's life but also indicate something of the breadth of its world. A family constitutes its own world, which is not to say that it closes itself off from everything else but that it determines what parts of the external world are admissible and how freely. The family maps its domain of acceptable and desirable experience, its life space. The outer limits of life space for any family are fairly definite and reasonably well marked. There are signposts for goals and signals for danger. But these metaphors fail because the boundaries lie within persons, and however firm they may be, there are always areas of inexperience not adequately charted. As new experiences occur, as new feelings arise, new actions are taken and are brought to the internal limits of the person taking them and to the limits which others help to set. In this back-and-forth of interaction is to be found the family members' mutual regulation. Each directs himself toward others by virtue of the representation they have in his mind; the others respond to him in terms of the way he is represented in theirs. Limits to experience—broad or narrow—are established in a variety of ways and along several dimensions. Some of the more important are these:

1. *The differentiation of individual personality.*—How elaborated individual personalities of the family members are; how self-directing individuals are and are expected to become. From the gross categories of infantile experience, comfort and distress, incorporation and expulsion, personality develops to encompass a range of emotional experience and more mature ego mechanisms. The complexity and differentiation of personality can proceed further in some families than in others.

2. *The intensity of experience.*—How deep or how shallow experience is; how detached or how involved family members are in their activities and one another; how controlled or how spontaneous their behavior is. The question involved here is how much of the self is made available to experience—the fulness of intimacy or the enthusiasm of commitment to something.

3. *The extensity of experience.*—The literal geographical scope —the range and variety of actions; the importance of neighborhood and locality as compared with communities of more abstract definition—"democratic society," "the legal profession"; how much of the world it is important to know about and be interested in; how far actual acquaintance extends. Thus, less literally, how many kinds of life and action are conceived of, known of, or understood.

4. *The tendency to evaluate experience.*—Families differ in their inclination to permit members to make unique personal evaluations of and responses to stimuli. The constraints of evaluation—the internalization of criteria—modify and translate stimuli and experience. Values create in the individual member emotional positions on definable categories of experience—jazz, sports, "classical" art and music, comic books, politicians, science and scientists, literature—the broad range of stimuli available in our culture. The family also evaluates experience initiated by the individual member and evokes from him modes of responsiveness to his own behavior and the behavior of others. A prominent element of this dimension is the tendency toward moral evaluation of experience. The freedom from or constraint by guilt and the freedom to range inwardly in thought, impulse, and fantasy, to entertain unaccustomed possibilities, are involved here. Moral evaluation also affects the freedom to range outwardly, to be at home in new circumstances, to find out for oneself. The central issue is the need, or lack of it, to condemn and repudiate or even simply to shun what is traditionally not one's own.

These are at least some of the most important dimensions which describe the boundaries of a family's world and the kind of life that can be lived within it. The characteristics of this arena help determine for each member how multiplex his life is, how close to himself, how close to others, how close to home. Establishing the boundaries of experience, in the terms just enumerated, is one of the principal processes of family life. It continues not only while the members live together but even after they disperse—even influencing how far and in what direction they will go.

In a final sense, the predicated states are never reached. What turns a life may take cannot be known, so that the pattern-establishing processes do not result in changeless solutions. While it may be possible to predict how a family of a given type will weather economic privation, if it should occur, the predicted kind of change will not take place unless the financial stress does. Similarly, in greater or lesser degree, the "establishing" processes are always in play, responding to the new elements introduced into the family's life. However, it is necessary to recognize that while in a literal, concrete sense, the boundaries of experience are never definitively established, it is possible to ascertain with high probability what they are likely to be for a given family. If the life of a family never reaches a final, unchangeable form—even for a delimited period of the family cycle, such as the child-rearing stage—it nonetheless gains a recognizably firm structure, as any human association must.

DEALING WITH SIGNIFICANT GIVEN BIOSOCIAL ISSUES OF FAMILY LIFE

The most essential structural characteristics of the nuclear family are well known and need not be extensively elaborated here. The fact that a family, unlike other voluntary groups, must be established by one member from each sex means that sex membership is a basic point of reference. In the study of any particular family it is necessary to investigate what it interprets male and female to be. What qualities are attributed to each sex? What is demanded of each? What is accorded to each? How important is the distinction felt to be? Is the sex difference minimized, or does it serve as a basis for proliferation of emotions and activities? Are the two sexes differentially evaluated so that rewards and penalties are distributed on the basis of sex membership? All of these questions have, of course, certain conventionalized answers provided by the larger social units to which a family belongs—social class, ethnic group, community. Yet each family also provides answers of its own; each family makes use of sex difference in structuring its own world.

While parents choose each other voluntarily in marriage, their children become family members without exercise of choice. This fact, together with the fact that they are helpless at birth and hence born into the care and authority of their parents, sets the question of how the differences between the two generations will be construed and handled. How much of family life is to be regulated by considerations of authority becomes an important dimension. Parental authority—its scope, the manner in which it is exercised—is one of the forces shaping the pattern of separateness-connectedness. Its potential is realized in such consequences for the child as self-direction, submissiveness, a sense of injustice, or a readiness to learn from those of greater experience.

In dealing with this gulf in power and capacity between themselves and their children, parents have to make a decision (not a conscious decision, in its essentials, but one arising from their own personalities) about how insistently they will impose their images upon their children. Families differ in how far parents interact with their children, amending or reshaping their own aims as their children become increasingly formed. Where they expect the children to do all the adapting, there is little room for negotiating, so that the process of self- and mutual discovery is compressed within narrow limits.

Families differ also in how the parents pace their children through childhood—whether they push, encourage, or restrain. Parents seek to shape their children in keeping with their own desire to achieve preferred experience. They stimulate the children in accordance with what they feel children should be, as a part of their activity in defining their own world. The nature of parental stimulation—its intensity, frequency, and diversity—expresses the aims of their care and authority. When we observe that one parent is eager for his child to behave as much like an adult as quickly as possible, whereas another regrets his child's loss of babyish ways, it is clear that different personal wishes or aims are operating in the two cases. But it would appear that different concepts of growth and different time perspectives also operate here. In some families there is an urgency to growing up, sometimes motivated by the parent's wish to be quickly relieved or what are conceived as the taxing aspects of child rearing, or by an anxiety that each "delay" or concession to impulsivity is threatening to ultimate development. This idea seems to include a notion of a fixed termination point, a time when development has reached its goal and is then essentially over. The happenings beyond this point are construed not as growth but simply as events, important or not, in the passing of time. In other families a sense of a long, indefinite time span prevails, together with a belief that growth cannot be compressed. Children are seen as moving slowly toward maturity, and it is felt that they have time enough to do so. Growth is intricate, not readily mechanized, and the forces of childhood are tamed rather than broken.

Implicit in these several aspects of parental feeling and action vis-à-vis their offspring is another decision: *how much of the child's world does not belong to his parents?* In part, this is a matter of authority. In exercising authority, parents not only choose among techniques of reward and punishment. They also may or may not restrict themselves from incursions into the child's domain. Whether a child is granted privacy in any sense —privacy of quarters, of possessions, of thoughts and emotions, of responses to others—or whether these are all felt to be subject to his elders' inspection and manipulation is a question decided according to how parents define themselves and children. Bound up in the decision is a conception of integrity, for the terms on which people have access to one another, while communicated earlier in the infant-care context, become increasingly defined and actualized during childhood.

The relationships which develop among the various members of a family do not follow simply the intrinsic lines of sex and age. They are shaped as well by the underlying family themes and images which impart meanings to sex and age and also to various other personal characteristics. On the basis of the meanings which the members have for one another, particular inter-personal ties evolve. The closeness between any two members, for example, or the distance between a group of three closely joined members and a fourth who is apart, derives from the in-terlocking meanings which obtain among them. Each family tends to have a characteristic distribution of ties or pattern of alignment (which may be negative or positive in emotional tone) among members. How these patterns are developed and sustained is, then, a matter of considerable significance in under-standing life within families as well as the course of any one member's life.

In these concepts we have attempted to provide a framework for understanding the family as an intimate group of members which functions in systematic ways. We have focused on the in-terior of the family, so that the framework is somewhat less use-ful for analyzing the relationship between the family and society. The case studies in this volume have been prepared in terms of the point of view advanced in the present chapter, though the concepts identified here are not reiterated with each detail of family life. At various points where it has seemed necessary, we have elaborated on some idea that seemed to us to illuminate the family being discussed. The frame of reference is intended to serve as just that—marking out the range of phenomena en-compassed and the terms in which they are considered.

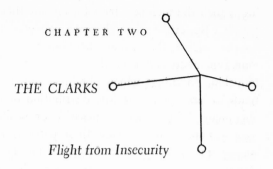

CHAPTER TWO

THE CLARKS

Flight from Insecurity

Sometimes a family's life draws its psychological theme from stark realities of the past. Two young adults, seeking in one another an escape from emotional deprivation, join in a mutual effort to establish a new family which will provide for themselves and their children a dependable source of security and gratification. Such a family attempts to effect a generational transformation in style of life and to surmount the childhood which still opposes them from within. In seeking to transform their own lives together, they develop an image of what they and their children should do and be.

The Clarks are such a psychologically mobile family. Their attempts to improve the family's circumstances are oriented toward avoiding some of the misfortunes, both economic and psychological, which the parents vividly recall as part of their own childhood. They have no aspirations toward the life of the socially elite: they would be content to become a secure, stable family with dependable income, respectable children, and moral behavior. However, their past leaves its imprint. It cannot be merely discarded; it must be warded off. The Clarks are in a phase of mobility that might be described as the formulation of a negative identity—the development of resources that are essentially defensive and protective in character, representing features which are important because they constitute opposites of the chaotic deprivation of Mr. and Mrs. Clark's early years. These resources echo the fears underlying the issues characteristic of this family group.

Henry Clark was six months old when his father died of typhoid. Henry remembers only the image of his father which was maintained by the family; this image was indistinct, sketchy, and uncomplimentary, but its impact upon Henry was profound. The memory of his father offered to him was of a carpenter who provided adequately for his family but who gave them no roots and no sense of stability: "My father wasn't a settled man. He liked to move around, following the rainbow." He was following an oil boom in a small Texas town when he died. Mrs. Clark immediately took the family to a small town in southern Indiana, where she worked as a seamstress to support Henry and his five brothers. Henry was placed with an unmarried aunt who lived a few blocks away.

Henry Clark recalls with ambivalence the maternal figures in his early life. He recognizes that poverty forced his mother to neglect her family, and he attempts to absolve her of blame for the circumstances that characterized his home life and for his unconscious feeling that she deserted him.

She tried to give us an idea of what was right, and she impressed on us the importance of honesty and things like that. She wasn't there to give us much supervision, and during the day we ran wild. We didn't have a normal family life at all—no father and with Mother out of the home all day.

He remembers his aunt dimly as a woman who "was good to me, and kind." This aunt, the warmest of the adults in his early years, died when Henry was five. His response to this succession of losses is apparent in his expressions of rootlessness and the sense of being left emotionally empty-handed.

Upon his aunt's death Henry moved back with his family. Several years later he went to Chicago to live with an older brother and his wife. In order to distribute the economic responsibility more evenly, Henry was shuttled from one brother's home to another until he was able to maintain himself.

Despite the discomfort of his memories, Henry Clark accepts and even finds merit in certain aspects of his early experience. One of the positive recollections that he has of his family is the feeling of responsibility that each son felt toward the younger members of the family and toward the mother. "It's always been like that—everybody helped everybody else when they could. We still help mother that way, too."[1] However, each individual's contribution toward the maintenance of the family was primarily concerned with economic and social necessities. The family was never unified psychologically; the threat of isolation and poverty did not foster close emotional ties or encourage interaction. Although the brothers still assist their mother financially, there is little contact or communication among the brothers themselves.

Thus Henry Clark's early experiences centered in emotional and economic impoverishment. The usual structure of family living was replaced by economic protection without emotional interaction. This protection was given as a matter of course, without reciprocal demands for gratitude, dependency, or affection. Economic assistance and other forms of basic support became symbols of family unity and obligation, apparently offered without resentment and accepted without guilt. Life itself was tough and threatening, and much of the energy at hand was expended in securing essential physical gratification. Mr. Clark's orientation toward his contemporary life draws heavily upon his inner responses to early experiences. He is engrossed with the need for protecting himself and his family from economic insecurity, from social isolation, and from uncertainty. He has developed patterns of behavior which ward off the external dangers he fears most and at the same time afford a partial resolution of his basic psychological conflicts.

Now, at thirty-five, Mr. Clark lives with his wife and two chil-

[1] This parallels the description in Allison Davis, "The Motivation of the Underprivileged Worker," in W. F. Whyte (ed.), *Industry and Society* (New York: McGraw-Hill, 1946).

dren in Gary, Indiana. The family moved to Gary from southern Indiana three years ago, when Mr. Clark was given a promotion and transferred to the Gary office of the soft drink company for which he works as office manager. The six-room apartment is of moderate size and gives the appearance of being well filled with objects of various kinds. Rooms are papered with patterned wallpaper; there are chintz curtains and slipcovers and chenille scatter rugs. A large Bible rests on the table in the dining room.

In this apartment Thelma Clark presides. She agreed immediately to participate in the research, without consulting her husband, and was pleasant and entirely co-operative throughout the period of interviewing and testing in the home. She is a tall, fair, attractive woman. Although she is occasionally quite informal in dress and appearance around the home, she exerts considerable energy in keeping herself neatly groomed and the apartment in order.

Thelma Clark also grew up in a broken home. When she was three months old, her father left; he has made no subsequent effort to contact Mrs. Clark or her mother. Thelma Clark reports that she knows little about him but his name and the occasion of his deserting the family. She adds, however, that he was handsome, worked irregularly, and "got in with the wrong crowd." He was a coal miner who left no financial resources or assets behind him. However, since Mrs. Clark was an only child, the economic strains were not quite so severe as those of her husband's family. Her mother went to work, first as a housemaid, then in an auto factory in Detroit. Thelma Clark was placed with two aunts—spending summers with one and winters with the other. She has little nostalgia for her early years:

I don't think it was happy. I wasn't mistreated, but I had no home life. Always moving from place to place, and I just didn't belong to my aunts.

In certain crucial ways her childhood parallels her husband's.

During the depression Thelma's mother married again and

took her daughter back to her home. Although Thelma, who was eleven at the time, had no difficulty getting along with her stepfather and mother, she never felt that her mother succeeded in making a home for her. She softens her criticism by asserting that her mother made a serious attempt to offer a home:

She tried to make a home for us. I didn't pay much attention to her. She disciplined me if it fitted in with her plans. She didn't care much what I did. I went to dances and things very young. I wouldn't want my children to do those things. She's living in Chicago now. It's remarkable how she has changed. She's becoming more like a mother. Mother wasn't affectionate— she is more now than before. One aunt was more affectionate, and I was to her also. I wasn't with mother very much. I didn't feel that anybody cared about me. She was a better mother to my stepsister than to me.

Thelma married at seventeen, during her senior year of high school. In retrospect, she feels that she married too young, though she quickly disclaims any wish to change husbands. There was moderate opposition to the marriage:

My principal at high school and my mother wanted me to wait. I think I got married because I felt in the way at home— especially after my sister came. At seventeen no girl realizes what she's doing. I wanted to have fun, but I became pregnant six months after we were married. I used to go dancing until I was six months along.

Thus the sober responsibilities of maternity befell Mrs. Clark prematurely, destroying the carefree excitement of adolescence. Thirteen years later she still carries some of the resentment she felt at being forced to relinquish teen-age fun for maternal duties. Actually, the marriage decision itself had been a complex one. Mrs. Clark wanted to be loved, to be an accepted member of a family, even if she had to establish one of her own. She also wanted to flee from the home that had never quite provided a family for her. Her decision, although firm, was immature. She now recognizes in part her motivation, but she is still concerned and wistful over her lost youth, wondering possibly just how much better and more exciting her life could have been had parenthood not pressed upon her so soon.

Lucy, the older of the two children, is a pretty, blue-eyed child in the very early stages of adolescence. Like her mother, she is polite, pleasant, and co-operative, and she makes an earnest effort to be a lady. Her manner and responses give the impression of a very proper girl who tries to avoid the slightest appearance of behavior or impulses that would be disapproved by adults.

Lucy is proud of her family and says she enjoys "all the things they do together," from annual vacations to spending evenings at home. She likes a fairly wide range of adults' and children's TV programs ("Super Circus," "Ramar of the Jungle," "Mr. and Mrs. North," "I Married Joan," and "This Is Your Life") and speaks with almost equal enthusiasm about school. She is a lively and active girl:

I like to swim. I've never really had a chance to do this, but I'd like to ride horseback. On Monday nights I have Girl Scouts. In the summer I swim—I took lessons last summer.

INTERVIEWER: Do you belong to any clubs?

LUCY: Girl Scouts. I have so much stuff that keeps me busy that I have a hard time fitting it all in. Then there's church, you know.

INTERVIEWER: What sort of activities?

LUCY: Junior training program—daily Bible reading and memory verse.

INTERVIEWER: Who do you go around with?

LUCY: Well, there's about three or four girls. Usually one or two. Once a large group went ice skating together. We play games—monopoly, hopscotch, basketball. We go to the library.

Lucy already has a strong orientation toward adult activities and has unusually definite ideas about her career. She wants to go to college and to secretarial school. However, her plans are always qualified by the possibility that she will feel impelled to devote herself to a career of religious endeavor. "I might like to be a missionary. If God calls me to be, I will be. Otherwise a secretary or a housewife. I'll do whatever I'm called to do." These remarks indicate that underlying Lucy's assertive approach to daily activities there is a wish to be a dependent, obedient part of a larger plan—a willingness to surrender her individuality in service of the needs and demands of others.

Jimmy, at eight, is a towheaded, good-looking boy, alert and serious and almost as co-operative as his sister. In many of his comments about his family there is an expression of pride—verbal testimony to the family as a source of satisfaction. However, he is of two minds about the family's service to him, and he indulges his ambivalence in open complaint:

INTERVIEWER: *How do you act when you're mad?*

JIMMY: *Well, I never speak to anybody, and if they say anything I sit there and act like I didn't hear them.*

INTERVIEWER: *Who do you usually get mad at?*

JIMMY: *My sister mostly. If she hollers, they tell her not to do it again, but they whip me.*

Jimmy's resentment about his place in the family is in part an extension of his belief that boys have a more difficult time in his family than do girls. Consequently, to a degree his problems have no hope of solution. The sibling rivalry revealed in his comments, while not unusual, has a significance quite apart from the antagonism itself. It points out topics and issues around which Jimmy's, and perhaps the family's, emotional conflicts are clustered; thus it provides initial clues about underlying family issues.

Jimmy is less enthusiastic than Lucy about participation in family and school activities. His preferred activities are school recess, playing with his "boy friends," and watching TV. He belongs to no clubs and lacks the range of leisure play behaviors apparent in Lucy. However, he has both a close friend, who lives next door, and a peer group, and he offers comments on the easy availability of playmates in the immediate neighborhood.

Jimmy follows a family pattern in his expressed desire to be helpful. He thinks of himself as assisting his mother in her household chores and clearly enjoys such participation. He displays less eagerness in helping his sister and occasionally feels that she attempts to take advantage of him.

Lucy is the better organized of the two children. She is more in command of herself, less troubled by the threat of violent feelings than Jim. Competence is part of her self-concept—she knows what to do and believes that she knows what she wants. Jim is more diffuse, less sure of himself. His energy is partially drained away by internal conflicts, leaving less available for active, overt expression. He wants to meet the stated family standards of unselfish giving and service, but he feels at a disadvantage and is unable to repress or deny completely the conviction that more people should be giving more to him.

The initial impression one gets of the Clarks is that they are an "ordinary" family. The children are conforming at church and school and are generally "well behaved"; economic support is adequate; the children are well provided with acceptable friends; the group is strongly attached to two major social institutions—the school and the church—and professes a feeling of satisfaction, emotional stability, and contentment. However, the relative stability of family life which this group exhibits was established and is maintained in spite of the parents' grossly unfavorable childhood experiences. Both Henry and Thelma Clark lacked a paternal figure with whom to identify; their relationships with female identification models were unstable and uncertain. This family presents an unusual opportunity to examine the processes and the resources that promote family stability. Although the desire to avoid insecurity and isolation motivated the Clarks, they see their goals in positive as well as defensive terms.

THE PATTERNING OF DAILY LIFE

The Clarks' household routine is predictable and to a degree consciously planned by the family itself. Mrs. Clark organizes the daily sequence of activities and assumes responsibility for maintaining it. Other members, although not as assertive as she in promoting family regularity, are grateful for her supervision and concern. She makes it clear to them that a firm schedule benefits the entire group. Only Mr. Clark's working hours intrude upon the orderliness of family events. Mrs. Clark reports the intrusion in these terms:

He's never home on account of his work. His job requires him to be there when the shipments come in. I'd like him to have a job where he works eight hours a day and then comes home. I never know when he's going to get here—never can plan to do things together, except church. It's been like this for thirteen years. Never been able to plan even dinner. I'd like him to change jobs but don't see any prospect of him doing that.

Thelma Clark, concerned and distressed by unevenness in the day-to-day schedule, has exerted significant pressure on her husband in an effort to move the family toward a more routinely organized life. Henry Clark is aware that the irregularity of his schedule creates a mild but chronic source of irritation in the family. However, he resists his wife's attempts to correct the situation that is so troublesome to her. The only criticism he has to make of his wife is that she "always wants to know exactly what time I'll be home. She makes me tell her a time and knows I can't do it really."[2]

Apart from his own timetable, Henry Clark is content to leave the control of daily activities in his wife's hands. He describes an "average day" in these words:

I get up sometime in the morning. If I work late, I sleep late. We usually get up from six to eight. Thelma gets me off to work. She fixes my lunch and gets the kids off to school. I'm gone to work all day. The kids are in school. Thelma is around the house. I'm usually later than the rest for dinner. Then we have TV and homework and then we go to bed.

[2] Even though his uncertain evening arrival presents practical difficulties, it is possible that, for different reasons, Henry Clark's schedule is emotionally so important because it is reminiscent of the chaotic psychological disruption of the past.

In comparison with many other husbands of our research group, Henry Clark shows an unusual reliance upon his wife to help him make the transition from sleep to work. This reliance on her contrasts with his resistance to her attempts at persuading him to change jobs in order to achieve a more routine work schedule. Perhaps Henry Clark clings to the apparent autonomy of his working day as a balance against his wish to depend upon his wife while he is at home.

Mrs. Clark's impression of the daily activities agrees in content with Mr. Clark's, but its tone emphasizes repetitiveness and boredom. Even her husband's unpredictability has become a fixture in her image of anticipated events.

It doesn't vary . . . getting up, getting children off to school, breakfast, lunch same time every day. Children come home; husband doesn't. At six we have dinner; sometimes it's six-thirty. Then two hours of TV for the children. We did have family devotions, but my husband is home different times. We read the Bible every day.

During the day I clean house, make beds, wash dishes. I bake every day, wash and iron every week. I like to cook. I bake every day—pies, cakes, desserts, hot rolls. I bake to please the family. They like homemade things.

Few women of the research group see their daily tasks as consisting so exclusively of activities designed for the welfare of the family and care of the home. Thelma Clark has other interests and activities that take her time and attention away from the home and her family, but she makes very little of these extra-family activities in her talks with our staff member. The image she presents to us is focused upon her roles as mother and homemaker. Her role as wife and her activities as a woman in the community are less important to her. It is as a homemaker that her most overt criticism of Mr. Clark occurs. Mrs. Clark invests a great deal in her ability to manage the home smoothly and efficiently. This is the core of her image of herself as a wife and mother. She is able to control and arrange all the major elements of the home schedule except her husband's work hours. Persistent attempts to correct this flaw have been without success, and she reveals a feeling of resignation to the situation. However, resignation has not silenced her; her objections continue, but now they serve the purpose of expressing discontent rather than a straightforward attack on a mutual problem.

Mrs. Clark regards the household chores as her own responsibility. She would like assistance from the other family members, but to insist that they help would be to compromise her own feelings of competence. When asked how the housework is divided among the family members, she replies:

Nobody helps. Father washes the walls in the spring, but I don't insist on them washing dishes. Lucy does things in the house to get badges for Girl Scouts. I let them do it when they come and ask me but don't make them. They'll do a lot more then when I do ask them. Or if I'm sick, they'll all do their part.

Doing things for the family and demanding little from them serve to bind the family to her, to insure their continuing allegiance and affection.

Lucy's account of the daily routine reveals an awareness of her father's activities. Her initial comments about the "average day" suggest a sensitivity to his presence and a feeling that his schedule is an important part of the day-by-day routine. In fact, she does not mention her mother until specifically questioned by the interviewer:

LUCY: *Well, Father is sometimes here when we get up for breakfast. Some days he leaves early when he didn't work later. On rainy days if he's here he takes us to school, then goes to work. Then we come home for lunch. Sometimes we have lunch in the living room and watch TV. At night when Jim and I come home, he goes and plays and I go to my girl friend's or watch TV.*

INTERVIEWER: *What happens in the evening?*

LUCY: *Everybody's home for dinner—usually me, Jim, and Mother. Father eats later when he comes home. I finish up* homework, watch TV until eight-thirty or nine-thirty. Fridays I stay up till eleven, then sleep late on Saturday.

INTERVIEWER: What does your mother do during the day?

LUCY: One day she washes and irons. She cleans the house and finishes sewing, bakes pies and cakes. Yesterday she baked a chocolate cake.

INTERVIEWER: What do you do to help around the house?

LUCY: Sometimes I help with the dishes or bake a cake or watch Jim while Mother and Father go to shop. When Mother is sick I get breakfast for me and Jim.

INTERVIEWER: Have you no regular jobs?

LUCY: I'd like to. Oh, yes! I have to pick up dirty clothes, mine and Jim's, and take care of the dog.

Lucy does not share her mother's irritation with Mr. Clark's irregular working hours. She accepts the daily schedule as satisfactory for her purposes. Her only dissatisfaction with her place in the routine comes from her feeling that she has too small a share in the maternal activities. Unlike the majority of children of her age in our group, she expresses no resentment over the chores assigned to her by her parents. On the contrary, she appears to enjoy a participating role, or at least believes that she would enjoy one if it were offered her. She is not inclined to see this as a severe issue, however; she views the day as orderly, moderately predictable, and unexciting.

Jim's summary of the average day is in agreement with the reports of other family members—it is not an exciting routine:

My mother, she works around the house. Lucy and I go to school. My father, he works in the office, and sometimes maybe my father will go out. While he's working, if Mother didn't fix lunch, he'll go out and buy lunch.

INTERVIEWER: How about after school?

JIM: If TV is on we look at it. If not, we go out and play. Sometimes I go next door and play in my friend's house.

INTERVIEWER: What about evenings?

JIM: The TV is on in the evening. Then we eat supper, then

more TV, then bed. I go to bed at nine o'clock. Everybody eats breakfast together, but for lunch there's Lucy, Mother, and me. Dinner, all of us are together, but sometimes my father is home later and we eat before he comes home.

In Jim's version of the day, everyone in the family has a place. The family members are together at conventional times—meals and television. Like his sister, he shows no indication of chronic complaint about the family schedule, nor does he seem particularly enthusiastic about any recurring event of the day. His opening glimpse of the family routine runs like a theme song of the middle class American family stereotype: The mother works around the house; the father works at the office; the kids go to school. Jim's comments are concerned with what the family members do as individuals, and he shows no interest in what they *are*. Contrast this with the response of Sally Littleton (chap. iv): "My mother usually screams at us, and Tabby [the cat] is always hungry, and the television gets turned off." Sally's statement reveals, among other things, a sense of the family atmosphere, of interaction, of persons affecting one another. All this is lacking in Jim's responses. While this difference reflects the difference between the two families' daily activities, it also reveals the extent to which an even, predictable sequence of commonplace family activities reflects the Clarks' image of the nature of the family.

The weekend for the Clarks is occupied with church activities and local trips to visit relatives or places of interest to the children. Neither parent shows much enthusiasm for these activities, but the children obviously enjoy them a great deal. In Mr. Clark's words: "Sunday is occupied with church, morning and evening. Saturday we do different things—go for a ride or visit relatives on the west side of town, perhaps stay in bed late." Mrs. Clark adds that on Sunday the family usually has guests and TV is taboo, although Mr. Clark is beginning to permit some viewing on the Sabbath. She also makes evident her dislike for the weekend family trips:

INTERVIEWER: *What things don't you like to do with the family?*

MRS. CLARK: *Going to the museum. I hate those places, and they love them. If I can, I stay home so it doesn't tear up their day. When the weather is good we take them pretty often, and often I'll go along, even though I think that when you've seen one you've seen them all.*

Lucy is openly enthusiastic about the weekend family activities. She likes the excursions to the museums and looks forward eagerly to the casual Saturday afternoon activities with her father. She is unaware of, or not concerned about, her mother's distaste for trips to museum or zoo. Jim sees the weekend as providing less opportunity for interaction than does Lucy, but he does mention the family trips and the fact that "Father watches TV with us."

One of the characteristics of the Clark's daily habits is that, other than church, no recurring event during the day or weekend has become a family ritual for supporting interaction and unity. Rather, the children have individual preferences for activities that hold particular interactional meaning. Mr. and Mrs. Clark express little if any preference; Lucy likes the unplanned minor activities that occupy a casual Saturday afternoon—getting the paper, shopping, tending the dog—and Jim prizes the things he does with his father:

Well, me and my dad do things together while Lucy and Mother are doing things, and when we don't have things to do we just sit around and watch TV. Usually we look at books and think of things we might get—something for my mother, something like that . . . sometimes Father reads to me while Mother is fixing dinner.

He adds that if he had more time he would "play with my sister, go for sled rides with Father, and go to the show with Mother."

Vacations are an extension of weekend activities. Occasionally the family takes an extended trip, but more frequently they visit relatives. They do not offer rationalizations or specific objectives for these actions. Like other activities, they appear to be in the category of "things to do" rather than part of a conscious plan for educating the children, providing stimulation, or extending family horizons. However, the evenness and predictability of the family affairs are sources both of satisfaction and of discontent to Mrs. Clark. She is gratified when the home and family run smoothly. She sets the family pace and is reassured of her ability as a mother and housewife when the family is in even stride. However, the very predictability that she has achieved for the group reminds her that much of her life is dull, that she has lost forever the opportunity for youthful glamour and fun, and that the comfort of security is the most likely reward for her efforts. Its rewards for Mr. Clark, however, are more satisfying. Where the household routine affords validation of role competence to Mrs. Clark, it offers her husband evidence of security, protection, and maternal care.

FAMILY IMAGE AND OBJECTIVE: THE PREREQUISITES OF SATISFACTION

The goals that a family has chosen and by which it attempts to regulate its façade of social behavior and its internal processes of communication and interactive affects, necessarily reflect both the assimilation of cultural goals and the psychological areas of deep concern to its dominant members. The desired image that each parent brings to the family they together create partakes of the image of the family that they knew most intimately. Some parents attempt to introduce into their family patterns certain themes that contrast with their early experience, but this very effort underlines the influence of the family of orientation in creating issues and areas of psychological moment for families of the next generation. Thus the desire for reshaping and reformulating the general pattern of family interaction itself tends toward perpetuation of central family themes, although the manner in which these themes are handled may be sharply divergent. Successful re-creation or mending of family patterns, as in the Clarks, perhaps occurs frequently; however, even when "success-

THE CLARKS

ful" it maintains concern over the issue under attack and passes this concern on to the children.

Mr. Clark feels that the family has been moderately successful in attaining the objectives that he believes to be most important. One of the family's most important assets is a competent mother: "My wife is an outstanding person in many ways. Compared to other wives she's way up on top. She's a good homemaker and mother." In his image she has a strong will, is able to make family decisions, and exercises strong and sufficient control over the children. The significance of maternal capability is related to Mr. Clark's desire that the family have a stable, normal pattern of interaction. In his view, the mother is primarily responsible for providing and organizing the family routine—a position obviously related to his comments about his own mother. The husband plays a minor, supporting role in rearing the children and caring for the home. However, he has an important, basic contribution—economic support—which permits the mother freedom to pursue her family obligations.

Considering its social origins, the family has relatively high ambitions for the children. Both Lucy and Jimmy want to go to college, and we may suppose that the expression of such a wish at the pre–high school level indicates an imitation of parental preference. But in its push toward mobility, the family has incorporated some indecision about the children's goals. For example, there are no clearly predetermined occupational objectives for Jimmy to follow.

INTERVIEWER: *What would you like the children to do?*

MR. CLARK: *What they feel like they ought to do. I don't have any particular desires for either of them. If they grew up and were good citizens and were settled and happy, I'd be happy. I'd like to see my boy in a profession if that suits him.*

INTERVIEWER: *How much education would you like them to have?*

MR. CLARK: *Well, as much as they need for whatever they're going to do. Regular college would be fine.*

In another context, Mr. Clark draws back from assertiveness and expresses a wish that Jimmy not be too ambitious. The virtues and achievements most significant to Mr. Clark are apparent in his essays about his "ideal" person:[3]

My Boy

I would like Jimmy to be honest and know the meaning of integrity. I want him to be a Christian. Would like him to learn how to use the intelligence he has in a way that would make this a better world and benefit mankind. Would like for him to learn to enjoy the simple things in life and not try to be too ambitious. Learn to control his temper and be a fellow all people like. I want him to know God's will for his life and live it.

My Girl

I want her to be happy. I would like for her to be industrious like her mother. I want her to be able to support herself if necessary and want her to know God's will and follow it. I want others to like her.

These essays show the desire for stability, security, and conformity that characterizes Mr. Clark's aims for himself and his family. He wishes that his life had been different, that he could begin again with the benefit of his adult experience. While he feels that he could have done much better for himself if he had been properly and wisely directed, he believes it is now too late. Opportunities were missed, and he feels unable to re-create them.

Interviewer: *What would you choose to do if you could?*

Mr. Clark: *I probably wouldn't know better than to stay where I am . . . but if I had it to do over again, and if I knew what I know now, I'd possibly be a lawyer . . . I'm natural-born argumentative. I like to tell my story so people will take sides with me.*

[3] Written in response to the instruction, "Please write an essay about the kinds of persons you would like your children to become." All research techniques are discussed in the Appendix.

In his essays, Mr. Clark introduces a family theme—commitment to a religious belief. Reliance upon the religious code has become an integral part of the family image. Thus Lucy is expected to receive her career plans from a superior sacred source; dependency becomes a prime virtue. Mrs. Clark also emphasizes the importance of sincerity and helpful service, but she sees Lucy's future as much more in her own control. "Her occupation depends entirely on her . . . I would like for it to be Christian work. . . . Her desire is to be a missionary . . . if not that, a teacher of some sort."

To Henry Clark, the family and the children could do no better than to maintain amiable, conflict-free relations with the outside world. The individual members should not wish power, wealth, or fame for themselves but should be likable and able to earn a sufficient living. The aim of effort would be to "benefit mankind" and thus earn the right to community acceptance and approval. The family's role in this, so far as the children are concerned, is to teach the importance and meaning of moral standards and to teach repression of selfish and other antisocial impulses. The family is subordinate to the church and draws heavily upon the church for help in promoting and rewarding moral behavior. In the family itself, the maternal influence should be dominant, extending to the husband as well as the children. Comfort, care, and guidance should be freely extended to all from the mother, and in return the children and husband should respect, revere, and depend upon her. The husband provides economic support, moral and religious guidance, and assistance in the necessary and inevitable task of punishing untoward behavior in the children. Home is a place where one may express feelings that are not acceptable in the outside world. In the family, acceptance and love are unalterable obligations.

Mrs. Clark's image of the family is detailed and firm, and she puts a great deal of effort into guiding the family toward it. The family that would most nearly meet her overt demands and covert wishes has several characteristics. It would be a well-organized, well-run, conflict-free group. Each member would be self-sufficient, needing occasional maternal care (primarily when such ministrations were most convenient for her). The children would inhibit exploratory urges, both geographical and sexual, finding sufficient gratification in conformity and routine activities. They would "know their places," behave properly and gently, not interrupt adult conversation or activity unless they had specific needs or problems to be handled. Interaction for the sake of personal enjoyment and companionship would be kept at a minimum in all relationships, except that the children would want and be able to entertain each other with little adult supervision.

Formalities of role behaviors would be strictly observed. Mother would have adequate meals prepared on time; the family would be present promptly and enjoy the food she had prepared. The house would be kept clean and tidy; family members would pick up their own clothes and wipe their feet at the door. From time to time, parents would be given relief from all family burdens and responsibilities. The family would be oriented toward and responsive to moral directive, especially to formal religious expressions of proper conduct and living. The role of parent would be largely given to transmitting divine expectations and administering punishment for waywardness.

Mrs. Clark is not enthusiastic over her success in shaping the family to conform to her image. However, she is satisfied that the job has been fairly well started. She sometimes feels that she signed the marriage contract in an uncomprehending girlish daze, but she is proud of her husband and her children and "would not trade them for the world." She continues to make persistent and determined efforts to effect her desired family image, and she tries to suppress her feeling of having missed something important (undefined and unknown, to be sure) by marrying so young.

In general, the children echo their parents' wishes. They emphasize their own desires, but these are never in basic contradiction to the family image. Lucy says:

THE CLARKS

I'd like to be a secretary. I think that is a nice job for a girl. Another reason is I like to write and keep books. There are a lot of secretary jobs open, too.

I'd like to be a kind girl so that everyone would like me and I would have lots of friends. Also, when I grow up I am going to try to please Jesus the best I can. I think I would like to be like my mother because she is all that I mentioned before. I just want to be a good Christian girl.

Lucy is a devoted girl. Her stated view of the family is that of a protecting group which she should strive to please:

There is no other family like them. I think they're wonderful. They're not strict like some kids' families. Some parents let their children out all hours; Mother tells us when to come in, and we do. . . . We aren't allowed to run around like some of the kids.

The intense desire to please and to avoid all suggestion of unacceptable impulses is illustrated by her description of an ideal girl her age: ". . . obey her parents—not do anything that they wouldn't like and not do things [just] because they've been unfair."

In Lucy's ideal family there would be no disagreements, no conflicts, no thoughtlessness, no autonomy. Life would move along serenely under the protection of a powerful God and understanding parents. Readiness to please is thus seen as the price of emotional tranquillity. With such a strong orientation toward doing things for others, Lucy's reliance upon a strict, external moral code to help define and guide her behavior is a virtual necessity.

Jim's ideas about his future are, at present, involved with industry and other affairs more practical than his sister's. He writes the following essay:

When I grow up I would like to be an office manager like my dad is, and when I grow up to be that old I would like to be young enough to do little things like I did when I was a child. I would like to collect stamps from different countries, and if I couldn't do that I would like to make model airplanes.

I would like to be a nice person and have enough money to pay for things, and I would like to be the kind of person who would give them to others.

Jim's place in the family does not seem as secure or gratifying to him as does Lucy's. He says that his is a nice family—one that takes care of him—but he frequently reveals a belief that he is mistreated. Like Lucy, but less intensely, he feels that the ideal person should be good, obedient, generous, and self-sacrificing in order to get along with others. Jim's view of the desirable family is one in which he would spend much more time with his father than he does now, would be treated as his sister's equal, and would receive much more of his mother's care. However, he is less convinced than Lucy that selfless living is the way to get what he wants.

The recurring theme of self-sacrifice for the benefit of others is one of the most obvious tones of the children's essays. The altruistic note is sounded more explicitly and more frequently by the Clarks than by most of the families of the research group. Unlike the Lansons (chap. iii), the Clarks' focus of helpfulness is directed toward the outside world rather than primarily toward the family group. It is a common theme that gives direction to behavior, but it does not emphasize family unity as its objective. The cohesion that is provided is a by-product of the effort to conform to an ideal or code that is seen as external and superior to family and individual needs.

Mrs. Clark demonstrates more clearly than other family members the tendency to deny one's desires for the benefit of others. She sees this attitude as a part of the maternal role, and while she resents it at times, she is committed to the self-sacrificing role as part of her life pattern. She says, "I'd like to dance, but I can't because I have to teach young girls the right things." As we have already seen, subordination of her own preferences to those of the family extends to the recreational activities of the group. This is not as she would like it, but she is ready to sacrifice her own preference if there is any suggestion that her own wishes are selfish or insufficiently maternal.

The elements of the Clark family ideology are closely related to three themes: the critical significance of a stable, predictable pattern of family activities, achievable only with the aid of a competent maternal figure and conformity on the part of children; the efficacy of self-effacing service in social interaction; and reliance upon an external, superior source for a code of behavior. In such a context the desire for autonomy is itself a threat. Strength is displayed by a demonstration that one "has the courage of his convictions." The convictions that this family has embraced assume the inferiority of the individual in relation to other members of the society. Sacrificing a measure of autonomy in exchange for group approval is, of course, a classical model of the socialization process. In this family, however, the price is excessive; sacrifice is extended beyond social necessity by inner fears of a situational vulnerability that no longer exists. To the Clarks the price does not seem to be high; they have achieved the rewards of social and economic stability toward which the two parents have aspired. In view of their early lives, they feel that their achievements are substantial compensation. The Clarks, like most other families of the research group, have developed patterns of behavior that tend to bring into congruence the images they have of the family and what they would like it to be. The ways in which they attempt to create and maintain consensus, while satisfying both individual needs and group demands, and the resulting patterns of interaction provide additional dimensions through which we can view their family world.

THE REGULATION OF SOCIAL BEHAVIOR

The limits of behavior for the Clark family members are defined by two distinct standards—the family ideology and the content of a moral code derived from formal religious beliefs. These ideologies complement each other and serve the family's common psychological needs.

The use of moral imperatives in controlling behavior is one of the central and significant features of the family. All the members are persuaded that the constraints they exercise upon themselves, or that are imposed upon them, are for their own benefit or for the benefit of the group. The controlling authorities, both parental and divine, are invested with a protective benevolence. The children illustrate this attitude by these comments:

INTERVIEWER: *What's your family like?*

JIM: *They're nice. They take care of me real good. They give me whatever I want, if they can.*

Lucy makes a more pointed comment:

INTERVIEWER: *How about your parents, do they measure up to your ideal?*

LUCY: *I think they're excellent. They give me just anything I want that they think I should have.*

These remarks echo the parents' religious conviction that life has been ordered by a superior design or authority and that it is in the best interests of the individual to follow this pattern.

The notion of benevolent control justifies harsh enforcement measures and strict conformity. Henry and Thelma Clark are firm in their enforcement of parental discipline, and they have succeeded in internalizing their standards in the children. They have no gross complaints to make about Jim's and Lucy's behavior. They are not problem children, and the minor deviations which crop up from time to time are not regarded as particularly troublesome by Mr. and Mrs. Clark. Mrs. Clark describes her impressions of the disciplinary process:

Everything has to be more thoroughly discussed with Jim. Lucy doesn't ask why; she just does what I say with no comment.

INTERVIEWER: *What kinds of things do the child do that you disapprove of?*

MRS. CLARK: *Any kind of back talk. I don't let it pass if I can correct it. I don't have any trouble with Lucy, but I do with Jim.*

THE CLARKS

Lucy takes correction and orders with no comment. Also, I don't approve either of them sitting in on adult talk. Lucy is worse than Jim in that. I don't like either one of them to correct adults —even if it's a small thing. Lucy is inclined to do that. Big things —big mistakes—we encourage them to point out, but small ones we don't like them to tell us about. Lucy is slow. I don't know what to do about it; it's very irritating.

INTERVIEWER: What do you do when they talk back?

MRS. CLARK: Well, I ask them why. Then give them another chance. If it happens again, I punish them in some way. I explain about how ugly tempers are. I think talking back is temper.

INTERVIEWER: Do they ever fight?

MRS. CLARK: No, they fuss, but they don't fight. If it's over something, I take it away. It's usually over food—desserts or something they really like. If it's over TV I turn it off.

INTERVIEWER: What do you do when they don't come home on time?

MRS. CLARK: She doesn't go anywhere for a week. If it's my son I go out looking for him. He never knows what time it is.

INTERVIEWER: What type of punishment do you use?

MRS. CLARK: According to their age. My daughter is too old to spank, so I take things away from her. Putting my son to bed is the worst punishment. I sometimes spank him. Putting him to bed works better, but sometimes I've spanked him before I think of that. Spanking is partly to let off steam.

For Mrs. Clark, and for her husband to some extent, talking back, lying, and verbal criticism of adults are all expressions of impulse indulgence on the part of children. They suggest a non-conformity of intellect—inner reservations and resources of autonomy. Thus they collide with the feeling that both parents share—inhibition of experimentation, adventure, and autonomy are absolutely essential for the maintenance of a stable, secure way of life.

Thelma Clark reports that she rarely loses her temper but suggests that her control has not always been as effective as it now is. She mentions an incident three years ago as an illustration of the "last time" she lost control over aggressive expression. In this incident it was Mr. Clark, rather than the children, who was the object of her outburst.

Mrs. Clark's efforts are directed toward keeping a home that is clean, orderly, and presentable to the outside world, both physically and emotionally. Her attempt to avoid disciplining the children in front of visitors indicates her desire to maintain a respectable front for the eyes of the world. This is not to suggest that she holds a double standard; her own norms for acceptable behavior are quite strict, but she prefers to keep disciplinary tensions and open conflict within the family circle.

While Mrs. Clark insists upon obedience, she attempts to provide her children with reasonable explanations for the punishments and restrictions that are imposed upon them. These rationalizations have had the desired effect—the children feel that the parents are exercising discipline for the good of the child. This way of justifying discipline disguises the exploitation of the generational differential in the regulatory process. The Clarks do not make a pretense at family democracy. The parents do show respect for the subordinate members of the family group, but they do not claim that every family member has equal voice in family affairs. Acceptance of a status hierarchy within the family parallels acceptance of the adults' subordinate relationship to a superior Being, with consequent dependency and obedience to a superordinate ideological system.

Mr. Clark is content with a secondary role within the family group. While he makes decisions affecting finance and some family activities such as weekend excursions and church participation, he is glad to leave the problems of family management and socialization in Mrs. Clark's hands: ". . . she's a good homemaker and mother. Except for me it's a fine family. There's not too much to be said for me. I'm not here enough. I leave a lot to her." In response to a question about his participation in household duties, he says:

Not too much. Occasionally I wash the dishes. I'm not a household man.

INTERVIEWER: *Do you fix things around the house?*

MR. CLARK: *Not too much. If it's bad enough, I call the landlord.*

Mr. Clark lends little firmness to the disciplinary tone of the family. He attempts to maintain a show of authority, but his underlying preference is for a home in which he is not called upon to assist in maintaining order, particularly in interpersonal frictions. Though he leaves most of the routine socialization to his wife, Mr. Clark has strong reactions to misbehavior that occurs when he is present. In fact, the children report that he is head of the house when he is home. His manner of dealing out punishment is harsher than his wife's and more impulsive.

INTERVIEWER: *What kinds of things do the children do that you don't like?*

MR. CLARK: *It's something they don't do. They don't brush their teeth often enough.*

INTERVIEWER: *What things make you mad?*

MR. CLARK: *Things that really make me angry—that I shouldn't do.*

INTERVIEWER: *But do you?*

MR. CLARK: *Yes, of course. When I feel like spanking them on the spur of the moment just because I'm mad, I shouldn't do that. They're not mean, really. My girl is poky—that makes me mad, but she comes by it honestly. I'm like that. He hasn't developed too many bad habits but is more inclined to answer back.*

INTERVIEWER: *What do you do about it?*

MR. CLARK: *I usually spank him. We don't do too much about Lucy being slow. I've encouraged Mrs. Clark to give her something to do every day to get her moving, but she doesn't do it.*

INTERVIEWER: *What would you do if they fought between themselves?*

Mr. Clark: *I'd slap them. I don't mind Lucy slapping Jim, but I don't like men to slap women. I want Jim to grow up with the idea that a woman is a lady even if she isn't. With other children I'd like them to stand on their own feet. I think they have to take care of their own scraps.*

Interviewer: *Do you ever lose your temper?*

Mr. Clark: *Not to the extreme.*

Interviewer: *How do you act?*

Mr. Clark: *Well, when my boy called me a liar, I slapped him real quick. But I don't get into a rage or go into a two-week sulk.*

Henry Clark is not altogether satisfied with his exercise of authority within the family group. He insists on obedience from the children and cannot tolerate impertinence or open rebellion. However, he is aware that his disciplinary behavior is sometimes harsh and selfish. "Fathers sometimes / treat families badly," he says on the Sentence Completion form.[4] He feels that he has suffered from lack of strict, close supervision and control as a child, and he is determined that his children shall not experience a similar disadvantage. His admiration of Mrs. Clark is rooted, in part, in her ability to discipline the children effectively, and he attempts to assist her in presenting a consistent disciplinary front to Lucy and Jim.

His awareness that he sometimes uses discipline as a means to express his own irritability is illustrated by this exchange with the interviewer:

Interviewer: *Do you get angry more at home or at work?*

Mr. Clark: *Possibly more at home.*

Interviewer: *Why?*

Mr. Clark: *You have more right to become angry at home. At home you expect people to overlook it. In business you might make other people angry and they wouldn't forget it.*

[4] The Sentence Completion form (SCT) used in gathering data for the project is reproduced on p. 298.

This attitude points up one of the internal discontents that characterize Henry Clark's expression of authority and paternal role. To him, home is a place of refuge from the standards and stringencies of the outside world, a place that also permits relaxation of internal standards without threatening withdrawal of protection and affection. He would often like to avoid the necessity for applying discipline to his children—not through distaste for the disciplinary act but through a desire to abdicate his responsibility in favor of dependency upon the family for gratification of his own needs. His discipline becomes at times an expression of irritation over events at home that force him to assume a dominant fatherly role when he is not in the mood for it. Thelma Clark complains that he leaves her to make the decisions about the home. His sense of surrender to her is indicated when he says of the children: "I would like them to be strong-willed like Mrs. Clark." These comments show his wish for a home that is not managed by him, but one in which his place is assured. His desire for a home that is well managed by a competent wife and mother is one expression of his ambivalence about independence and assertiveness. His reponses to two TAT cards are further indications of his concern about dependency and self-assertion:[5]

CARD 2: *Can't figure it. Well, this fellow's mother over there is watching him plow. It looks like the girl is on her way home from school, and this neighbor boy, she would like him to notice her, and probably he will after his mother goes away. She doesn't want him to go fooling around with any of the girls. And after he gets off from work he will go and see her, and it looks good. I think he will probably marry her and have a farm of his own. That country life appeals to me anyway.*

CARD 6BM: *Oh, brother! You know this is a boy and his mother, and he is the last of the lot, and love has come into his life at last. Mother thought the son would never leave her, as some mothers do, and the son came home with the news one*

[5] See p. 297 for a description of the cards used in this phase of the data collection.

night that he had found a girl and was serious about it, too. Nice-looking fellow . . . nice boy . . . nice mother, and she had this boy to herself for several years and learned to enjoy it, and if he gets married, what is she going to do? And she is thinking about it, and she thinks about her life and how she had to live without his father, and now she will have to live without him. This boy knows that she will be hurt and is sorry for her. And she's made up her mind that whatever will make him happy, that's what she wants, and she is consenting to him following, whatever course he thinks is best. And do you know what happened? They had three children, who brought joy into the old lady's life, and they adored their grandmother. So the normal course of events is about the best way.

Several similar elements emerge from these two responses. The image of women in both stories is of dominant, protective, controlling figures. The male's problem in each instance is to achieve a satisfying degree of freedom from maternal control. However, he is uneasy about the reaction that such efforts might create in himself and so attempts to disguise his motives. Unable to acknowledge his own fear of assertion, he portrays the mother as the clinging member of the pair.

Mr. Clark's internal conflict between his desire for protection and his desire for self-reliance is more apparent in his feeling about himself and his attitudes toward the children than it is in his relation to Mrs. Clark. With his wife he has resolved his conflict by placing her in a maternal role with respect to himself as well as the children. She is at once the symbol of his independence from his own mother and an expression of maternal control. However, he has engaged his children in his ambivalence. He worries that his children may be too ambitious and hopes that they will not set their goals very high in terms of material achievements; thus he projects onto them his own fear of self-assertion. Nevertheless, he expects them to achieve in school and to display responsibility and self-control in the home. He wants them to be strong-willed, like Mrs. Clark, but he imposes upon them the constraints of his religious beliefs in a manner that thwarts self-expression and self-interest. His own reliance on conscience and religious institutions appears in some way as a substitute for a father on whom he could not depend. Conformity to a moral code also relieves the guilt he feels over his desire for autonomy and the discomfort he feels over some of his unconscious impulses. He has a sense of frustration in not reaching goals for which he must at one time have wished. In the interview he expresses a desire for a red and black Mercury car, but at other times he rationalizes his sense of failure by depreciating material gains. At the same time he is thinking of improving the effect he makes upon others, by making public speeches and gaining public acclaim. These fantasies of self-assertion serve him as a substitute; he tells us that work (the realistic assertive mode for males) tires and depresses him. Ultimately, he places the conflict in the background; he manages his feelings of deprivation by striving for moral values, being the "good man," and by a sense of worthlessness that checks his feeling of guilt.

Mr. Clark's attitudes toward autonomy and control apply differentially to his children. He holds distinct standards of conduct for Jim and Lucy, as his comment about Jim's slapping Lucy reveals. His attitudes toward his own mother are not sufficiently differentiated from those toward his own daughter to permit rational disciplining of the two children in certain areas of behavior. Lucy has a special place by virtue of the fact that she is a female; Mr. Clark permits himself to transform his feeling about women into unequal discipline toward his two children.

It is on this point that Mr. and Mrs. Clark have their sharpest divergency over control and disciplinary techniques applied to the children.

INTERVIEWER: *What disagreements do you and Mrs. Clark have over handling the children?*

MR. CLARK: *When she gets tired and worn out, they're my children. When I do spank Jim I'm too hard on him, and I never touch the girl. We don't have many disagreements because she's pretty reasonable about the way she treats them.*

This excerpt illustrates his reliance upon his wife for controlling the children and his disappointment and irritation when she attempts to transfer the responsibility for discipline to him. It reveals also his awareness of greater severity with Jim than with Lucy. Mrs. Clark's comments show that she also recognizes this tendency in her husband:

INTERVIEWER: *Have you and your husband had differences of opinion as to how the children should be treated?*

MRS. CLARK: *Just over my son. I'll take explanation from my son quicker than he will. It's usually over eating. "Eat up your vegetables," and that sort of thing. I know what he had for lunch and whether he is hungry or not. Mr. Clark believes the plate should be cleared.*

INTERVIEWER: *Anything else?*

MRS. CLARK: *TV on Sunday. I don't see any harm in it. He does. In that he's stricter than me. Otherwise we're about the same.*

Mr. Clark's tendency toward inflexibility in discipline and adherence to rules is curious in view of his desire to permit Mrs. Clark to manage the home and discipline the children. He relinquishes his disciplinary and decision-making authority; yet he is more strict and more severe than his wife in demanding conformity to regulation and in reprimanding the children for misbehavior. He is dimly aware that his harsh approach, especially to Jim, creates resentment and division in the family. However, he seems not to understand himself the sources of his autocratic outbursts; they lead him to depreciate his competence as a father. When asked to compare himself to the ideal father, he says, "If he was about six feet, I'd be one foot."

It seems likely that Mr. Clark's insistence upon conformity to rules for their own sake is an expression of his lack of confidence in himself as a parent. He believes that he had inadequate supervision as a child and is determined that such loose control shall not be permitted in his own home. However, the affect underlying his disciplinary manner suggests a strong component of rivalry with his children, especially Jim, and the exploitation of discipline as a way to put the child in his place. To a degree, Mr. Clark competes with them for Mrs. Clark's attention and care, and he uses his status position to maintain his advantage. Thus his disciplinary approach combines several elements: feelings of competition with his children, a wish to drive them along rigorous paths that he missed as a child, his image of the superior position of females in the household, and his own anxiety over wishes for autonomy.

The children are not unaffected by the complex mixture of emotions that are blended into parental discipline. Both children attempt to offer an accepting, pleasant report of disciplinary practice in the home. Lucy carries this effort off better than Jim, possibly because she has less to complain about.

INTERVIEWER: *What do you do that your parents disapprove of?*

LUCY: *Nothing that I can think of.*

INTERVIEWER: *Nothing that makes them mad?*

LUCY: *I can't think of anything. Well, they don't like the dog to jump on me, and he does. They don't like to hear me say "yeah."*

INTERVIEWER: *How do you know when your parents are mad?*

LUCY: *Sometimes Mother hollers if we're doing something she doesn't like. Father is calm. He just talks to us. He don't get real mad at us.*

INTERVIEWER: *Who is head of the house?*

LUCY: *Father is. Mother is when he's not here, but when he's here, he is. . . . Father is stricter. He don't like for us to watch TV on Sundays.*

INTERVIEWER: *Who makes the decisions in the family?*

LUCY: *I think Mother and Father talk it over and usually agree.*

INTERVIEWER: *If there were a difference of opinion, who would win?*

LUCY: *I don't know exactly. They might each do what they*

wanted to do. If it was buying a car, father would do it. They'd compromise. There's never been a disagreement like that.

The ideal, happy, reasonable family scene pictured by Lucy, with only the dog and an occasional grammatical lapse marring the harmony, also appears in her fantasy material. In that, however, expressions indicative of inner tension and conflict are apparent though essentially consistent with her overt behavior. She is aware of some hostile feelings, but expression of hostility toward her parents is almost nil; when it does occur, it is very tentative. All hostile situations are ended by an abrupt reversal, usually implying repression of the hostile affect. She recognizes quarrels in two TAT stories, but in both instances one person is arbitrarily convinced and conforms to the wishes of the other. Lucy is generally conforming in her TAT responses. Especially in relation to her mother and to mother figures—like teachers—she is anxious about getting recognition and a positive response. This feeling provides much of the motivation for conformity and for behavior which she believes will please others. Her impulses toward autonomy and rebelliousness are forsaken in favor of continued dependency.

To a degree Lucy feels that parents do not sufficiently understand their children and that punishment may be arbitrary or unjust. Hostility and punishment from adults is somewhat unpredictable, and one must be constantly looking for ways to meet the threat or appease the authority. In Card 2 of the TAT series she sees the older woman as unreasonably hostile:

... this school girl walks by, and this farmer's wife don't like her much, and she starts saying things that aren't very nice, and the girl don't say nothing but keeps on walking, and she gets to thinking that when she grows up she is not going to be like that woman is.

The story continues on this theme and ends with the aggression unresolved.

The strictness and harshness of her father's discipline appear to be related to her response to Card 4.

Well, this couple, they have one child, and sometimes they don't agree on the same things. Now he thinks their child has done something wrong, and she is trying to stop him. So she tells him why she doesn't think he has done wrong, and he tells her why he thinks the child has done something wrong, and she tries to persuade him not to punish the child, and it ends up when he finds out that she is right.

To Lucy the relation between punishment and behavior is not generally predictable; adults mean well, perhaps, but they do not understand children and may mistreat them. There is a diffuse sense of guilt and vulnerability underlying her stance toward adults. Her replies to the instruments are often defensive—arguing that she is misunderstood, that she does not deserve the guilt of her conscience or the disapproval of her parents. Some of her Sentence Completion comments deal specifically with her feeling that parents are not sufficiently understanding and are too strict; in view of this circumstance, conformity is the safest route to interpersonal harmony:

My father / understands.
My mother / understands.
Children / have to be understood.
Children would be better off if their parents / could under-stand them better.
Fathers sometimes / are strict.
Mothers sometimes / are too stern.
To get along with people / I try to act right.

Lucy has attempted to resolve her doubts about the benevolence of authority and the uncertainty of harmony by becoming involved in religious ideology and by conformity at home. These goals she translates into explicit behavior, indicated by her description of an ideal twelve-year-old girl:

Keeps herself neat. I try to do that. Obey her parents—not do anything that they wouldn't like and not do things because she thinks they've been unfair, and be nice to her little brother, and have good manners, and try to be a little lady.

INTERVIEWER: *How do you think you measure up?*

LUCY: *I try just as best I can to measure up. I sometimes have bad manners and things, but I try real hard.*

Jim has not been able to achieve for himself the degree of inner resolution or outer harmony that his sister exhibits. While he openly expresses his need to appease others and win favor by showing co-operative behavior and by attempting to buy positive response with gifts, he has not been successful in repressing his resentment over his father's tendency to punish him more easily and harshly than Lucy.

INTERVIEWER: *What things do you do that your parents disapprove of?*

JIM: *Well, mess the house up, and if I get out in the car they don't like for me to jump around in it.*

INTERVIEWER: *How do you know when they're mad?*

JIM: *They usually tell me not to do it again, and they act kind of mad. They kinda holler at me, and when they walk away they walk like they're mad.*

INTERVIEWER: *Who gets mad at you most?*

JIM: *My mother, because my father is never here very much.*

Jim expresses directly his chagrin that Lucy "gets away with everything."

INTERVIEWER: How come?

JIM: *Well, if she hollers they tell her not to do it again, but they whip me.*

INTERVIEWER: *Is that because you're younger?*

JIM: *Yes. Maybe they think I should learn because I get older.*

INTERVIEWER: *Who whips you?*

JIM: *I get whipped more by my mother.*

His responses to the Sentence Completion Test offer evidence that Jim sees his father as the more feared of his parents and looks to his mother for protection. Whether correctly or not, he sees himself as providing an important issue of conflict between his parents. His underlying feelings over punishment which he regards as unjust arouse considerable anxiety and guilt. Like his sister, he attempts to assuage his guilt by conformity "To make people like me / I try to act nice"), but the rewards for compliance are more frequently self-protective than gratifying.

Jim's compliance is a response to a generalized fear of threat and catastrophe as well as to specific concern about his position in the family. His fantasies in the TAT are recurrently taken up not only with death but with the dissolution of the family, generally in the absence of the father. Tragedy comes frequently to children in his stories, especially when they display autonomous or impulsive behavior. It is this uncertainty about his position in the family and in the world that acts to constrain his impulses and prevent behavior which his parents disapprove.

Jim is, in a sense, the victim of a complex of circumstances whose net effect is to restrict his development as an assertive male. Considerable data indicate that Mr. and Mrs. Clark are not sympathetic toward assertive masculinity. Both feel that they suffered from fathers who wandered, following their own bent. Further, it seems likely that Mrs. Clark holds her husband partly responsible for her exchanging adolescent irresponsibility for early parenthood, even though at the time she felt that her marriage helped her escape from the conflict relationship with her mother and stepfather. Finally, we note repeatedly how Mr. Clark demeans himself and his own masculinity. He wants his children to grow up to have the strength of his wife, not of himself. Jim, seeking to identify with his father, is confronted by a man who tells him in effect that he does not wish to serve as a model for his boy.

The nature of social control that appears in the Clark family is thus a transformation of the uncertainties and threats of affective dissolution that characterized both parents' early childhood. They have struggled hard and effectively to defend themselves against their own recollection of emotional disaster and to protect their children from the trauma that they knew so intimately. In doing this, they have conveyed, perhaps unconsciously, some of their own fear and diffuse anxiety to the children. For the children this anxiety is comparatively unrealistic and may be less adaptive than it was for Mr. and Mrs. Clark. As with the parents, the conformity generated by this diffuse concern affords provisional emotional security at the expense of spontaneity.

In few of the families of the research group did we see a family so tightly and explicitly related to the institutions of the community. In a significant sense the family leadership has been deposited in the church and its ideology, and the family has become subordinate to it. To Mr. Clark religious affiliation is a family characteristic of great significance: "I think our church life is the most important thing to all of us." We have already seen how entwined are the religious values with the children's stated ideals and career plans. The mutual reinforcement of family and sacred requirements is remarkable. The church has helped the Clarks establish and maintain a way of life that meets their image to a satisfying degree; they in turn contribute loyalty, money, and effort to the church. In one sense, Mr. Clark provides leadership for the family by pointing it toward the church and by exemplifying as well as insisting upon the subordinate relationship for the family that he has adopted for himself.

Since neither parent was reared in a stable two-parent home, both were without the advantage of parental example for the conduct of a family and home. The change which they have insisted upon in their own family has been greatly assisted by the clear statement of rules which the church offers. These religious expectations, reaching into the particulars of daily living, have defined many aspects of life for the Clarks and have given them confidence and a realization of welldoing which they would otherwise have lacked. However, the family's reliance upon the church for ethical and behavioral standards does not detract from Mr. and Mrs. Clark's effectiveness in applying these principles to themselves and the children. By overt behavioral standards they have done well.

The conventionality of social behavior evident in the Clark family was not easily achieved. Emotional deprivation complicated the process of establishing and maintaining a stable family life. Although these effects have not precipitated obvious or open family crises, they have to a degree directed or limited the interactional patterns both within the family and between the family members and community institutions. The family's contemporary stability has left unresolved certain psychosocial issues that arose as residuals of childhood relationships to the family and through the family to the broader social group. We may understand the Clarks more completely if we examine both the dominant family issues and their relationship to Mr. and Mrs. Clark's psychodynamics.

Much of the emotional structure of the Clark family can be understood if considered as an underlying theme of conflict around growing up and becoming an adult. Adulthood, with its implications of antonomy and initiative, is felt to be impossible of attainment and threatening if attained. Autonomy and initiative are fraught with fearful consequences, resulting in injury to someone else or to oneself. Thus Mr. Clark wants his boy to "not try to be too ambitious" and to "control his temper and be a fellow all people like." However, he accuses himself of lack of ambition, claims that success is limited only by ambition, and he says he would aspire to be a professional man if he had an opportunity to live his life again. Lucy's response to Card 6BM offers another illustration:

Well, this is a boy and his mother, and he is coming to tell her that he is going away and going to see if he can find him a job, but his mother don't want him to because she thinks that he might get in trouble there in the city, and she tries to persuade him to stay. But he is sort of stubborn, and she is looking out the window as if she is seeking help from looking out in the clouds like. Well, she keeps arguing with him and trying to get him to stay, but he leaves anyway. And in a couple of hours, she has been crying because he has left, and he walks in and tells her that when he got down to the bus he got to thinking about what she said, so he decided it would be best to come back.

The conflict between a desire to leave, to assume self-direction, and fear of the possible consequences of initiative is prominent in Lucy's story. The desire for autonomy is strong but threatening; a great deal of psychic energy goes into restraining and inhibiting efforts. Jim, too, offers dramatic evidence of his fear of autonomy in his TAT responses, where the open exercise of initiative frequently ends in disaster. Card C is an example:

Well, this family they were sitting around, and the older boy came in and said he had a problem, and they asked him what was the problem, and he said all the other boys were going somewhere, and he asked if he could go, and they said he could. So he went, but they didn't know he was going to take the car, and they heard there was a wreck on the highway, and five boys was in it, and he found out that one of the boys was his, and that was the one that was driving the car.

In response to a concern over autonomy wishes, the family has developed an emotional climate in which there is concerted effort to hold oneself in, to refrain from attempting too much, and the family becomes an elaborate system for limiting aspiration. This in turn brings despair of ever coming into one's own. Lavish fantasies of "showing the world" are employed to counter this conviction of ultimate despair. Mr. Clark would have been a lawyer "if I had known then what I know now," and Mrs. Clark often thinks of herself as a model and dreams of what life might have been if she had not married so young. The family emphasis upon moral correctness, and a firm religious conviction in the eventual triumph of personal virtue, is not unrelated to these compensatory fantasies.

Allied to the fear of autonomy is a recurrent effort to become disencumbered of responsibility. This wish leads to a search for someone who can take responsibility and provide protection. In actual behavior, this wish also promotes a determined effort to assume and adequately exercise responsibility in denial of the wish for help. The search for protection follows many paths but leads most repeatedly to an attempt to find a mother who will protect and offer care. The surrender of autonomy is offered as a price, but the price is felt to be paid in vain, because deep doubts remain and no one is convinced that dependable protection is forthcoming. Mrs. Clark is relatively stronger than other family members but has difficulty in her attempts to give warmth, comfort, or protection; she is no more eager than the others to accept responsibility in the affective functions of the family. The children turn to their father from time to time. Although he offers temporary satisfaction, he is unable to meet the more basic problem because of his role and because he, too, is looking for a protector and is unable to conceive of himself as having strength to offer others. Mr. Clark's comments about his wife and about himself illustrate the degree to which he sees her as the central figure of the group:

My wife is an outstanding person in many ways. Compared to other wives she's way up on top. She's a good homemaker and mother. Except for me it's a fine family.

INTERVIEWER: *Why do you say, "Except for me"?*

MR. CLARK: *There's not too much to be said for me. I'm not here enough. I leave a lot to her. . . . If he [the ideal father] was six feet I'd be one foot. I don't spend enough time talking to them about the important things in life. I don't have the patience to explain things as we go along. Possibly I don't provide as well as I could.*

Henry Clark's comments speak of his self-image, but their basic point is the definition of his own place in the family vis-à-vis his wife. To exert himself and assume a more dominant role would change the relationship between them in a direction not to his liking. By assigning himself a subordinate position in the family, he leaves the major responsibilities to his wife and simultaneously neutralizes his anxiety over his own hostile feelings. His saying that he is unworthy is best interpreted as a reversal of his feeling that he really merits more gratification than he received in childhood.

Jim's response to TAT Card 3BM reveals his concern about the constancy of maternal care. His view of the mother parallels his father's emotional position:

Looks like he's crying. Looks like his mother has whipped him and he's crying in his bedroom, and he went outside and started to play, and when he came back in his mother is gone, and he thought she had left him, and so he went to his dad's office and told him that his mother had gone, and they both came home and she was there and she said she had just gone to the store. And she said when she found he was gone she had gone looking for him, and they all got together that night, and all of a sudden it started to rain, and after that they went out and made up for their troubles and had a good time.

Disappointment at the failure to find dependable protection is always close to awareness. Mrs. Clark deals with her early disappointment by attempting openly and consciously to compensate to her children for the lack of love and care that she associates with her own childhood. She also confesses to the interviewer crying fits and feelings of loneliness. "Most people don't know that I / am lonely," she says on the SCT. Achievement in her maternal role is one of her defenses against the pain of feeling lonely.

The apprehension of violence and threat that appears in the fantasy material is another indication of the intense desire for protection. Emotional violence or physical catastrophe appears as a threat in over half of the two children's TAT responses. These apperceptions are related to the sense of guilt that characterizes this family. They feel themselves to be endlessly struggling with temptations posed by impulsivity, which is defined as evil. The parents' responses to TAT Card 7BM provide an illustration of this feeling. Mr. Clark says:

Old Albert Einstein. An old man and a young man. That old man is giving the young man some advice. He came in and asked him for it. It's just a matter of business, and there's a question in the young man's eyes as to whether it is honest. This is a merchant, a Jew, and he and the young man have become friends, and he sees a chance to make a fast buck if he can forget the things the old man has told him about integrity. He can make a lot of dough. And he has come to the man to talk him out of the honest urge, and he is trying to sell the old man on this ideal of dishonesty. And the old man goes back on his own experience and tells him that he could have done the same thing fifty years ago and could have made a lot of money if he had been willing to say something that wasn't quite true, and he goes on to tell the boy that the thing he has found to be worth more than money is to be able to stand up and look everyone straight in the eye and know that you haven't cheated anyone. This boy still longed for the money, but he made up his mind that possibly the very thing he admired most about the old man was that thing he had been trying to make him give up. So he remains honest.

This story indicates the need for a father figure to help stabilize personality and behavior, to provide standards of conduct and thought. These standards at the same time offer a rationalization for lack of success and a view of the world as a place where the virtuous man is at a disadvantage. The relation of this response to Mr. Clark's own experience is clear. Of particular relevance here is the tendency to see moral disintegration as the alternative to the presence or availability of a source of wisdom, guidance, and control.

Viewing the same picture, Mrs. Clark says:

Well, let's say they are cooking up something that is not very honest. They might be whispering about it, and the younger man is trying to put over a deal with the older man in their business, and maybe the younger man is trying to get the older man to be a little less honest in his work, maybe to make a little more money. And the older man looks like a kind man and maybe trying to set the young man on the right way, and he will talk to the young man and will persuade him to go on the right way and make a greater decision.

The similarity of the responses offered by Mr. and Mrs. Clark is obvious. Like her husband's, Mrs. Clark's story presents a theme emphasizing dependence upon external control for moral behavior. Both parents see the younger man as wanting to be dishonest and the older as offering friendly moral assistance. The parents appear to share the feeling that people assist one another in part to help fortify against impulses toward antisocial behavior. This attitude forms a part of parent-child relationships in the Clark family and appears, for example, in Mrs. Clark's comments that she would like to dance but ". . . I can't, because I have to teach young girls the right things."

The children's fantasy responses deal often with wishes or behavior that they fear will be unacceptable to parental figures. Even the desire for autonomy arouses feelings of anxiety and guilt, as if the wish for autonomy were itself a cardinal psychological sin. There is an additional element of vague and uncertain guilt which the children are not yet able to relate adequately to the code of behavior which their parents present to them.

Lucy's response to TAT Card 4 (p. 53) indicates her feeling, which is shared to a degree by other family members, that moral standards are external demands and that they depend upon the judgment of a person or group rather than upon an impersonal or absolute code. In this story, as well as others, there is apprehension that one's actions may eventually be punished or that they will result in disharmony within the family group.

Jim, too, has incorporated much into the framework of bad things which he feels he should control. His SCT responses reveal his fear of wrongdoing and his attempt to conform in an effort to avoid guilt.

> I am sorry when I / do something I shouldn't do.
> What gets me into trouble is / when I do something bad.
> I don't like the sort of kids who / play games with knives.
> If I had my way / I would do the things that are right.
> If they tell me I shouldn't I / won't do it.
> To make people like me / I try to act nice.

Like other family members, Jim carries a sense of being under the scrutiny of omnipresent observers who might pass moral judgment on behavior and thoughts. The family members wish they were pure enough to have nothing to hide, but they constantly fear exposure. The children attempt to alleviate guilt by conformity and a show of acceptable, virtuous behavior. There is little possibility for negotiation with their own parents, however, since they share the feelings of guilt and are unable to provide for the children the forgiveness and assurance they seek.

Significant for the control system of the family is a sharp contrast in the evaluation of males and females. Females (not femininity) are idealized, accentuated, and regarded as having extraordinary prerogatives; males are devalued. They see themselves as having to gratify females; the females see males as limiting their rightful self-indulgence.

Mr. Clark's image of women is perhaps the key to the family attitudes toward females. Apparently he considered his mother a controlling influence and felt keenly the need for her presence to make this control effective for himself. ("She wasn't there to give us much supervision; during the day we ran wild.") Her absence and lack of attention are in part responsible for his feelings of ambivalence toward her and toward women in general. On the one hand, he has extreme respect for women, putting them on a pedestal and thinking of them as far superior to men: "Compared to men, women are / wonderful." His contrasting description of his and his wife's competence in the parental roles illustrates this feeling vividly. On the other hand, he complains about the possessiveness and irritability of females and has some doubt about their ability to manage problems. His expectations are that women have some sort of perfection. He does not complain openly about his mother but accepts his childhood situation as the result of unfortunate circumstances for which she was not to blame. His response to TAT Card 4 reveals his feelings about both males and females and about the nature of heterosexual interaction:

I can't tell exactly what that fellow's thinking about. Can't tell whether she's trying to restrain him or hug him. He looks as if he might be angry at somebody, and he's afraid he might go and get into a fight. Somebody came along and insulted this girl, and her boy friend got mad and is going to go and sock somebody in the nose. She don't think it worthwhile and she's holding him back, and he's going to stop and think it over. I don't think he will sock him; it isn't anything much anyway. She takes him in and feeds him and he's all right.

Mr. Clark's comments in the interview amplify the theme of Card 4. Both carry the appearance of a desire and attempt to protect females. However, it is the female in the TAT story that is the more sensible and more able to control situations and relationships. The ultimate psychological objective of the story is achieved when the female becomes the nurturing maternal figure and protects and feeds the male.

We have already seen Jim's responses, which are indicative of a similar wish for protection and reveal his anxiety over whether maternal love and care will be consistently forthcoming. In a sense, the responses of Jim and his father, though similar, are not comparable because of the great difference in age, status, and role between the two. However, Jim appears to be evolving an image of females as favored, as obtaining protection from punishment which is not extended to him, and as the source of comfort and love.

Jim feels at a disadvantage with his sister; perhaps more significant, he sees his father as offering gifts only to the women in the family. In another context in the interview, Jim recalls some of the things he and his father do together: "Usually we look at books and think of the things we might get—something for my mother, something like that."

The tendency to depreciate men appears in Mrs. Clark's SCT and TAT. This is a completely understandable stance in view of her father's desertion of the family and the circumstances associated with it. Mrs. Clark offers these SCT responses on the topic of sex role differentiation:

Most women / are nice.
Most men / drink.
Mothers sometimes / cry.
Fathers sometimes / are helpless.
Compared to men, women are / wonderful.
When Father comes home / he does nothing.

Mrs. Clark's TAT stories add substance to the image. In her response to Card 2 the male is ignored; all interaction takes place between the two females. Mrs. Clark's image of the female as relatively more competent and possessed of superior personal characteristics frequently takes the form of specific criticism of her husband ("I think sometimes he could do better [on the job]"). She is displeased with Mr. Clark because he has started smoking again: "I don't like the smell. I think it's unclean." In spite of the fact that she complains about her husband's absences from the home and criticizes him for not spending more time with the children, she describes Mr. Clark's absence during the war with the comment: ". . . with no man around the house it was easier—my mother-in-law helped." This was during her second pregnancy, when she was in bed most of the time.

Mrs. Clark sees men as obstacles to self-gratification. They cannot always be persuaded or manipulated; sometimes one must simply put up with them. In part, her constellation of attitudes springs from her own deep wish to be a sufficient mother, as compensation for her own sense of loss and as protection for her children's emotional development. She would like her husband to join more actively in this reconstruction effort. However, he draws upon her resources, as do the children, and she has inadequate supply.

Lucy's image of males and females contrasts with those of the other family members. She expresses admiration for both her father and mother and selects characteristics of each with which to identify. She says that she doesn't like her father to smoke, then adds, "but I think he's entitled to that." She also speaks of her father as having "patience and understanding." Her SCT responses offer typical attitudes:

> When things go wrong, Mother / or Father usually straightens it out.
> My mother / understands.
> Most women / do not smoke.
> Most men / are good.
> When Father comes home / we have a good time.
> Compared to women, men are / good.
> Compared to men, women are / good.

Lucy's desire for conformity and her repression of hostile impulses and critical comments account in part for the favorable terms with which she portrays both her parents. However, her TAT responses include situations of negotiation between adults of opposite sex in which each is persuaded and influenced, in turn, by the other.

The critical emotional and interactional issues in the Clark family, while they possess a continuity with the adults' early experiences, have an autonomy of their own in the family's emotional organization. Although these issues are not consciously recognized or openly faced, they have become a part of the total pattern of family living and interpersonal communication.

AFFECTIONAL INTERACTION: THE TRAGEDY OF
PSYCHOLOGICAL DEFICIT

The attempt to construct normal, stable, and satisfactory family interaction upon immature and emotionally underprivileged psychological foundations can probably never be completely successful. This is the hazard of the Clarks' efforts toward emotional and social mobility. That is not to suggest that such efforts are pointless. The emotional dissatisfactions that characterize the Clarks' family life would still be present if no attempt had been made toward reconstruction. Indeed, the gratifications that derive from the degree of stability and normalcy that the family has achieved enable them to live in reasonable comfort with echoes of their past.

It is in affectional interaction within the family that the consequences of the past become most readily apparent. The Clark family is well cared for, well run, thoroughly socialized, and actively participating in community affairs, but it is a family characterized by a low degree of emotional warmth and affection. This is not, however, a consequence of unusually ambivalent or hostile feelings among family members, nor does it indicate a major interactional flaw of the group, in the sense that the group is divided and lacking in co-operative efforts. Many of the internal strains spring from a lack of affectionate resources and poorly developed interpersonal skills.

The Clarks are concerned with finding some way to gain a sense of connectedness. But closeness is difficult, and the family is not hopeful of achieving the feeling of unity that they desire. Other aspects of normal family life are obviously theirs, but family warmth and unity are not so easily emulated. The Clarks recognize the external signs of family unity in the homes around them and strive to duplicate these behaviors, but underlying their efforts is an awareness that the warmth they see in other families is missing in their own. Like the need for protection, chronic emotional insatiability has become a lifelong problem.

The family members make deeply motivated and repeated efforts to approach each other. However, these attempts occur within the context of the dominant family issues. Wishes to relate more closely to one another typically become transformed into attempts to establish symbiotic relationships or to obtain narcissistic gratification. Thus the interpersonal emotional approach is so charged with family and personal issues that it becomes subservient to alien purposes rather than an experience in itself. Jim speaks of his interaction with his father by recalling that the two of them look at books and think of things they might buy for Mrs. Clark. This is the model for emotional interaction in this family. Two family members are drawn together by a similar dependent relationship to the mother, interacting with each other not in terms of contact between two personalities but in terms of a common fear of isolation, seeking to find a technique for communication not with each other so much as with the third and absent party, and relying upon gifts as a substitute for emotional interaction.

Both Mr. and Mrs. Clark are essentially withdrawn people, with a sense of isolation from others. Their own affect is limited, and neither has much capacity for empathy. Also, Mrs. Clark is readily antagonistic in the sense that she tends to structure interpersonal encounters as a conflict of wills. She frequently makes comments about wanting to help others, especially her children, but these take on specific significance in the following TAT responses:

CARD 7GF: *Well, let's say the little girl's doll was hurt, and she was very concerned about taking care of it the right way, and so she asked the help of her mother, and the mother, being kind, got the doctor book down and told her how to take care of the doll. And the doll wasn't too badly hurt and got well.*

CARD 9GF: *Well, by the looks of the picture I would say the girl running has done something that in her own mind hasn't been very nice, and the girl watching her has seen what she has done, and she doesn't want this girl to see her at this very time, but she looks like the sort of person that will go to her later and tell her that she has done wrong and will help her in every way she can. . . .*

Mrs. Clark's desire to help others is a conscious, highly valued motive that she cultivates in her children. She does not recognize the underlying tone of moralistic control (evident in the above stories) that frequently characterizes her attempts to be helpful. Her determination to give her family a normal life and to be a competent mother has a coercive quality that acts to substitute specific behavioral demands for mutual respect and tender feeling. She bakes every day in order "to please the family," but she complains that her life is dull and routine. She believes that a good mother is not too strict and that a child should be persuaded with reasonable arguments, but she is proud that Lucy "doesn't ask why, she just does what I say with no comment." This is not to deny Mrs. Clark's habitual care and concern for her family. She sees clearly the need for a firm, reliable, nurturing woman in the home and would rather make sacrifices of her personal preferences than violate this image of herself, but she feels that to a degree family stability is achieved at her expense.

In the Clark family, mother-son and father-daughter alignments are apparent. Mr. Clark concedes that his punishment of his son is harsher than that of his daughter; Mrs. Clark has more patience with her son than with her daughter. The children's comments confirm this pairing. Lucy, in revealing a preference for her father, reports that she confides in him rather than in Mrs. Clark, that she likes to go on local family outings (which Mrs. Clark dislikes), and that she likes to think she has her father's features: "I always say I look like Father, but once I saw a picture of Mother at fourteen. It was just like me, so I guess I look like her." The following comments about her parents are perhaps the most informative of her feelings for them.

INTERVIEWER: *What about each person in the family do you like best?*

LUCY: *I like it that Mother can make out with what she's got. She's a good cook, too. I just like everything about her, not any certain thing. I like everything about Father. . . . I'd like to be able to cook and keep house as good as Mother. I'd like to be like Father in things we do at church and have as much patience and understanding. . . . Father understands more than Mother. I think Mother is just as good at understanding some things, though.*

And in another context she talks of her father and his work in these terms: "I like it just fine. He's been in it for a long time. I always said I'd be in it too, if I could. Whatever he likes I like. I always said I'd go and work for Daddy some day."

Although Jim would like more love from his mother, he sees

her as offering a source of protection that is not supplied by Mr. Clark. Jim seems to feel that his mother expects him to spend time with his father while she is with Lucy. In this situation he turns to his father but is frequently disappointed. Jim's fantasies are recurrently taken up with a twofold theme: the absence of the father for long periods of time and exposure to physical danger or a dissolution of the family while he is away. The father's presence thus serves as a protection, but it does not fulfil Jim's deep wish for closer contact with both parents. His fear that family ties are tenuous is a profound source of anxiety.

In her relationship to her children Mrs. Clark shows a preference for Jim. The boy is like her, she says, in such things as clothes habits and taste for music. In the dialogue that follows her enthusiasm for her son is evident:

INTERVIEWER: *In what ways are they different from you and their father and from each other?*

MRS. CLARK: *I don't know if I can answer. I think Lucy is more serious about everything in life than Jim. Sometimes I think she's too serious for her age. I worry about that. I don't think they look alike. They both have blue eyes.*

INTERVIEWER: *In what ways is Lucy different from you?*

MRS. CLARK: *She likes to read and study; I don't.*

INTERVIEWER: *How about her father?*

MRS. CLARK: *I guess she likes to go places and she likes sports and he doesn't. I guess she's more like me really, in the things she likes to do.*

INTERVIEWER: *In what ways would you like them to be like you and their father?*

MRS. CLARK: *I'd like Lucy to be a good mother and housekeeper when she gets married, if she does, like me. I'd like her to be honest and sincere like her dad.*

INTERVIEWER: *How about your son?*

MRS. CLARK: *Being as he has so much life, it's nice to have him around. I'd like him to be like me in that. My husband and me have different ideas. He doesn't know how to have a good* time. I'd like Jim to stick to a job like my husband does. . . . I think Lucy is like her father and Jim takes more after me. Maybe it's inherited.

Mrs. Clark's response to her husband is perhaps best described as bland. She recognizes the importance of a father to the family but has not as clear an image of his role as she has of the constellation of maternal activities that she attempts to maintain. Overtones of resentment creep into her comments about him—objections to his working hours, his smoking, his lack of ambition and of interest in the home. He performs his parental role with considerably less competence, in her eyes, than she does.

INTERVIEWER: How do you think you measure up to your ideal of a good mother?

MRS. CLARK: Anybody would have to say not so well, but I think I do all right. I do put my children first. I'll do without when there are things they want. I fall down in not knowing how to sew. That's important when you have a girl, but I'm always here when they need me.

INTERVIEWER: How do you think your husband measures up in terms of your ideal?

MRS. CLARK: I don't think my husband spends enough time with the children. Sometimes two or three days go by without his seeing them. I think he's more interested in church and work than the house.

In general, however, her criticism is modified by the fact that her feelings and affect are not characteristically intense. She tends to withdraw from both positive and negative intimate interaction with all members of the family. Still, it is clear that she feels that Mr. Clark's interaction with the family and his emotional commitment to her are not his central interests. Although he takes only a secondary role in the activities of the home, she needs his attention and interest to confirm her own identity.

The world that the Clarks have fashioned for themselves is founded upon stern inner constraint of affect and upon a network of formal regulations and deliberate role performances. This family leans upon the evidence that overt behavior and observable testimony provide. A sense of basic mistrust of the future, as well as of the past, demands continual validation by concrete display of allegiance to the family image of normalcy, stability, and security. Affective expression is a mode of interaction that the parents failed to learn well in early family experience; their psychic adaptation to emotional deprivation makes more difficult the relatively late attempt to learn new expressive techniques.

Neither Jim nor Lucy has learned to accept and express affective components of family interaction. They are shadowed by a vague anxiety about possible threats to security; unlike their parents, they know only the shadow, not the substance, of life circumstances that justify such apprehension. It is thus the more difficult to manage. The uneasiness of the two Clark children is less related to external and obvious reality than was that of their parents. The changes that the Clarks have effected were accomplished to deal with fear of deprivation, but the disquiet remains as an inner state concealed by the routinely stable life of an "ordinary" American family.

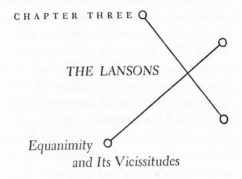

CHAPTER THREE

THE LANSONS

Equanimity
and Its Vicissitudes

Being in the Lanson home for a short time, one gains a feeling that here life is tranquil and subdued. No forceful sounds are to be heard, no visible assertions arrest the eye. Care and containment are suggested in the plastic coverings on the conventional furniture. People speak quietly in this house, with an evenness of tone that extends into the physical surroundings. Walls, carpet, and furnishings are in pale neutral shades. In talking, the Lansons maintain a steady posture, shifting placidly, gesturing minimally. The modest but new five-room house is, in almost all respects, a suitable setting for family life as the Lansons believe it should be: harmonious, quiescent, and unspectacular. For such a life few paraphernalia are necessary, and few are immediately in evidence. The visitor in the living room sees no books, pictures, or magazines—only yesterday's newspapers. The absence of cultural artifacts does not reflect lack of intelligence. Neither, in this family, is it a sign of lack of interest in the house itself or in its embellishment; when the Lansons moved into this house five years ago, as soon as the builder completed it, they were realizing a long-cherished dream for a home of their own.

Mr. Lanson and his daughters enjoy working in the garden, Mr. Lanson often staying there until ten o'clock in the evening. Something of his feeling about the house is also apparent in his enjoyment of doing the decorating himself. The Lansons' dedication to a home of their own as the only right setting for family life has not diminished, and their pride of ownership has not abated. The absence of articles must be understood, then, in another context. In this family there is little room for whimsy, stray impulsivity, or careless disposal. Nor may one encroach on a space that belongs to all. Shaping of taste into a distinctive form that bespeaks individuality and privacy of experience does not occur among the Lansons, and the display of idiosyncrasy is not an acceptable form of expression. Only those actions and experiences which openly and evidently subserve the good of all are suitable for all to see. Activity may not spill out undirected; although the Lansons have a good time, sprawling is not part of it. Consideration for others requires that one not intrude oneself forcibly into their awareness and so shatter the calm that prevails. Donald Lanson, his wife, and his two daughters all feel this way, and they like their house to show how they feel.

THE FAMILY MEMBERS

This house, with its small, tidy front lawn, was the destination of an unassuming yet clearly conceived journey. The Lansons are both of English ancestry, but their families have been in this country for three or four generations. Donald Lanson, forty-four years old at the time of this writing, was born in a small midwestern rural community where his father owned a feed and farm implement store. The family was in comfortable circumstances financially. His father had only a grammar school education, but his mother attended a teachers' college and subsequently taught school. Both parents not only were devoted churchgoers but were also active in a variety of church organizations.

Donald completed high school in the town of his birth and then went on to obtain a Bachelor's degree from a midwestern state university, where he took a general liberal arts course. An only child, he recalls his family as close, though he is uncertain whether he was closer to his mother or his father. He inclines to think that he was closer to his mother, and we may note that he also began his work career as a teacher. Though remaining in teaching for several years, he was dissatisfied with it and went to work for a business firm when the opportunity presented itself. He has progressed to become head of the purchasing department of a chemical products company. Until recently he also was assistant editor of the purchasing agents' trade journal, writing some articles of his own, rewriting some submitted by others. He does not seem to have regarded this as an outlet for self-expression or as an opportunity for prestige or influence, for he tells us that he took on this extra work "partly for the contacts I could make and partly for the money, which was very useful before I got my last promotion." The side job is no longer necessary, and so he has given it up.

In his career Donald Lanson is now contented. "I am in the work I enjoy. I have found myself and am very satisfied." He does not regard the interlude in teaching as having been a false step during a period of self-exploration. It was, rather, a sober necessity. "I taught because I was in need of a job when I graduated. I always wanted to be in business." Thus, an objective clearly in mind since youth has been attained. In his career there is no place else he wants to go. He has attained status-complacency.

But it is not only in his work that Donald Lanson has arrived at his destination. The sense of being where he wants to be, the feeling that now in middle life there is nothing of great importance to want is true of his home life as well. "I think both my wife and children are ideal. I wouldn't change them in any way even if I could." He is content to have his children live as he has lived. "I want my children to / have a happy normal life and homes of their own as happy as ours has been." Caring for and improving his home is one of his favorite activities. "I like to do things around the house with tools. . . . I enjoy painting and decorating and gardening." He is also a man who proceeds with care in whatever he does. As he characterizes himself:

I perhaps am very methodical about how I do things. I am very systematic. My wife works faster, maybe accomplishes more in a given length of time. I think possibly the children are like their mother in that and different from me. They don't figure out what's the reason for the thing they're doing.

The orderliness of his life is apparent in his response to the interviewer's question about whom he goes to when he has a problem.

My wife and I would talk it over if it were a personal family problem. If work, I would go to the president of the company. If it were a personal problem that we couldn't solve, I'd probably go to our minister. If it were financial, we'd probably go to friends. We have no family secrets.

Mary Lanson, with a few minor variations, has traversed a route that is a close counterpart of her husband's. Her background, too, is rural; she and her sister, who is four years older, were born in a small town not far from her husband's birthplace in a neighboring state. Both of her parents were high school graduates, and both were devoted church members who tried to apply the teachings of the church in their everyday lives. Her father was a salesman who provided comfortably for his family until his death when Mary was preadolescent, shortly after the family had moved to Chicago. Financial circumstances were strained thereafter.

Mary completed high school and then took further training in a commercial institute. After working for nine years for an old established company in various clerical and secretarial capacities, she met and married Donald Lanson. She continued to work until her first pregnancy. During this time they lived with Mrs. Lanson's widowed mother, but when Angela was seven and Alice four, the family moved into the house they now occupy. The quiet pride Mrs. Lanson feels about this is evident as she volunteers that her older sister, also married, is still living at home, i.e., with her mother. "She has never had her own home. She has three children, older than mine." When, in another context, Mrs. Lanson observes that "my sister was always more domineering than I," we sense that she has some feeling of having been more successful than her sister and that she has in this fashion righted some childhood wrongs.

It would be erroneous, however, to conclude that Mary Lanson gloats as though having carried out a successful coup, for neither in her tone of voice nor in her manner nor in the train of her own associations is a competitive spirit indicated. Nothing could be farther from her mind than the notion of besting another or taking comfort from someone else's lesser fortune. Mary and her sister are on very close terms.

They come here all the time. We go back and forth a lot, more than once a week. The relationships are very close. The whole lot of us seem like just one big family. My sister and her husband and Donald and I go out together a lot while the kids stay with my mother.

For Mrs. Lanson, outstripping her sister contributes at most a secondary meaning to this house. Primarily it is significant as a physical and symbolic representation of an attained goal. Like her husband, she feels that now, at forty-three, she is at her destination, and the future can bring only anticlimax. As she herself puts it, "We don't have too many high ambitions. We're satisfied with what we have." Most satisfying of all is her family. "I looked forward to having a family for so long I'm thoroughly enjoying them now before they grow up and leave us."

Although her family is her paramount interest, Mary Lanson enters into a few outside activities, and she does so with forcefulness. She is second vice-president of the PTA and president of the women's league in the community church which the family faithfully attends every Sunday. The family are also members of an organization of their extended kin called the Cousins Club, and Mary and her husband are members of a bridge club which meets irregularly and a dancing club which meets in a hall once a month. But when asked what she most enjoys, these activities clearly take second place.

I'm happy to have what I have now—a husband and children. I just like to be where they are and doing what they're doing. . . . We hardly ever go to a movie except all together. . . . We do most everything together.

Angela and Alice are both tall girls, in this trait resembling their parents. Angela, twelve years old, is already five feet, seven inches, and her nine-year-old sister has passed five feet. The girls are clearly of this family in other ways as well. In demeanor they are placid and soft-spoken. Their greeting to a visitor is courteous, and they have proceeded well beyond the rudimentary skills of a hostess. They were pleased to co-operate with the interviewer, and, unlike the majority of children studied, they sat still throughout. In further contrast to other children studied, when the interviewer was seeing one or another parent, the children's play in another part of the house was scarcely audible, and they did not enter the room to interrupt. Moderation and consideration are the way of life in this family, and both girls are full participants in it.

When Angela is asked what a good twelve-year-old is like, she answers:

She should be courteous and know how to act when meeting strangers. She shouldn't be greedy at teas and parties, like when she was younger. She'd know how to dress appropriately for what was going on whether she was working or going out. I think she should be able to enter into things but not be too noisy and greedy so that everybody would be talking about her.

And when the interviewer inquires how well Angela feels she measures up, she replies, "I try to dress appropriately and try to be courteous and not greedy. I try to be like that." She reveals no sense of strain or protest. What she should be is right, and she is congruent with what she should be. Of her parents she says, "I don't think I'd want them different in any way." She, too, is where she wants to be.

There are no rebels and no black sheep in the Lanson family. This family and this life are Alice's choices, just as they are the choices of her parents and sister. The interviewer's opening question is, "What is your family like?" To this, nine-year-old Alice replies:

I think it's nice. They all treat me well and everything. Some people have more money and aren't as happy as we are. I don't think I'd want very many changes at all.

An hour and a quarter later the interviewer presents her concluding question: "Are there any ways you'd like to be different?" If the interview has aroused any anxieties or uncertainties, they are not apparent at this point, and Alice remains steadfast in her answer:

No, I think I'd be just the way I am. I wouldn't like to be rich. If I were, I'd probably be spoiled, and I'm happy just the way I am. I think work prepares you for when you get older and get married, and that's good. So I really wouldn't want to be different.

All the members of this family give voice to their sense of the rightness of their lives and their satisfaction with the family as an expression of personal fulfilment. Expressions of satisfaction, however, are the end products of a series of antecedent events and circumstances. In attempting to understand the workings of a particular family, we obviously cannot stop with the observation that all are happy here. We want to understand more fully what kind of life a family's members are content with and how that contentment is attained. Having seen the Lansons as they appear in public, to themselves and to an observer, we turn to a more detailed scrutiny of their involvement with each other.

THE QUALITY OF PREFERRED EXPERIENCE

As we have suggested in chapter i, it is useful to look for those central, pervasive tendencies in a family's life that can serve as an over-all characterization, enabling us to say in broad terms what kind of family it is. It pays us to inquire into the family's basic stance toward the world and their experiencing of it. For most families of our study we find that there is a quality of preferred experience which the family seeks. They want to experience life in a certain way. Families put differing investments of energy into this effort. Some strive with single-mindedness to fashion all their activities, relationships, ideas, and feelings into forms that will be consonant with preferred experience, and they are concerned to exclude whatever is not congruent.

Above all else, the Lansons seek to maintain and preserve equilibrium in their lives. They are, in fact, comfortable only when there is an ongoing sense of harmony and when there is a sense that everything is in proper balance. Circumstances are appraised according to whether they promote equilibrium or disrupt it, and people are evaluated as co-operative or not. In a multitude of contexts the quest for equanimity is renewed and reaffirmed. As Mrs. Lanson puts it, the greatest satisfactions from family life are "to have things run along smoothly and with happy expressions on everyone's face." Freedom from strain and disjunction is for her the touchstone of the good life. If we contrast this with another woman's response, it is apparent that Mrs. Lanson's feeling is not simply the vague generality that anyone might offer to such a question but a clear emotional choice which guides many more specific choices. Another woman in our study group expressed what are for her the main satisfactions from family life in these terms:

Loving and being loved—by people you admire and respect. The understanding and sympathy you have with children and a husband, and the affectionate gestures they make. Like at Easter the two of them put together all the money they had and bought me a big box of candy. I was really touched. It's a real bounce when you get something like that. . . . Having people close to you who care and who you care about makes the world so warm and satisfactory.

The concentration of affect in the "bounce" that this woman describes is unwelcome to Mrs. Lanson. For her a less intense and less fluctuating level of pleasant feeling is a more satisfactory state of affairs. Insofar as possible, the more homogeneous the stream of experience, the better. Accent, difference, peak, and trough—these are incompatible with her view of stability. But the choice of a tensionless world is not without its grayer overtones, and afterthoughts of discontent cannot be banished. As she puts it in two of her sentence completions: "The weakest part of me / lack courage in experiments. I often think of myself as / too meek and dull."

While Mrs. Lanson is perhaps the most explicit exponent of smoothness and equanimity, the other members of her family share her feelings. It is probably not accidental that she is the most articulate in this area, because she has experienced more painfully than the others the lack of evenness which all value together. During both of her pregnancies she was constantly nauseated. "They tried everything on me and nothing worked. Our chiropractor told us that it could be adjusted and it isn't necessary to be so ill. But I didn't know." For her first delivery, "I went to the hospital not expecting to bring home a baby at all." In speaking of the illnesses which members of the family have had, she reports:

I have had nothing except the children's diseases and an appendectomy. I have had two nervous breakdowns, one after my father died when I was about ten. Then I had a spell right after I graduated from high school. Since then I've learned to control my nerves. I have neuritis at times.

Contributions to this achievement come from the other family members because they too maintain an equable tone. In Mrs. Lanson's own words, her children are dependable. And she married a man who was retiring in manner and has mellowed with the years. As she puts it, "I have no fault to find with my husband. He has grown more confident and sociable since we have been married. He's even-tempered and a real family man." Donald Lanson also thinks that part of his own merit in others' eyes is due to his equanimity. "What people like most about me is / my even disposition."

If equanimity is a principal point of emotional reference for the Lansons, how, then, do they conduct their lives so as to remain within hailing distance of it? Wishing things to go smoothly is a definitive cast of feeling, a commitment of emotional energy to a range of experience that excludes other ranges. There are paths that lead in a desired direction and paths that lead astray. A family, like an individual personality, attempts to organize the release of energy in ways that are compatible with how they want the world to feel and that are also, at some level of generality, consistent with one another. In the admission of impressions to the self, in expressive manifestation, in the construction of activity, tendencies to patterning are to be found, and these can be grouped together in the concept of life style. In the following sections we turn to some of the ways in which the Lansons fashion a life together.

SELF AND FAMILY: THE SYMBOLIC DIALECT

Which path is sanctioned right and which leads astray is dramatized within the Lanson family in a pair of antithetical symbols that recur in the interviews. We have found that many families make use of key terms to express a large area of striving or conflict. The symbols a family selects serve as guides to its major areas of concern. For the Lansons, the way to equanimity lies through *co-operation* and the threat to stability arises from *selfishness*. For them, the good of the family is central; every act must be tested against this standard, and whatever cannot be construed as a positive contribution to the family is unacceptable. This canon is actually applied far more broadly than to acts of selfishness, so that almost any act in which an individual member claims a private gratification is frowned upon. The centrality of the family is clearly set forth by Mr. Lanson in answer to the question, "What are the important things about your family?"

We have always agreed that we should try to live within our means at any time. We have never gone into debt heavily to have things we wanted, except for the purchase of this home, for which we did take out a mortgage. I think that we are con-

siderate of each other. We have all tried to consider the feelings of all other members of our family in any important decision or any policy of behavior.

His greatest avowed fear is "that some unforeseen crisis might break up our family unit prematurely." And, later, in speaking of the qualities necessary for an ideal father and an ideal mother, he proposes:

First of all, to be a good father you have to want and like children; you need an even disposition, an ability to put yourself in the child's place. If you love them and want them, you can make a sincere effort to be a good father. Every father would like to be able to give them the necessities and education and a few refinements.

And a good mother is "the same as my wife, I'd say. Someone who is even-tempered and kind, who knows how to run a house and who is utterly unselfish." If in some ways he sees the mother's role as involving greater self-sacrifice than the father's, it is nonetheless worth noting that the stress on unselfishness distinguishes him from many of the parents we have studied who feel that the greatest necessity for a mother is patience. Patience is a much less extreme call for self-surrender and reflects a more realistic acceptance of the vagaries of human nature.

All the Lansons expect a high degree of merging of the self into the family pool. Not only is sublimation held out as an ideal, illustrated in the father's comments above and in Angela's characterization of a good twelve-year-old, but it is also assumed as a fact. When Angela is asked to describe the important things about her family, she states:

Alice and I don't argue at all. We try to work together co-operatively. When we're working or talking co-operatively we offer our views to each other in a nice way without hollering at each other.

Restraint of self-assertion in all its forms is the practice as well as the precept. There must be no unseemly pleasure in eating, for this is greed. Anger is an individual's naked attack on the structure of co-operation and hence on the well-being of the family. Noisiness is a selfish infringement of proper regard for others.

The demand for sober constraint is also evident in Angela's omission of any reference to play. Instead, she talks of working with her younger sister. Alice, in her own statement of what a good nine-nearly-ten-year-old should be like is more childish, but her picture of appropriate childishness is a description of the classical latency-period girl:

> By the time she's ten I think she should know how to help her mother and be courteous and have good table manners. I don't think she should be rowdy or noisy, and should be a young lady. She should be free to play but not too rough.

In this context we can also recall Alice's statements of satisfaction with her family quoted on page 79. There she speaks of the dangers of being rich, of having too much; it is easier to be happy if one can renounce demands. With parental voice she warns herself of the danger of being spoiled; she would become unacceptable in her own eyes and would lose the feeling of contentment she now has. Curtailment of longings is thus one of the keys to the attainment of self-esteem, which in turn yields the pervasive contentment the Lansons share.

Finally, we can add Mary Lanson's words. An ideal mother should "not be selfish in her own wants all the time. The family should come first. Treat them fairly, not be partial." And in writing of the kind of persons she would like her children to be, she concludes, "I surely hope they will never be selfish and self-centered." The danger of being too demanding is not only in her need to control her own wants but in her projection of this restriction into the outer world when dealing with the wants of others. Fairness and impartiality in gratifying others serves to render the others into external representatives and guarantors of her own self-control. There is no self-admonition here to give to each what he or she particularly needs but rather equal portions of the same to all. Evenness of disposition in the sense of controlling one's temper and one's self-seeking is extended to become a requirement for measure in all dealings. It is important to note, also, that Mrs. Lanson gives no really positive prescriptions for what a mother should do. Her emphasis is on what a mother must not do if she is to fill her role satisfactorily. She must not withhold and she must not give too much; she must take care to restrain and not indulge herself. But there is little implication of actively providing one or another kind of experience. Adequate containment rather than expansion to the greatest possible limits is the implicit aim of child rearing.

To exorcise selfishness requires not only maintaining co-operation but also, for the Lansons, forswearing open conflict. There is, in fact, freedom from avowed conflict. Both parents are emphatic on this point. Concerning disagreements over how the children should be dealt with, Mr. Lanson says, "None. Not even a little one, ever." And his wife echoes, "We have never actually argued in the sixteen years we've been married." Angela is only a little less totalistic: "Not too many. Father sometimes thinks Mother is too fussy about us having jackets on or something. But no real arguments." But Alice's affirmation reasserts the parental emphasis: "They don't do that. They're happy together, and they don't yell at all at each other." Nor do the children fight. Says Mrs. Lanson:

I just haven't allowed it. We find out what they're fussing about and then usually nobody gets it. But they're good. Each gives in to the other some of the time. . . . The children don't push and shove one another.

Not only must every visible sign of conflict be blotted out, but conflict must under no circumstances bring private gratification. Mrs. Lanson comments, "The children share everything. They aren't selfish. We have watched that carefully." Nobody ever is allowed to win a dispute. The family is concerned that no differentiation of status into a victor and a loser shall appear and that no one shall even for a moment experience alienation from the family. There is no bribery—one child given her way and the other offered a consolation prize. The children are expected and largely expect themselves to conduct an entirely self-equilibrating relationship, and the relationship of the spouses is offered as the model which they are to internalize.

It would be quite remarkable if even such assiduous efforts were completely effective. And, indeed, though open conflict is minimal, elements of dissension remain. This is indicated most clearly by Alice, who as the youngest has had the least time to fully acquire the controls demanded by this family. Of her relationship to Angela she comments, "We don't fight, but she doesn't think what I think. She does things I don't like." This statement was in the specific context of a question asking what things her sister did to make her mad; seen in the context of the entire family, it is little more than a ripple in a sea of concord. And Alice's attunement to the niceties of social control can be seen in her comments about her own anger. She avers that she never loses her temper but that she does get mad. Queried for an illustrative occasion, she provides an instance that occurs away from home and that is thoroughly suffused with social sanction:

I don't like poor sports. At school there are a couple of girls who are bad sports. They won't take ends at skipping or get hit out in games, and I don't like that so I get mad. . . . If it's real bad I tell the teacher or say I won't play with them. They aren't like that all the time, and if they see we don't like it they catch on.

The socialization of aggression so that it is harnessed to suprapersonal ends is also manifest in Angela. When she is asked whether she ever loses her temper, she replies, "Well, not exactly, but I get pretty mad when the kids in school push and shove. I'm a monitor, so I holler at them and make them stay in during recess." It is apparent, then, that the children's contribution to family concord is supported in part by their acting-out of aggression in school and on the playground—arenas away from home. But the aggression is not randomly displayed. The impulse is released in an institutionalized context and entirely in the service of positive norms. Even the sibling rivalry is locked into the family co-operative structure. Pressed for another instance of things that make her mad, Angela adds:

Sometimes Mom or Dad ask me to do something and Alice grabs the chance to do it before I get a chance to. There are so many little kids, they're always around over here and they get in the way. I tell them to go away, and after they've gone, I do what I was going to do.

The competition is to see which child will be the most co-operative.

From statements quoted earlier, it will be recalled that no conscious complaints are leveled at this regime or its consequences. All members are in accord that this family and its way of life are not only satisfactory but the best possible. There is no open conflict and no apparent reason for any. One of the principal techniques for attaining this accord is the concerted effort to prevent status differences from arising. As we have just seen, tendencies that lead to a differentiation into victor and vanquished are reversed as soon as they appear and not allowed to develop to conclusion.

Likewise, differences of authority are minimized and even alleged not to exist. Not only does Mr. Lanson say that all members' feelings are taken into account in any important decision, but he further refuses to attribute decisions to any one person or pair of persons. "All of us" make the decisions. "Anything that has to be decided for the children is done by all of us." When he is pressed to describe "who would win" if there were a difference of opinion, he replies, "A fifty-fifty proposition. Sometimes I'd win, sometimes her." Finally, it appears that decisions are a parental prerogative and responsibility, but equally shared between them. Unlike many families we have seen, no division of spheres of authority is acknowledged. And Mrs. Lanson concurs. "Either Father or I, whoever gets the question first. For a while it was always me they asked, but I make them ask Father."

We have here another view of the self-equilibrating process in the family. When there is an imbalance, it is corrected; the differentiated status is de-differentiated and merged in the communal pool of authority. Though the parents are reluctant to acknowledge that most decisions are theirs and that the children cannot share in them, it is clear that the distinction between generations is maintained, though external marks of it are kept as inconspicuous as possible. Both daughters see themselves as full participants in decision making; they are scarcely aware of the inconspicuous indicators. The parental image is, on one level at least, the image which the girls accept as true. Angela says, "We all do really. Everybody says what they think. We all have a fair chance, and we take the majority vote." If there were a difference of opinion, "I don't know. Maybe we'd do something different." In almost identical terms, Alice sees the decision process as democratic: "We all do. We talk about things and do what the most people want." Like her sister, she is at a loss to explain who would decide in the event of difference of opinion: "Gee, I don't know. Father, maybe, but I don't know."

The foregoing material may be viewed from several vantage points, all based on the overriding importance of the family group as a devotional object. It may be that the extent of consensus between the parents is so great that the girls have no image of how differences can be resolved. While it is likely that, in comparison with many other families, this is actually so, it is more likely that what differences do arise between the parents are settled out of range of the children.

Another possibility is that the principle of symmetry and balance which we have seen in a number of contexts governs the settlement of differences either consciously or unconsciously. In this event, one spouse who has influenced a decision previously may in some manner concede the next to the other. This equilibrating process may be sufficiently random—i.e., neither literally one-for-one nor assigned to exclusive spheres—to prevent the development of a stable, crystallized image of resolution.

Yet another possibility is that the girls themselves do not venture opposing opinions about a course of action either because such alternatives do not occur to them or because they are self-suppressed or repressed. Angela and Alice are votaries of the family fully as much as are their parents, and a proposal tinged with individuality is easily stigmatized as selfish. Self-limitation in proposing alternatives is a prominent feature of the equilibrating process, and we must ask how it is possible to reduce conflict to nil and difference in outlook to such infinitesimal proportions.

The answer to the question is, on one level, clear and simple. When Mrs. Lanson is asked to tell what her family is like, she speaks willingly and at some length:

> When the youngsters were young we taught them no meant no, and now we have no arguments. Each has her say, but we have no big disagreements. The children don't push and shove one another. We've brought them up not to. Each gives in to the other some of the time. I love them to have a holiday and have them home. They work along with me. I try to teach them to take care of the home. We work together and play together. Donald had taught school, and I had watched my friends have their children. Donald said they weren't going to be brats. We thought if we corrected more when they were very young, we'd have less to do when they grew older, and it seems to be working out. I only say no when I feel I should, and we have been happy around them.

From the information in this statement we cannot explain why the girls did not become openly hostile and negativistic, an outcome which would seem at least as possible from such training as the course their development did in fact take. But it seems clear that the training has had the functional consequences anticipated by the parents. Both daughters have become highly sensitive in discerning the limits of behavior open to them, having been shown those limits in unmistakable terms when they were young. They now limit themselves.

Behind this statement of training procedure we discern an

implicit aim of child rearing and an implicit image of childhood. The parents feel that the most quickly attained and the most complete self-contol is the best. Childhood is the best preparation for adulthood when the former most nearly approximates the latter. Independence is viewed as the ability to handle for oneself those very tasks which initially others must carry out for one; it does not include the responsibility to construct new possibilities for action or to form judgments at variance with the existing order.

This image of childhood which the parents held at the time they began rearing their children is of immense importance to the structure of interpersonal relations in the family. Since the girls' behavior gives full testimony to the parental image and thereby legitimates it, overt authority and status differences can be minimized. The children need no longer anxiously concern themselves about who is boss and how he will make his authority felt. And, since the children early "learned their place," the parents need now spend little effort confining them to it, and the children do not attempt to alter this set of status arrangements. In a sense, the issue has been settled once and for all, and the children now operate within a framework of trust of their parents, since the questions that arise do not challenge the fundamental order. As Angela declares:

A good mother ought to be like my mother. She's always looking after her family in some way. And Dad is a good father, too. He always thinks of the family. I think they're pretty good. They listen to me and don't start to answer till they've heard all about it. I guess I have good parents.

That the overt status order is not so securely stabilized as to dispel all parental concern is dramatically demonstrated in the following exchange between Mr. Lanson and the interviewer:

INTERVIEWER: *What kinds of things do the children do that you disapprove of?*
MR. LANSON: *Really not too much that I could tell you.*
INTERVIEWER: *Any little things that annoy you?*

MR. LANSON: *Chewing bubble gum loudly.*

INTERVIEWER: *What do you do?*

MR. LANSON: *Ask them to stop.*

INTERVIEWER: *And do they?*

MR. LANSON: *Yes, as a rule.*

INTERVIEWER: *What other things?*

MR. LANSON: *I really can't think of any.*

INTERVIEWER: *Who has most to do with disciplining the children?*

MR. LANSON: *I think that's shared equally. If there's any question, my wife consults me.*

INTERVIEWER: *What method of discipline do you use?*

MR. LANSON: *We have never had to resort to spanking since the youngsters have gotten older. We did when they were smaller. But we believe that you should reason with them and have them understand what we were doing and why.*

INTERVIEWER: *What would you do if they didn't come home on time?*

MR. LANSON: *If they were gone too long we'd deny the privilege of staying out after that, if they didn't phone or have any explanation.*

INTERVIEWER: *What if they got poor marks?*

MR. LANSON: *It might not be the child's fault. If they did their best, nothing would be done. We'd encourage them every way we knew. We'd try to help. If it were simply laziness, it might be necessary to insist on more homework.*

INTERVIEWER: *If they fight?*

MR. LANSON: *They don't fight. If we had boys, I'd teach them to stick up for themselves but try to have them understand that fighting is not the way to settle everything.*

INTERVIEWER: *If they talked back?*

MR. LANSON: *I have strong feelings about that. I wouldn't stand for a sassy child or one who doesn't respect parents and elders. I would take harsh and severe measures for that.*

INTERVIEWER: *If they lost or broke things?*

MR. LANSON: *If it's just normal, nothing much would be said.*

But if often, we'd call it to their attention and have them use more caution, and if that didn't work, maybe make them pay out of their allowance. But only if it happened often.

In dealing with all but one of this catalogue of children's misdemeanors, Mr. Lanson is patient, easygoing, understanding of children's lapses. But, in dramatic contrast, he is dire when confronted with the prospect of assertive rebellion against the established order. The rationality and co-operative inquiry which suffice to govern the system in equilibrium are inadequate to cope with such drastic disequilibrium. The Lanson family system does not allow for renegotiations of status, particularly when these are attempted through outright challenge. Parental status will be safeguarded by a display of power.

Mrs. Lanson, though believing that her basic work with her children was finished early, cannot quite rest secure that this is indeed so.

I enjoy taking the children out because I'm sure they'll behave. Of course, some day I may get a jolt, but I think they're pretty good children. . . . The problem will be after they get older and go out on dates—how fast they'll want to travel. I don't know what to expect, but we've always tried to teach them right and wrong.

She is concerned that the future may dismantle the structure so carefully built and devotedly maintained. After a life in which contingency has been reduced to insignificance, alternatives disallowed, and aspirations forsworn, the ultimate irony for her is not to know what to expect.

Mrs. Lanson's apprehension of the possibilities of waywardness in her children is matched by her dismay at her own loss of control. Asked whether she ever loses her temper, she replies, "Very seldom. But I'm normal." Questioned about instigations to anger, she confesses, "Well, I get nervous every now and then, and then I say cross words. When they get careless about picking up things, if it goes on too much, I get mad." The interviewer then asks how she acts, and Mrs. Lanson reveals, "I lost my temper when I was trying to teach Angela how to keep from telling lies. I spanked her about that, and afterwards I cried." Unless aggression can be completely contained, total collapse threatens. The need for perfect family balance, involving conflict avoidance, minimal interpersonal differentiation, muting of authority, and submergence of self, is an externalization of the effort to maintain inner control. If the need is most urgently experienced by Mrs. Lanson, she only sets a pace that others find it desirable to follow.

In this section we have described in some detail the symbolic dialectic of selfishness and co-operation as it is lived out in the family. The tension of opposition in these symbols reflects the family's tension, which is contained by the particular structure of interpersonal relations they have developed. The basic characteristics of the structure are minimal differentiation of status and authority, and precedence of communal aims over any private or individual gratification. This structure describes the terms on which the members encounter one another. But no structure of interpersonal relations is fixed once and for all. It is maintained through processes which renew it and counteract any tendencies to alteration.

The major processes we have considered are individual self-restraint on the part of all members, so that strong impulses and strong feelings are kept in check; socialization of hostility, so that it is acted out only in the service of communal aims; restriction of conceivable alternatives in action; renunciation of aspiration; and application of the principle of balance in any potentially disjunctive interpersonal encounter, which is always perceived as an incipient imbalance. These processes as we have described them express some of the ways in which the members relate to each other. But the system of relationships is also affected by and involved with aspects of the world which are not personified. These, too, are structured by the human psyche and provide a covert groundwork for action.

Time is an ingredient of all human action. The Lansons make use of it as a major support of the family's life style, and to conserve what they have attained. They strive to relate the present to the past and to the future in a way that is relevant to their conservative aim. For them this means that the family must have stability, and, in turn, this means that it must have continuity and an even tempo. If we consider Mr. and Mrs. Lanson's stories to Card 1 of the TAT, we see something of how they locate themselves in the flow of time:

MR. LANSON: *We have here a picture of a boy who evidently is taking violin lessons and faced with the prospects of practice. Studying his facial expression, it would appear that he would much prefer to be outside playing ball with the boys than spending the time indoors practicing on the violin. . . .*

INTERVIEWER: *Well, then what do you think he will do?*

MR. LANSON: *He probably in the end, uh, he will get around to the practicing perhaps against his own desires . . . possibly with the thought of someday becoming a great violinist. Is that sufficient?*

MRS. LANSON: *Oh, my. This little boy has studied a long time. He's quite a musician and he's tired, but he still wants to keep on. And he's sitting there dreaming and, of others that he's seen play. Is that enough or do you want some more of the story?*

INTERVIEWER: *That's fine, but what do you think would happen to him? You know, an end for the story?*

MRS. LANSON: *Oh well, he keeps trying, and in the end he becomes quite a musician.*

These stories yield material in several areas, but we wish here to confine attention to the time characteristics. Both spouses open their stories by immediately setting the depicted scene in a chain of events that has no ascertainable beginning. This lesson is but a unit in a series that stretches back limitlessly. We can say, then, that the outer world tends to be experienced as continuous and repetitive. Any situation newly encountered is likely to be regarded as a version of something that has been seen before. While the two stories are fairly commonplace, and also differ, they have in common the assumption that this situation is not new. The boy has not just been given a violin he has always wanted, nor is the situation one in which the boy finally terminates the lessons he has always hated. This is a picture of the usual; the boy is placed in a circumstance long familiar and one which in no way departs from what he has always known. (We should note that the circumstance is also one essentially lacking in interpersonal contact.)

The sense of temporal continuity is reinforced by a systematic censorship of the past which modifies its unpleasantness and tailors it to the pattern of acceptable repetitive units. For example, when Mr. Lanson talks of his family of origin, he observes, "It was a close family. It's hard to say whether I was closer to my mother or my father, possibly my mother. It wasn't strict for those times." In this statement we see obliteration of the sharp painful edges of the past, smoothed to fit less obtrusively into the temporal flow. This operation is carried out by withdrawing the affect attaching to the events as experienced, and this, in fact, is what must be done to keep the sense of time homogeneous. The personal color that would highlight one's special attachment to this or that portion of time and mark one's disappointment in another is painted over with a neutral shade that makes time impersonal. Any special claims upon time are relinquished; there are no "good old days," nor will the future return miraculous dividends.

We have only to cite Mrs. Lanson's account of her own childhood home to observe the same process occurring.

I didn't realize it at the time, but I never heard Mother and Father have a fuss. It was a very congenial home. It was fairly strict. We didn't roller skate or things like that on Sundays, but we didn't complain. All homes were like that. No noise on Sundays. It wasn't considered right.

These are familiar events, undoubtedly occurring in many homes of that period. Our purpose here is not to explain the effects of some unusual childhood background but to point out how the past is represented in the present and serves to maintain a way of life now in process. Unresolved leftover feelings are disallowed and rationalized. It is as though they were saying, "Since all homes were strict, my discomfort was nothing, and I have no complaints." The withdrawal of affect from the painful past is observable in Mrs. Lanson's answer to the interviewer's question about the changes that followed upon her father's death: "It was such a blow to Mother, it took quite a while to adjust. We had to learn to think before we spent." She gives no indication of her own feelings here, placing emphasis, instead, on her adaptation by practicing self-restraint in a new area.

The censorship of the past extends to the more recent past, as well. Past annoyances and frictions are quickly forgotten. This is seen in the statements by all members of the family that they have no real faults to find with other members. We are here describing but one possible way of managing the past that is available to normal people. This differs from, for example, the management of the past described for the Clarks, or for business executives who have been socially mobile.[1] These men who have left behind an unsatisfactory past maintain a clear recognition that it was unsatisfactory and do not lose sight of it as a circumscribed period which is now alien to them.

The Lansons do not wish to leave the past behind; they want to carry it with them in the present in a form that is ego syntonic. This involves smoothing the past and simplifying it in other ways so that it is confluent with the present. For example, when asked what the children were like as babies, Mr. Lanson says, "They were different. Each had her own little ways and mannerisms." The interviewer next queries whether he remembers any of them, and the answer is, "No. You'd have to ask their mother." We might interpret this statement as resistance to the inter-

[1] W. Lloyd Warner and James Abegglen, *Big Business Leaders in America* (New York: Harper & Bros., 1955).

viewer; he just didn't feel like trying to remember what the differences were like. But this would also be consistent with the interpretation that the past is simplified. Mr. Lanson was a co-operative informant, so that even if this be regarded as one of the few points of resistance, its selection is consistent with the general framework we have proposed. The interpretation is also consistent with our observation that characteristics which could be used to heighten distinctions among persons and between eras are minimized.

Time functions in yet another way. It is meticulously organized and then articulated with other forms of organization. This fact can be illustrated by considering the fashion in which Mr. Lanson met the interviewer's request to describe a typical day in the family.

We start with the alarm clock in the morning. We prepare for work or school and get breakfast. I'm usually ready for breakfast before they get up. My wife and I have breakfast, and I leave then before the kids have breakfast. The rest of my day is work. The kids are in school till three. They come home for lunch. Mrs. Lanson is busy with duties as wife, mother, housekeeper. When I arrive home from work, we eat. Then the girls do the dishes or help with them. Then we do many different things after dinner. The kids do homework. On Friday or Saturday we go out, so that the kids won't be up too late on weekdays. Mrs. Lanson's mother acts as baby sitter for the children. We try not to impose on her.

Two interlacing principles of order are prominent in this description of a typical day: the explicit location of events in time and in sequence, and the explicitness of tasks. What draws our attention here is the underlying conception of the day as consisting of closely articulated segments joined together by temporal connectives. The only feeling which is introduced is the expression of consideration for Mr. Lanson's mother-in-law. No other sentiment about the day or any of its parts is suggested; one cannot tell if there are any highlights that enliven his day.

It is a sober day, in which each person carries out his duties. The sense of orderliness is notable.

Mr. Lanson tells us nothing of waxing and waning, of energy mobilized and abating, of a period when he tapers off. The principal co-ordinates of his day are time and duty. Relaxation is not easily accommodated to this framework. He says of his work:

I supervise all materials that go into products, also office equipment. There is considerable responsibility. We spend millions every year of the company's money. However, it's varied and a pleasant kind of work so I enjoy it.

His sense of personal worth is enhanced by the significant occupational role that he fills and by the knowledge that he can carry out the high responsibilities it entails. But whatever relaxation he finds in gardening, decorating the house, and visiting with relatives is not sufficient to remove the sense of constraint that girds him. On the SCT he reveals a heartfelt wish: "There are times when I / would like to 'duck' the responsibilities of modern-day living and lead a simpler life." But while his involvement with the outer world is draining, relaxation is a threat. An unconscious concern about giving in to his inward passivity is one of the sources of Mr. Lanson's energy, his steadiness in keeping going. We suggest that among the functions of such a formally structured day for Mr. Lanson is its service as a bulkhead against the pressure of his passive wishes. If he were to let go and depart from structure, it would be not to challenge the tried and true with a new and original form of organization but to sink into disorganization. The fact is that he does not let go. His self-organization and the pattern of life he has constructed are firm, and they serve to keep him steady, upright, and responsible.

Time as a harassing yet also organizing principle appears in Angela's account of a usual day:

We get up and make our bed while Mother and Dad eat. Sometimes we practice the piano. Then I and Alice eat and then practice some more if there's time. At noon we eat and do the dishes if there's time and then go back to school.

The repeated phrase, "if there's time," tells us something of Angela's efforts to learn how to fit into the family's requirement for being orderly with time. She communicates her awareness of the goal, as well as the recognition that she has not yet become proficient in pacing herself as she should.

Mrs. Lanson fills us in on the evening: "About ten, Dad reads the paper. He's busy till then in the garden. I iron and sew and mend. We keep busy." Here is a satisfying program, and yet subtending it is a concern lest any time be empty and unaccounted for. Aimlessness and slack are uncomfortable states. Time demands filling.

Our best informant on the weekend is Angela.

We sleep late, then we get up and make beds, practice, dust, clean up our room. I mow the lawn, clip the shrubs and things. We go out and play. Sundays we go to Sunday school, and Sunday afternoon we read. We don't get real rambunctious on Sunday. Go out for a ride or go visiting; other people visit us.

Alice gives an almost identical account, though in less detail, concluding with, "We don't do anything very rambunctious on Sundays." We seem to have come upon another family symbol of the negative set that includes "selfishness" and "pushing and shoving." Propriety and self-control are reaffirmed. Time is well managed.

Of considerable interest in understanding the Lanson life style is the way it is expressed in vacations. Donald relates:

We haven't had too many. So far we've gone touring—visiting different sections of the country we decided we wanted to see, historical spots for the children's education. We feel that travel is broadening.

Initially, it is somewhat puzzling to explain why Mr. Lanson chooses this kind of vacation rather than a cottage at a resort to which he returns year after year. The same comfortable, familiar, rustic surrounding situated on a small inland lake—say in Michigan, Wisconsin, or Minnesota—would appear to gratify vacation demands for a man of his personality structure.

At this point we must note, however, that his wife has given us a bit of information of which he made no mention. Mrs. Lanson, in her interview, says:

We used to go to our home town or to Mr. Lanson's home town always. Last year we drove through the Black Hills and part of the Rockies. I think from now on we'll try to take the girls somewhere when Donald has his vacation.

We see, then, that there was a time when vacations followed the pattern of a return to the familiar, in fact the most deeply familiar in the archaic, literal sense of the word.

But a significant change has now taken place in the family vacation pattern. In suggesting something of the functions which this pattern serves, we may point out, first, that it entails no involvement with a new human community. It is a vacation in which the Lansons interact with an essentially impersonal environment. Second, in place of the return to the actual past, the old home town, there is substituted a return to the past in a symbolized form—historic sites. Third, this type of vacation allows an experimenting with space, a cautious yet important moving beyond the boundaries which circumscribe everyday life and which Mr. Lanson so frequently symbolizes in spatial terms. He looks for some way to move beyond the circumscribed life space he has constructed, some way to feel that he is not imprisoned by stability. The sense of roaming at will about the country in search of historic sites provides that blend of structure and spontaneity which satisfies both demands of his personality, and it accords with the needs of the other family members. Finally, we note that the vacation is also conceived in terms of its utility: it is a rational measure on behalf of the children and in no sense a free indulgence. It has its place in the family psychosocial order. When Mr. Lanson is asked what he would do if he had more time and money, he proposes, "I'd travel more, first of all become familiar with this country before traveling abroad." His fantasy, too, prepares for a gradual and orderly release from constraint rather than any bursting forth.

Before considering the role of spatial symbolism in more detail, let us complete our account of the temporal order. In citing Mrs. Lanson's reply to the question of what she would like her children to do, we see an essential aspect of how she conceives the future:

Just so they aren't a stewardess. They talk about teaching. I don't know what they'll settle on. They both want to go to college, and we'd like them to go, if they want. If they're going to get married right away, I'd just as soon they worked a bit. I wouldn't force them to do it. I wouldn't like them to be airline stewardesses because of the unsettled kind of life. I want them to be stable.

We have at several points alluded to the dilemma which the construction of a stable equilibrium engenders. The world feels more comfortable—easier to cope with, conducing to equanimity. But a great deal of inner life has to be sacrificed to maintain such a stable psychosocial order, and the Lansons are not oblivious of the cost. Mrs. Lanson feels she is "too meek and dull," criticizing herself for "lacking courage in experiments." Her husband feels that in this style of life perhaps he misses something: "Maybe I'm too meticulous and a stickler for details. I've always been a bit retiring, not aggressive. I'd like the girls to be a little more aggressive, but not obnoxious."

This sense of being held in and the possibilities for release are often symbolized in spatial terms. In Mr. Lanson's TAT story to Card 1, not only are his own wish and the task demand in opposition—a very common story plot—but the opposition is explicitly projected into the world beyond himself and expressed as the difference between "indoors" and "outside." The solution is felt to lie in the manipulation of physical space. His preferred vacation expresses the resolution of the feeling of being unduly contained, and the fantasy of what would be done with more time and money carries this theme further. He proposes two courses; one of these is additional travel, first in this country, then abroad. In addition:

We'd enjoy having a home designed after our own plan and in a location more to our liking, outside Chicago. I'm too much small town to ever be really satisfied living in a city, but maybe a suburb.

All the family members share the wish for a larger home in the suburbs, feeling dissatisfied with their present house because the girls must share a bedroom. This circumstance is certainly a realistic confinement and hardly needs interpretation beyond a notation of the middle class norm that ideally each child should have a room of his own.

If Mr. Lanson is the family leader in formulating spatial solutions to the dilemma of confinement, either because he experiences the dilemma most keenly or because he is most resourceful in constructive fantasy that moves beyond the limitations of the present, the children also express the play between impulse and control in spatial terms. Angela describes her vacation in this way:

We go away for a week or so. We help around the house more and the garden. We clean and wash and iron. We go on weekend trips, and Mom and Alice and I go to the museum or downtown, and sometimes we take Grandma along with us.

Tasks at home alternate with movements to other areas which symbolize freedom for impulses. When she is invited to express her wishes for things she would like to have and do that she cannot at this time, Angela mentions learning to play tennis and to swim well and having a dog, and she adds, "I'd like to have a bedroom of my own. And I'd like to have a fence around the back yard to keep the dogs out."

Alice describes the summer vacation period in similar if more expansive terms:

We do our work in the morning, and we go out and play. It's mostly the same as any other time except no school, and I'm glad of that. We go downtown with our grandmother, and I like that. When Daddy gets a vacation we go on a trip. We've had two trips last year and this year. We went to the Rockies once. Then we take day trips and go to see places we like to see. We just take it easy and do what we feel like doing. If we like a place, we stay there a day or two, and if we don't like it we don't stay at all.

When asked what she likes to do best, she replies:

There's lots of things I like to do. No special thing. I like to go to the movies and play outside at volley ball or go to people's houses. Especially I like to go on trips, that's probably what I like best.

When Alice is asked how she feels about her father's job, she expresses her contentment with it in terms of its being a satisfactory spatial solution: "I think he has a nice job. I think he likes it. He has a nice office and building."

It is abundantly evident that experimentation with the boundaries of space is a highly gratifying activity. Students of child development have long been aware of the psychological significance of locomotion in the very young child. The shifts from the boundaries of the crib world to crawling and from crawling to walking are accompanied by an increase of autonomy and great spurts of exploratory activity, leading to expansion of the experienced world. Climbing, first onto people and furniture, later over fences and up trees, adds another dimension. In all of these types of movement, impulse and control are involved: the wish to negotiate a particular space becomes integrated with the knowledge of capacity to do so and the dangers that must be considered, whether those of gravity or those presented by the parent who declares certain areas foreclosed.

From our analysis of the Lansons, it would appear that the functions of locomotion in later childhood and adulthood may also be similar in kind to those of early childhood, with this difference: with the increasing differentiation of personality, the possible functions of space as an object increase in variety. To suggest this, we have only to cite another man in our study whose idea of a vacation is to drive six hundred miles in a day; space for him is a one-way avenue of flight. By contrast, the Lansons have structured space in such a way that, moving through it, they expand their world without ever leaving their way of life behind, without actually altering the structure of self-constraint in any fundamental way. They steer a middle course: they do not cut loose with a reckless binge in an effort to repudiate their way of life; neither do they remain transfixed in immobility. Their vacation represents a complex blending of many components. The importance they ascribe to remaining together is realized in this annual excursion. The trip is not aimless but has an intellectual function in expanding the range of information and acquaintance with phenomena that lie outside their daily compass. While indulgence for its own sake cannot be sanctioned, it is yet permitted in the form of relaxing the timetable. It might be said that vacation for the Lansons is not an occasion for becoming casual with others but for becoming casual with themselves. Their choice represents, then, continuity with their everyday life, yet provides sufficient contrast to be rewarding.

HARMONY, INTIMACY, AND IDENTITY

The Lansons have fashioned a way of life that we have seen to be outwardly smooth, well structured, and facilitated by a number of processes that renew and reaffirm the paramount sense of harmony. We have seen, too, that though outward harmony is a definitive choice, it is accompanied by a sense of constraint and limitation. The family members are variously aware of this; they recognize that harmony, too, has its costs. Harmonious interpersonal relations require the participants to forbear from some of their individual ends and wishes. What these abandoned aims are determines in part the character of the group life.

That the Lansons place great store in outward evidence of concord is clear from many of their own comments and observations. Though the parents grudgingly concede that all normal people sometimes become angry, they can but regard anger as a threat. In addition, all conflict is subsumed under the rubric of anger, so that it is always seen as disruptive of good relations and never can be viewed as promoting growth. It would be incorrect to say that the family is content with only outward signs; they do seek to safeguard a sense of inward stability, for which unflagging mutual bolstering is conceived as the only possible course. By the adoption of this course, however the conflicts forestalled between members are hedged within individuals, there exerting effects on the form of relatedness they are able to offer one another. In general, the brunt of the inner conflict falls upon the children, Angela and Alice. It is not possible to say that this consequence is inevitable in this type of family organization, but it is the case in this family. In the present section, we shall explore this point in some detail, setting it in the context of the various interpersonal relationships that prevail.

The Lansons are an energetic group; every member of the family has considerable drive in the solution of emotional issues. They do not use energy in spectacular ways, but in steady, sustained effort they persevere. They live neither haphazardly nor indolently; rather, each grapples with the stresses life presents. They often do not meet with easy success, but they do not allow themselves to drift. Though Mrs. Lanson has twice, in childhood and adolescence, been overwhelmed by emotional conflicts she could not master, in adulthood and through the medium of a family she has attained, for a considerable period at least, a viable solution. Her husband, too, has found ways of coping with his conflicts and integrating his solutions into a supporting social structure. Both daughters, hard pressed by the terms of the parental solutions, have not surrendered to despair or confusion or diffuse open aggression but have struggled to find a way to order their experience and assimilate it.

In the relationship between the parents, certain characteristics stand out. The harmony which they sustain between themselves is predicated on maintaining sufficient distance so as not to confront each other with the more demanding or more intense aspects of their inner selves. Donald Lanson is a man who protects himself by not becoming aware of his impulses and feelings and who extends this self-protectiveness by avoiding interaction that does not have a public, standardized quality. He tends to be secretive and noncommittal, to withhold himself and keep distant. He sets up a barrier such that no strong feelings may flow outward from him nor any kind of decisive influence penetrate. As he observes of himself in a sentence completion: "The strongest part of me / is my ability to say 'no' when necessary."

In fact, he is a man who would prefer not to have to say no; this is, so to speak, a second line of defense. He relies upon it only when his reserve is challenged. His predilection for holding himself apart is further expressed in his story to Card 9GF, potentially a stimulus to competitive feelings:

> Apparently one girl is trying to avoid being seen by the other who is evidently running. One girl is trying to hide behind the tree so that she perhaps will not have to meet the other girl and talk to her.
>
> INTERVIEWER: Why would they be in that situation, do you think?
>
> MR. LANSON: It's quite possible that they have been friends at one time; perhaps one has said unkind things about the other. . . . And the girl behind the tree is just trying to avoid the other one to keep from getting into more trouble.

It is consistent with what we have seen of his approach to people that in this story he would identify with the woman hidden behind the tree rather than with the woman running in the open. (His identification with the figure behind the tree is indicated by the fact that he provides a full account of her motives, suggesting thereby that he understands why a person might choose to be in that situation. In contrast, he does not explain why the other woman might be running.) To reveal himself, to expose his feelings—this is a danger, and his preferred solution is to recoil and to shun affective contact. In his reference to "unkind things" between erstwhile friends he seems to be conveying a feeling of having been burned in the past, so that emotional reserve is his guide now. To let well enough alone seems to him the wiser course.

Further insight into his reserve is provided by his story to Card 4:

Apparently the lady in the picture is pleading with the man for some reason or other unbeknownst, uh, unknown to the observer. . . . From the faraway expression on the man's face, it appears as though she might have difficulty in persuading him to give up whatever ideas he has in mind. He seems to be strong-willed enough to want to carry out whatever objective he has in mind, even though it means disagreeing with the woman, possibly his wife, shown in the picture.

INTERVIEWER: What sort of situation might lead them into this kind of activity?

MR. LANSON: Well, it possibly could be the . . . man's desire for drink. The woman's pleading with him not to give in to the situation.

INTERVIEWER: Do you think he would go on and do it anyway?

MR. LANSON: It's quite possible that he would.

In this story the man is represented as not initiating action, not engaged in any active purpose of his own, interacting only in response to outside stimulation—in this case from the woman. Curiously, in the story as distinct from the inquiry, Mr. Lanson insists that the man is firm in his purpose; yet three times he is unable to say what it is ("some reason unknown to the observer," "whatever ideas he has in mind," "whatever objective"). This suggests again how much he keeps his needs and feelings from awareness. In the context of the story, it suggests that a more free and open interaction with a woman carries the implication of submission for him and would represent a temptation to yield to passive inclinations. This seems borne out in the inquiry, which suggests that for Donald Lanson active self-assertion would mean a more insistent reaching for passive comfort ("desire for drink"). From the determined stance he gives the man, we know that Mr. Lanson has long since repressed self-indulgent promptings. The fact that these responses of reserve and withholding appear in his stories to cards depicting interaction with or between females suggests that emotional exchange with his wife will not be extensive, that so long as outward events run a smooth course he will be content. The likelihood that emotional freedom and spontaneity will open the way for passive gratification, which he fears, conduces to emotional restraint.

Avoidance of intimacy in the interest of harmony is not a one-sided affair. Mrs. Lanson, too, keeps a barrier between herself and her husband. Her story to Card 4 suggests how strong her feelings are:

This must be a movie. It looks like one of the moving pictures. Perhaps he has been fighting, trying to protect her in the picture, or perhaps she's trying to hold on to this man when he knows he should be leaving. Thus, several kinds of story flash through your mind when you look at this picture. I have a notion to say that she's holding on to him in a manner in which she shouldn't, and he realizes he must leave and go back to his own family.

INTERVIEWER: *Where do you think this takes place?*

MRS. LANSON: *Well, it must be in, perhaps, her dressing room; maybe she's an actress due to the pictures on the wall. Possibly it is in one of these so-called houses. It could be. But I believe in the end she will lose and he will win. I hope.*

To this card showing a man and a woman, she projects an image of intimacy as evil and illicit. Clearly, she wishes that she could allow herself the pleasure a close relationship might hold ("she's holding on to him"), but the desirable ending for her story is that the man should keep distant. Her feelings are underscored by the fact that she singles out this card as the one she likes least of the TAT series, almost railing at it:

Because I just haven't much consideration for weak people and especially along morals. God gave us will power, and we should use it. He has been weak, and the fact that he was weak to begin with gives me a distaste for the person. I hope that he will pull out of it all right. But the fact that he was easygoing and thought he could do what others do I have no patience with.

The issue raised by this card in her mind elicits such vehement repudiation that she loses distance from the card and treats the characters of her fantasy as though she were dealing with actual people, an indication that the card has touched upon a conflict area of some importance. But in Mrs. Lanson's denunciation of the man's "weakness" there is an element of too much protest, and a glance at her story arouses a suspicion that the female character is in fact felt to be the weaker, strongly tempted to yield to wishes that are against her better judgment. In her resolution of the story, Mrs. Lanson is unable to do more than hope the man will leave of his own accord; her own wish to have him remain is too urgent to allow the female a more decisive stance. The intensity of her own longings for affection is a weakness Mary Lanson feels in herself and which she must keep under control. Actually, she does maintain firm control; even in more disguised fantasy the capricious longings are not given full rein. In response to Card 19, she portrays a simple wonderland which both fascinates and repels her:

This is a fairy tale. It's one of those weird things that come out of a fairy book. The pictures may be sugar or candy land or something of that kind with the bunnies running around and the owls and the kitties, a make-believe story. Little boy or little girl dreaming this as they're sleeping after hearing some of the weird tales. You can tell that I don't like them.

Although establishing a dominion in which unfettered impulse gratification holds sway, Mrs. Lanson dismisses this realm of childlike capering as "weird." The land of sugar and candy is consigned to the same fate as other representations of "selfishness"; it is conquered by morality. We are here perhaps in a position to understand one of the important functions of religion for her. Toward God an adult woman may present herself as acceptably childlike. He will understand how deep a person's longings can be, but in accepting the mandates of the Deity in return for his understanding and forgiveness, she also receives support in resisting temptation.

However, while Mrs. Lanson can accept a provisional child-like status for herself in an other-worldly context, she is manifestly unaccepting of childishness in its mundane locale, whether in herself or in her offspring. She is an earnest woman who demands commensurate purposefulness from her family. In this regard she and her husband are admirably suited to one another, for both feel more comfortable with a relationship founded on compatible earnestness than with one based on expressive intimacy. A relationship in which passion is subdued and all affect muted makes it possible to avoid unwelcome disclosures and leaves both parents free to pursue their tasks with dedication. Mary Lanson tells us on her SCT: "Most people don't know that I / am easily hurt. Most men / are considerate." We are perhaps not amiss in concluding that her husband presents himself to her in a way that is gratifying—careful, considerate, asking little for himself.

Donald Lanson, for his part, is content to realize closeness to his wife through the medium of his children: "Children / make a happy home and bring husband and wife closer to each other." The partnership of parenthood is the form of relatedness to his wife that he finds most satisfying. In this connection we may recall also his story to Card 1 (p. 94), in which he reveals that his need for responsible effort conflicts with his wishes for affiliation with others in a context of play. The story concludes with the suppression of the affiliative wishes in order to carry out the assigned task. He is a man who feels his responsibilities keenly and who construes many of his life situations in terms of meeting his obligations.

The marital bond is based on an avoidance of emotional confrontation and interpersonal engagement. In their place is an exchange of tranquillity. This version of the good life has been transmitted to both daughters, as we have seen in earlier sec-

110

tions. We have also seen how both parents are cognizant of the defects of their virtues. Are the girls merely carbon copies? What place do they as individuals occupy in the family structure? How do they come to terms with the personal definitions offered by their parents?

Angela, over the threshold of puberty, is now having to deal with impulses that do not immediately find their place in a co-operative scheme. They have to be tamed anew. The struggle is difficult, and she has moderate feelings of depression: "There are times when I / wish I were dead. I often think of myself as / a failure." The undertone of sadness is perhaps nowhere more evident than in her story to Card 7GF:

Well, this girl looks like she might have been sort of sick and everything, and her folks had sent her to a, it might have been a farm, where she could run around and get more color in her cheeks and play instead of just sitting inside, and get a lot of sunshine or something like that instead of sitting inside and be in dark rooms where the shades are pulled. She, it looks like this other woman here was trying to read her a story, and she wasn't much interested in it because she wanted to be back in the city or to her home where her other friends were because out here she didn't know any of the girls or boys. And I think eventually she will come to like for some, come to like it out here because this woman might have convinced her it was for her own good and she had a lot of things, and she, to enjoy out here, and she would meet and make the friends and they would be just as nice as the other boys and girls were where she'd come from.

In her contrast of dark rooms and outdoor sunshine Angela tells us, in characteristic spatial imagery, that her life is lacking in the warmth she wants and needs. But it is also a story of vitality and struggle, of striving to cope actively with her problem instead of surrendering to the gloom. And the story has another important structural feature that recurs in five additional stories: a contest between two competing versions of reality, one which arises from her own perceptions and wishes, and one which is presented by an adult in authority. In the instance given, the woman convinces the girl that enjoyment will follow from accepting the woman's advice, and "eventually she comes to like it out here." But in Angela's mind this is not yet the definitive solution, for repeatedly in succeeding stories she raises the issue. Yet in all cases she accepts what is tendered in the name of her own good.

But the story points also to her own conflicting wishes to diminish the tie to home and mother and to cling to it. On the one hand, home and mother are stunting in their effect, and she is kept closed in from the world. On the other, they represent the comfort of what is familiar; on that account the new environment is unsatisfactory, yet not completely rejected. The story concludes with the inclination to try the new surroundings.

Similarly active effort is displayed in story 3BM, where "she might straighten herself out." In 7BM the older man "could be a judge or his father here trying to convince him and clear his mind of what really happened." Her story to Card 19 concludes: ". . . he'll realize that he's only being a more or less a baby or sissy, imagining these things when there's really nothing to be afraid of." The sense of difficulty that pervades her effort is indicated in her sentence completion: "The weakest part of me / is my brain." Perhaps she is here testifying to the formidable task of arriving at a perception of the world that has inner validity in the face of the highly systematic front of rationalization presented by her parents. The impulses she senses arising within her—of hostility, competitiveness, sexuality, dependency—are treated by her parents as nonexistent, because the parental relationship does not allow for testing impulses in interpersonal behavior, nor does it provide even for open verbalization.

Perhaps it is the relative privacy of the sentence completion that allows Angela sufficient openness to observe: "Fathers sometimes / can be a nuisance. Mothers sometimes / ruin their children's plans." When she completes a further sentence with "Nothing makes me madder than / ignorance," her feeling may be directed to the lack of adequate understanding all around—

her parents' and her own. Her own ignorance is frustrating because she feels she must comprehend for herself; what she feels to be her parents' failure to comprehend leaves her no alternative that she sees. She must not let herself be a "baby or sissy." How far she has succeeded is apparent in her projection, "Most people don't know that I / am only twelve and a half years old." She appears to be commenting that her behavior is more mature than might be expected for her age. There seems also a protest here, as though she were saying that she is, after all, still a youngster. It is difficult to be so reasonable, so mature.

This difficulty has another, more particular significance. Angela's notion that her "brain" is "the weakest part of her" not only reflects the parental premium on self-control but especially echoes her father's observation that he is different from the other family members in that "they don't figure out what's the reason for the thing they're doing." Reasonableness and understanding are the basis for relating to her father, but she cannot quite live up to what he seems to expect. In the light of this it is interesting to note her explanation of the person she takes after: "My father. We both like to be outdoors. We both work in the garden and with handicrafts. Mother and Alice are more the quiet type."

This is one of the few occasions in this family when paired alignments between members are indicated, and it suggests something of Angela's wish. Not only does she quickly indicate her interest in being close to her father, but she proposes, in effect, a basis that is easier for her to realize. Common interests of this kind are not, as Angela knows, of comparable significance to her father. In her own mind, the solution of these several facts and aims is that she places her faith in his judiciousness and understanding, accepting perforce the implication that her special claims will not hold, though she will be included as part of the group. And so she says, "He's a good father. He always thinks of the family." Once again we see that more personal and more differentiated aims give way to the good of the family group.

Nonetheless, Angela is the one who least accepts the dissolution of self into merged group. Of all the family members, she exerts pressure against the stable boundaries that define a homogeneous region. We have seen the push of inner force against the rationalizing adults in her TAT story to Card 7GF. And we see it again when she is asked what kinds of things she does that her parents disapprove of:

Father doesn't like me to ride Alice and other kids on the back of my bike. They don't like me to get hot and sweaty in the hot weather. Sometimes I don't want to go to bed just when they want me to, and they disapprove of that.

When the same question is put to Alice, she reflects a struggle that takes place more completely on the parents' ground:

I don't know. Once in a while I do something they don't like. Like not getting my work done right away or not getting it right on time. I really can't think of too many things. They don't get mad at us very often.

Alice stays closer to the shade of parental protection, and we are not surprised to learn that Mrs. Lanson finds her easier to handle than her older sister. "Angela has been moody, but she's getting to be adolescent now." Mrs. Lanson suggests, however, that the difference goes back to infancy.

Alice was premature. She was much easier to handle. I was very worried about her till she got a start. And then when we brought her home, Angela said, "Don't pay any attention to her. I'm your little girl." I nursed Angela for ten months, finally weaned her on chocolate milk. She was very difficult to wean. Alice was only nursed for six weeks. She was so weak she couldn't suck, so we had to pump the milk and feed it in a bottle.

Adolescence appears to be accentuating a difference that has its origin in infancy, and Angela is the source of what impulsivity there is in this family, testing, though tentatively, to see how firm are the limits that have prevailed. So far, Alice remains more conforming in behavior. Whatever inner pressures she feels, consequently, will be handled somewhat differently from her sister's mode, though we have already seen the considerable similarity in their basic psychological stance. We must ask ourselves what significance these differences have, for we can anticipate that they will enter into the structure of interpersonal relationships.

An important element of the structure is made manifest in Alice's answer to the question, "Who do you think you take after, your mother or your father?"

Well, my eyes are like my mother's and Angela's are like Father's, and the rest of me is like Father. So I guess I look like both of them.

INTERVIEWER: And what other ways?

ALICE: I think I take after my father a little bit. I'm not too sure. I can do things like he can do. I like the games he likes to play and that kind of thing. I take after Mother, too, but more after Father.

In comparing her statement with Angela's, we see her greater caution, her careful effort not to show open preference for one parent or the other. But she concludes with a fairly clear-cut, if hesitant, choice of her father. (Though the form of the question suggests that it deals with identification, both girls' replies may also be understood as expressions of object choice. They implicitly choose to affiliate with their father, but the material presented earlier in the case study affords the outside observer ample basis for seeing many ways in which the daughters have identified with their mother.)

Both girls indicate a preference for their father, though this is not coupled with a rejection of their mother. Nonetheless, they experience some slight anxiety in their relationship to their mother, as we would expect. Angela, in her story to Card 7GF, a stimulus to this area of concern, shows something of her orientation. Despite the fact that the card depicts a woman and a girl holding a doll, she devotes much of her attention in the story to a fantasy of establishing ties with age mates, thus revealing her impetus to grow up and away from the tie to her mother, to establish independent relationships. It is instructive to examine her younger sister's story to this same card. Alice says:

This looks like the mother is reading a story to her little daughter, and the daughter's holding a doll, and it might be an interesting fairy tale or it could be any kind of story. Or she may be talking to her daughter. Looks like she has a book in her hand, though. She may be reading the Bible or a book or, and the doll, I mean the girl, is listening carefully. It's sort of hard to tell what the end will be in this one, though.

Alice introduces no outside characters, showing instead a preoccupation with what her mother is saying or telling or reading. It is as though she were exhorting herself to pay close attention, while suggesting, inadvertently, that she wishes the doll could do the listening instead of herself. Whether Alice will later be able to move as far as her sister has we cannot say, though the potential is there. For the present, she is clearly less able to propose even in fantasy a more autonomous direction. Her psychic activity is more introversive, more intellectualized. Her story is concerned with different kinds of books; Angela's was concerned with different kinds of boys and girls.

We are not surprised when Mrs. Lanson tells us:

Angela is more active than Alice now. Alice keeps trying to write a book and writes a chapter or two now and then. Angela would rather play outside. . . . Alice likes to read more than Angela, and Alice also does better in school. I think Angela feels she has to try to keep her grades up to Alice's.

The girls have developed different styles of dealing with their problems, Angela trying to shape a more active and outgoing form, Alice finding a resource in intellectual activity and intellectualized fantasy.

Grouping several facts here, we are led to consider one further problem. We recall that both girls indicate a preference for their father, that he is a man who values a reasoned approach to things, that Alice is more proficient in school than Angela and shows more interest in intellectual activity, that Angela complains about the "weakness of her brain," and that Angela, according to her mother, feels the need to keep up to Alice's grades. These are the ingredients of a competitive situation, and strong feelings do indeed exist. Here is Angela's story to Card 9GF, depicting two women:

Well, here it looks like this woman, something had made her mad and she was running out, and this other woman behind the tree, looks like they might be enemies, and she is trying to more or less to spy on the one running out to see just exactly what she's up to. I think they might have both liked this one man pretty well and been more or less fighting for him, and something that this other girl behind the tree did made this one girl mad, so she ran out. And this other girl behind the tree thought she'd look and see just exactly what she was up to. Then I think something will happen to the one who was, the one behind the tree trying to be, well, it looks like she might be sort of a snob and might get—this other girl had really been going with this man and she had tried to win him. I think somebody will realize that she is in the wrong, and the other two will be happy.

Here are Angela's competitive feelings, not allowed much open expression at home but displaced, as we have seen, to playground activities, where she is a monitor during recess. We see, too, in this story the persistence of her individual aims and her hope of eventually winning the competition. Alice's story to this same card, also dealing with rivalrous interest in a prized possession, bears the stamp of the family image:

Well, this looks like a girl up in a tree, and another girl is running past. I don't know if that girl's going to drop something on the girl's head that's running past, or looks like this girl is sort of hiding from the other girl. It could be her sister or somebody that was mad at her, and she went to hide. Looks like the girl that's running is sort of dressed up, though. Looks like she might have been ready to go to a dance or something. Maybe the girl that's running wanted to borrow something of this girl's to wear, like a necklace or something and this girl wouldn't let her. It could be a lot of little things like that. This girl that's running sure looks mad. It's kind of hard to tell. In the end, if they were sort of sisters or something it'd turn out happy. Or maybe, it looks like this girl has something in her hand. Maybe she took this from this girl. I can't figure out what it is. It looks sort of like half of a book or something. And maybe this girl's running after her because this girl sort of stole it or something. In the end, it's probably nothing that the girls should get mad about, but I can't tell what that is. If it's something expensive or something, these girls should be mad for it.

We shall not analyze this story in detail, but simply point out how Alice veers back and forth over how legitimate it is to feel angry, recognizing that the competition for something valuable does arouse strong feelings, yet feeling the pressure of her belief that sisters really should not get angry with each other. She does not allow either character in her story decisive possession, nor does she attribute to either definitive blame.

Both girls are struggling with the problems of growing up, trying to integrate their personal emotionality with those feelings and standards that have come to prevail in the family. Alice, timidly, and Angela, more venturesomely, are trying to find the ground where self-assertion can prosper, where they can grow into themselves and not simply be external representations of their parents' images of them. They are engaged in testing the strength of the limits of harmony, wondering whether they dare move beyond. How far they will be able to proceed in transforming their own lives will depend on many factors not now ascertainable.

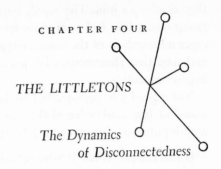

CHAPTER FOUR

THE LITTLETONS

The Dynamics
of Disconnectedness

In one sense, the Littleton family is fragmented; individual members go their separate ways, and there is relatively little communality of emotional worlds or overlap in the routine of their daily lives. In another sense, the family is tightly bound together with affective ties and mutual needs so intense that avoidance of intimacy and contact has emerged as a protective necessity. For this family, avoidance has become a mode of relating to each other—a means of coping with tensions and minimizing frustration. This fact and its implications are the most distinguishing features of the group. Strong centrifugal pressures, both physical and emotional, are easily apparent. These are balanced by less apparent but equally significant cohesive forces. The impulses and motivations underlying both sets of forces are powerful but threatening, and the equilibrium achieved by avoiding intimacy is an uneasy one.

THE FAMILY AND THEIR SEPARATE WORLDS

The separateness that characterizes the Littleton family is first apparent in Joe Littleton's daily schedule. Toward evening he leaves for work. The closing door of his small apartment seals him off from the activities of his wife and three children and temporarily relieves him of family obligations. The children come from school as he eats his breakfast and hurry off to the Y before he finishes. He feels lethargic upon awakening—ill prepared to show interest in their conversation or in the schoolwork they display to him. The rapid, impulsive conversation of the group makes him feel even more fatigued and arouses a mildly eager anticipation of the more congenial and predictable social exchange that characterizes his job as short-order cook on the five-to-two shift.

Not a good job, perhaps, but he believes that an uneducated man has few marketable skills. The long, inconvenient hours and unpromising future of his job are at times depressing:

INTERVIEWER: *What is your schedule on weekdays?*

MR. LITTLETON: *Work, work, work from five until two every day and five until three every Saturday, go home, go to bed, and then get up and go back to work.*

INTERVIEWER: *Have you always done the kind of work you're doing now?*

MR. LITTLETON: *All my life, except from '42 until '45. Then I worked in a defense plant. I started out as a dishwasher, then bus boy, and now I've been a cook for fifteen years.*

INTERVIEWER: *Do you work for someone else?*

MR. LITTLETON: *Yes, I work for someone else. I'm the manager. It's as if the place were my own, but it's not.*

INTERVIEWER: *How do you feel about your job?*

MR. LITTLETON: *Not too well. It's the one thing I know how to do—that I'm good at. I'd be happier doing something else.*

INTERVIEWER: *Have you thought of doing something else?*

MR. LITTLETON: *Not lately.*

The feeling of being caught, of having no alternatives, is evident in these comments. In spite of his distaste for his job and his belief that he would be more satisfied in another occupation, Mr. Littleton feels that there is no way out, no realistic hope for significant change; making plans is futile since he has already exhausted his possibilities.

Joe Littleton is a fairly tall, stockily built man of forty, the third child in a family of five. His father, until his retirement, worked as a coal miner. In addition to rearing a family, his mother kept a boarding house for miners. Joe was born in a small town in the Midwest, completed grammar school, and left for Chicago at the age of fifteen. Although he recalls his mother as the disciplinarian of the family, he speaks of her with fondness and admiration:

She was a well-liked woman. At the moment she's very ill. I've bought her a television set. She always has a lot of friends. She knows everything. She was a good mother. The children turned out well—no crooks or thieves. None of them are successful as far as money, but they turned out well. We were no problem to her. She has done very well with what she had—holding the family together and bringing them up.

Mr. Littleton's concept of personal and family effectiveness and of success is essentially negative. His comments reveal in part his own level of self-esteem and the basis for it. Averting personal and moral disaster is his foremost standard of achievement, and a level of aspiration for the family is offered in the same terms. It is sufficient to be able to prevent disintegration, to "hold the family together." This view suggests that Joe Littleton sees life as a struggle to maintain the minimum, a defensive effort to prevent an already dreary life from becoming tragic.

He mentions his father briefly and with moderate, perhaps ambivalent, feeling:

Generally, my mother was the disciplinarian in our family, not my father. When he did, it was a cuff of the hand. He had our respect and I have theirs [his own children]. All he had to do was whistle and I came. He's retired now, but he's still active.

He adds on the Sentence Completion Test: "My father is / one of the finest men I [have] ever known." A mixture of fear and admiration for his father's position of strength in the family is suggested by these remarks, and a sense of uneasiness and intimidation shows through his recollections.

It seems now to Joe Littleton that staying home and doing chores were the customary activities of his childhood. He recounts that his play and recreational activities consisted in going to a show once a week. In his opinion, his own children have more freedom and more activities than he had. To him, this is the greatest difference between the two generations.

Discontents of several kinds press in upon Mr. Littleton. He is unsatisfied with his job, both because of the hours and because of the nature and status of the work itself: "There are times when I / wish I had completed my schooling and taken up some other profession." This admission is related to other dissatisfactions—the lack of time he has for the children, the cramped living space for the family, and possibly the "nervousness" and "illness" of his wife. However, his efforts toward resolving such problems have been limited.

Karen Littleton is a housewife. Her domain is a furnished apartment of living room, two bedrooms, kitchen, and bath. All the rooms are very small. The apartment is one of eight in a building located on Chicago's south side; the building and the surrounding area are deteriorating, although they are situated near an upper middle class residential section of the city. The Littletons have lived in this apartment since they were married eleven years ago.

Mrs. Littleton is the only child of a marriage that was terminated before she was born. Her father left their home in Denmark four months before her birth; she has never seen him. When she was five, her mother came to the United States and left the child with her grandmother. Karen Littleton describes the situation:

My mother married a man against his parents' consent. From the time I remember, I lived with my grandma and mother. I was accepted in my dad's family. Mother was not. I was the only one who went to my grandpa's funeral. It was a real conflict. I don't know why. My mother always sent money to Grandma after she left. She had money. I was never in need of anything. I looked upon my grandma as my mother more than my own mother.

It was ten years later that Karen joined her mother in this country. She resisted when her mother wrote, urging that she attend school in the United States. The daughter won the argument against further schooling and got a job as a maid shortly after arriving in the States. However, the two stayed together for only two years before Mrs. Littleton left her mother and made her way to Chicago. Her drive, ambition, grasp of social reality, and self-sufficiency are apparent:

I went to work for a lady and her fourteen-year-old son. I learned English. The work was simple enough. I looked older. There was a [Danish] hall. I went there, and I met up with some smart people. I had in mind to get away from my mother because she made me do things I didn't want to do. Finally, I left and came to Chicago with some people. I got another job as a maid. That's the only thing you can do when you're in a country two years without schooling. I learned English and worked there two years. By then, I did not feel I had to do housework. I met people at dances and got a job as a cashier.

An atmosphere of interpersonal conflict, family disruption, and the struggle against odds characterized Mrs. Littleton's personal life until her marriage. She responded with an assertive and deliberate attempt to improve her own position, and these characteristics are still prominent in her manner and approach to life. She is a woman of thirty-five with attractive appearance and carriage who likes to talk and does so with ease. There is a sureness to her approach and an obvious attempt to be engaging and charming. Her approach to other family members shows a determined effort to force confidence and capability upon those about her. An example appears in remarks about her husband's qualities:

Bobby, my youngest child, is always much more sure of himself. His father has always lacked self-confidence. I don't think he'd admit it. He never had any responsibility. I tried to make a point of giving Bobby responsibility. When my husband was working at a small counter, I thought he was capable of a better

*job. He said he couldn't work there—he wouldn't know how to
act. He doesn't feel up with the next one. I did get him to
change jobs, however. What he lacked was just being sure of
himself. I've been all over Chicago. I've never lacked self-confidence. If I want to go to a certain restaurant, he'll say, "I
wouldn't know how to act there." I always came to decisions
about insurance. He left everything to me. . . . I noticed in Bobby that he was slow. I pushed him in among people. I gave him
jobs to do. Now he's very sure of himself.*

Karen Littleton's readiness to push her small son into social
interaction is in part an attempt to solve her own problems
through her children. She informed us that before she met Mr.
Littleton she had determined not to marry. "I always said that
the man could never be that I wanted to marry." Although she
had an active social life, by her account, she maintained a protective guard against friendships even after she was married; she
still harbors a mistrust of emotional commitment. She refers to
this in her comments about her second daughter:

*I have changed since I've been married. I was hard to get to
know. I was indifferent toward people. I didn't go out of my way
to make people like me. That's one reason why I try with Sally
to get her into groups. I recognize it because I was much like
her. She has few friends in school. You're better off if you like
everybody and are not too fond of anyone.*

This excerpt illustrates a significant characteristic of Karen
Littleton—the tendency to use the lives of her children as arenas
in which to correct her own misfortune and reconstruct her life.
For Mrs. Littleton this represents, among other things, a feeling
of dissatisfaction with herself and a conviction that the events
of her life and the personalities of her children can be shaped
by determined effort.

She attempts to keep in active contact with the community in
which the family lives. Her out-of-home activities are typically
invested in groups organized to provide services for children.
Her daughter reports that Mrs. Littleton agreed to work with

the Girl Scouts when most of the other mothers had professed to have too little time. Karen Littleton says, "I like to belong to groups that in some way or other help children—really help them, not just have teas." Many of her social exchanges with other women are related to her participation in these groups.

In many significant respects, Karen Littleton and her husband are sharply contrasted. He comes from a stable, apparently compatible home and is still attached to his parents; she is alienated from her mother and has never seen her father. Joe Littleton is disinclined to utilize any opportunities available to him; Karen Littleton has fought to improve her own situation. She is highly responsive to stimuli and reacts with wide emotional fluctuations; his emotional life is a monotone. Her daydreams often involve fantasies about her lost childhood and the lack of support from others; his revolve about his lost future and his own failure to take advantage of opportunity.

Three children were born to the Littletons within the space of three years. Betty is nine, Sally is eight, and Bobby is seven. Betty is a dark, bright-eyed, lithe girl who displays alertness, imagination, and a sense of humor in abundance. She is highly motivated to achieve, especially in artistic pursuits. Betty looked upon the TAT as an opportunity to demonstrate her proficiency as a storyteller, and she confided to the interviewer that she may some day be a writer. Her interests are varied—ballet, swimming, drawing, and writing—and her parents believe she has talents that may develop into a professional career.

There is a clipped, brittle quality about her conversation that is not evident in the other children's. An air of independence characterizes her approach to the interviewer and to other family members, but an underlying tone of sarcasm and bitterness suggests a reactive quality to her show of autonomy.

Betty's mental agility is demonstrated not only in scholastic achievements but in clear perceptions of the family relationships and the motivation of family members. Mrs. Littleton reports that for a treat she often takes the children to a local drugstore for lunch after Sunday school. Betty interprets this bit of family routine as an evasion of maternal responsibility: "Then we meet Mommy, and she takes us to the drugstore and gets us something so she doesn't have to fix lunch." Her self-possession is illustrated by the following incident:

I beat up my brother for fighting two little girls. I settled it. I did not tell my mother. I'll probably end up telling her if she is in a good mood. And if my little brother gets into trouble or if somebody is beating him up, he'd come to me. He says, "Boy, my sister can beat you up." I can beat him up, so he thinks I can beat everybody.

Self-confidence, assertive control, and candor add effectiveness to her intuitive talents and social techniques. A few of her SCT responses illustrate her straightforward approach to herself and to others:

What people like most about me is / that I am ahead in almost everything.
Our family / is a very common family.
If they tell me I shouldn't I / still want to.
When somebody makes fun of me / I don't like it.
Sometimes I feel like / I want to kill my sister.

Betty shares her mother's feeling that her environment is responsive to the persistent application of talent. This attitude represents in part her view of an appropriate feminine role. Her stories to TAT cards attribute to females the ability to control heterosexual situations and to assist the male in making major decisions. An excerpt from her response to TAT Card 2 shows her feelings of having ample resources and her readiness to make and effect decisions:

. . . this girl is in love with this boy that works in the fields . . . and he could not marry her because he did not have money. . . . She told him that he should run away with her. . . . She said he'd get another job. . . . She told him that she had a lot of money and they could both buy fares. . . . Finally he found a job in an office, and he didn't know anything about it, so she told him

126   THE LITTLETONS

that she would lend him some of her study books and he learned about his job . . . and got to be a manager. . . . She came back from the visit; she told him that there was work in that town he could do . . . so they went back and lived happy there.

Betty displays self-sufficiency and a certain amount of detachment in viewing her family. In the interview she claims that she does not take her personal problems to her parents: "I worry about my own troubles." Her tendency to assume a disciplinarian role with the younger children—which she feels it best not to report to her mother—further indicates the hesitation Betty has in involving herself in certain aspects of the family interaction. While she believes that she did the correct thing in disciplining her brother, she is convinced that her mother will not easily understand. The situation must be manipulated—she must find her mother in an approachable mood. In these instances Betty reveals an unchildlike quality. She assumes a precocious manner of maternal responsibility that places her for the moment as her mother's peer.

While Betty's resemblance to her mother is largely psychological, Sally duplicates Mrs. Littleton's physical features. Sally is a well-built girl with an attractive, round face and long, honey-colored hair. She is a spontaneous, affectionate girl with an air of femininity that is less apparent in her older sister. She is bright and alert, although possibly less so than Betty.

A heavy sense of duty and morality appear to inhibit her use of imagination and energy. Her TAT and SCT responses are heavily loaded with moral imperatives and interpersonal obligations. The repeated theme of these fantasies is self-management in order to deserve acceptance by the family and the outer world. The basis of negotiation with authority is irrational conformity to a moral code which she only vaguely comprehends. Nor is she convinced that acceptance necessarily follows conformity; however, she has not yet adequately developed alternative techniques.

Sally takes care of the cat, and other members of the family speak of her affection and care for her pet. She refers to him at one point to observe that he is always hungry. On another occasion when the interviewer asked, "What do you like best about each person in the family?" Sally replied, ". . . I like Tabby because he comes in my bed in the morning and keeps my feet warm."

A sympathetic sensitivity to the feelings and reactions of others is more evident in Sally than in other members of the family. However, she feels considerable competition with her older sister and her brother, and she has adapted her femininity toward defining a place for herself in the family group different from her sister's. She invests less than Betty in developing skills such as dancing and art; her vocational fantasies seem to favor more maternal, nurturant roles—nurse or singer—than Betty's—dancer and designer.

Bobby, less than a year younger than Sally, lacks her health and physical vigor. He is a small, thin, weak-looking boy. Although he strongly resembles his father in facial characteristics and coloring, he is unlike him in body build. Bobby's health has never been consistently good. He had feeding difficulties, presumably because of a stomach ailment or obstruction, and was fed special foods as an infant. Corrective shoes were considered necessary for a number of years. He has generally been more susceptible to disease and to minor respiratory ailments than the other children. His school work, too, has not shown the sparkle of Betty's able performance or Sally's solidly good scholastic achievement. He has frequently needed help from his parents.

In manner, Bobby is more co-operative and compliant than his two more independent sisters. He shows little interest in competing with them in the tasks set by the research staff members. His tone is less vivid, more subdued than theirs, though he occasionally engages in impulsive, playful exchanges with them. He belongs to the Cub Scouts and usually goes to the Y after school and on Saturdays.

The Littletons seem a disparate group, with greatly uneven capacities for living. They look in different directions and move with varied pace. While Mr. Littleton sinks deeper in his circumscribed track, his wife pushes restlessly to keep from being similarly caught. Betty meets the challenge of the parental discrepancy by being more self-sufficient, while Bobby and Sally feel disappointed over their ungratified wishes for contact. It is scarcely surprising that the issue of intimacy and separateness is more crucial for the Littleton family than for most of the families of the study. Mr. and Mrs. Littleton bring to the family interactional context widely different backgrounds of family experience. They approach family problems with different objectives, incongruent personal needs, and discrepant images of what is desirable in parental roles. These differences between the parents create an unusually high potential for conflict within the family, both between husband and wife and between parents and children. It is difficult for the children to discern group-approved images of self and family. Without communality of a desired image the children are hard pressed to demonstrate adherence to the family values and to affirm their rights to group approval and acceptance.

THINGS THAT ARE AND THINGS THAT SHOULD BE: THE
AMBIVALENCE OF RESIGNATION

The Littletons offer a fragmented pattern of family goals and standards. Preferences and ambitions affecting the family do not constitute an image upon which the group has achieved consensus. The image is lacking in clarity; it is not explicit; it is not shared. The goals that any one member has for another are typically not the goals the other has for himself. The separateness of the family members from one another affords little that might be called communality of family aims; the data suggest that the family feels it is not working together as a unit toward group objectives.

One manifestation of the outlines of a family image is the nature of the day-to-day expectations presented by parents to their children. Through this socialization process the children come to have a sense of what the family is and what they should and may do in it. To the Littleton children what they should not do is often expressed more clearly than what they should. They are also aware that the parents do not mean what they say. Betty's comments are indicative:

She doesn't spoil us. We're not to tell lies or do something she tells us not to do. . . .

INTERVIEWER: *What happens if you and the other children fight?*

BETTY: *She ignores it for a while until she gets so burned up that she separates us and screams at us, and then we know when to quit.*

In the Littleton family, definition of sanctions and taboos often follows the formula expressed in Bettys' comments. The content of the taboo—no fighting—need not be taken seriously; it is the emotional reaction of the parent that must be watched. These reactions often differ from the announced code. The code as seen by Betty may be phrased as follows: "fighting is all right until it irritates Mother." Moods are less easily predicted than behavioral standards, so the child's task becomes one of sensing the emotional mood of the moment and adapting to vagaries of temperament. Discipline becomes largely a function of frustration and threshold tolerance in the mother.

The Littletons have an uncertain and incongruent image of the kind of future that they prefer for their children. Mrs. Littleton says she wants Bobby to be a doctor, but she assumes that her husband has different ideas: "I'm sure his dad wants him to be a football player. What daddy doesn't?" Mr. Littleton actually appears to have nothing definite in mind:

It's up to them. I can't plan anything for the children. If they have natural ability and they want to do the thing, the thing to do is exploit it. As for planning, it's not wise. At this age they change so much. One week it's one thing; one week it's another. They're not at the age yet where they know what they want to do. According to what my wife tells me, Betty is a pretty good dancer. I've seen her in shows, and as far as I can tell, I can't see where she stands out. How much education can you provide? That's the thing. Nowadays if you don't have a college education, you can't get anywhere. It used to be high school.

In this reply, Mr. Littleton reveals again his awareness of his own inadequate training. His discouragement over the increasing standards in the world about him make his own level of qualifications and performance seem even lower. He recognizes the economic utility of education but shows little drive and little interest in assuring his children of the advantages he now wishes were his. He minimizes his daughter's ability and sees little value in encouraging the children's ambitions and attempts. There is almost no trace of the Newbold attitude (chapter v) that children are trained and encouraged, that youth is a period of rehearsal for adult activities. Rather, it is a matter of "Let them do what they want—if they can." Mr. Littleton makes little effort to provide explicit direction or guidance.

Karen Littleton has higher and more definite aspirations for the children, and her interest is more active and more intense.

Betty always wanted to be a ballerina since she could talk. I really feel that she will go into it some day. She's artistic. She has ability in drawing. Her poems are good, but she can't dust a table. Some girls play house, she, never. So far I can't see anything specific in Sally that's encouraging. She takes dancing, but she goes because she's told. She likes to play. She has more fun out in the mud. She's just a very average youngster, where Betty has been different. Sally says she wants to be a nurse. I want them to have all the education that's possible for us to give them. Not just sending them to school. It's often just a wasted education unless it's a special course. I can't see sending them to college. We'll do our best. We'll do what we can.

This statement reveals the ambivalence and unevenness that characterize the Littletons' attempt to formulate goals and aims for the family and its members. With no apparent realistic basis in financial or mental resources, Mrs. Littleton has selected a high professional occupation for her son, and she has high hopes for Betty; however, Sally's stated desire to become a nurse—a realistic goal—is depreciated and her ability minimized. Mrs. Littleton has ambitions for her children, but they are applied selectively and on grounds that must, at best, strike the children as arbitrary and obscure.

Not only do Mr. and Mrs. Littleton lack a common image of what the children can become, but they are both caught up in their own personal situations and can find little common ground in their relationship to each other. Both feel a sense of frustration, of having been bogged down in the pursuit of their inner aims.

We have mentioned Joe Littleton's dissatisfaction with his job. While he blames himself on the SCT ("The fact that I failed / I can only blame myself. The opportunity is always there"), he assigns some of the responsibility to his family's low economic resources. He has limited economic ambitions which he believes he cannot achieve: "I'd like to buy the place where I presently work. It's impossible as far as finances are concerned."

His reluctance to predetermine his children's occupational goals may be related to his regrets that he did not follow the interests he held in his youth. He says that he secretly wanted to be a singer or a musician and that, even now, he thinks of himself as a singer. The plausibility of these fantasies is impossible to determine, but the striking difference in the nature of the gratification that accrues from his desired and his actual occupation is apparent.

Mr. Littleton is painfully aware of his lack of authority in the family. He would like to be the head of his household, with a status role similar to his father's—non-participating yet respected, loved, and obeyed. He says:

The children feel their father is the head of the family. They tell me, "On Sunday, you're boss." They still think their father is head. If I'm not present, they turn more to their mother. She's more the disciplinarian because I see very little of them. When they see me, it's "hello" and "good-bye" and away to the Y.

When Mr. Littleton speaks of his own father's authority and of the prompt obedience the children showed, he adds, "My children are like that." And again, when asked which parent the children came to with their troubles he reports, "They go to their mother if she is here. If I'm home, to me." He supports his desire to be master of his house by disciplining the children with moderate severity when he is with them. However, they see him as more lenient than Mrs. Littleton. Betty says, "He is not as bad as Mother when she punishes, like when we come home from the show late we wouldn't have supper, except when Daddy's home that's different." And in a later comment, "Bobby is softhearted like my daddy. He'll give in to anything you want."

Joe Littleton's attempts to be authoritative are softened by his feeling that he is not living up to the accepted standards of fatherliness and companionship with the children. From time to time he tries to re-establish a position of dominance for himself in the group, but, knowing that he accepts so few of the other responsibilities of fatherhood, he questions his right to assume authority.

I fall short like anyone else. I feel that I do not have enough contact with the family. I don't participate in their activities as much as I'd like to. I am sort of neglectful. Some say you can do it if you want to. I don't know. With my working hours—I can't rearrange my schedule. I think I could be closer.

Occasionally Joe Littleton relives and reconstructs his life in his fantasy. He takes comfort from his sincerity in his dealings with his fellow man and in the awareness that they think he is a "pretty good fellow." But the tone that permeates his assessment of things as they are is expressed by a single SCT response: "Sometimes I feel like / I'd like to get away from it all."

As Mr. Littleton's self-reproach reveals regret over things he has not done for himself, so Mrs. Littleton's reproach is concerned with things other persons have not done for her. However, she tries to resist becoming cynical and bitter over the emotional and economic tragedies that she associates with her child-hood and adolescence. Her defenses against depression and despair are tough and stubborn, and her active, persistent search for a better life for herself and her family indicates the resilience and resourcefulness of her personality. "The strongest part of me," she says on the SCT, "is a strong will. No one can make me change my mind." Yet the discrepancy between her present circumstances and the life she would like is enormous. She is attempting to close the gap through her children. "I want Bobby to be a doctor. That's my ideal. I wanted to be that when I was little. I never tell him because he will be what he wants to be and is able to be." However, we learn from Bobby's interview that he wants to be a doctor because his mother has chosen that goal for him.

Karen Littleton's primary feelings of deprivation spring from her recollection of being deserted by her parents. She does not dwell on this topic in her interview or display excessive self-pity in discussing the circumstances which left her emotionally orphaned. She confesses to daydreaming about Denmark, and upon seeing Card 2 of the TAT for the first time, she cried:

Denmark! That is Denmark, so help me. The lake, the mountains, the field, the farm. . . . The lady standing on the side is expecting another baby, looking across the mountains, dreaming like all mothers would . . . and, naturally, the man is working, plowing fields, which I think is the most wonderful thing in the world. . . .

The SCT draws more reality-oriented responses. There she expresses her regret that her father has never seen her and that she has never seen him. "My mother," she says, "is far away." Reality, however, has not dimmed her image of the ideal family relationship—the warm, contented love of mother for child and the secure strength of a responsible father who tills the fields. This image is at once her strength and source of discomfort in dealing with her own children. She says the thing she wants most for the family is ". . . not anything special—just be together." But she has become resigned to the fact that her husband's work acts to separate the family. She is also aware that the family activities separate her from the children. Saturdays the children leave after breakfast for various places and activities; in the afternoon they go to a show and she does her weekly shopping. If there is no show available that meets her approval, the children "play out, visit friends, or watch TV." Even on Sunday, when Mr. Littleton is home, she sometimes takes the children to an afternoon show, leaving Mr. Littleton to prepare dinner.

The difficulty Karen Littleton finds in living up to her own ideal of a good mother is most clearly revealed, she believes, by her impatience with her children:

I'm probably too strict. I expect more than they are capable of remembering. Certainly I try to take a genuine interest in all their activities. No matter what they do, I think it's very important. What's not so good is that I yell at them, which I know is the worst thing in the world to do with children. If I didn't know it would be different. A lot of times I don't take time enough to explain things. In a mother as in anyone else, you just sometimes don't feel like it. It's hard to keep your temper all the time.

Mrs. Littleton is determined that her children will not grow up with the lack of self-confidence that she sees in her husband or with the inertia that Mr. Littleton shows and upon which she places the blame for most of the family's difficulties. It is likely that she has not concealed from the children her feeling about Mr. Littleton's lack of confidence and initiative. The extreme measures she takes to assure herself that the children will be self-sufficient are shown by her comments about her son:

As far as problems with Bobby are concerned, he didn't have self-confidence—like his daddy. That's remedied. It helped to shove him away. In the park, when he was little, he wanted to sit on my lap. I made him go and play. When he was older, I sent him to the store to buy bread. He was scared. I made him do it anyway. He is now a boy that works very hard in school. He

*works for the honor roll. I don't have to worry about his infe-
riority complex any more. He is up there. Maybe some mothers
would have loved it. I didn't want a boy hanging on to me.*

Mrs. Littleton's urge to create independence and vigor in her
child appears to be an effect of defenses against her own unful-
filled childhood dependency wishes and her disappointment in
Mr. Littleton's performance as husband and father. Eleven
years of attempting to arouse her husband's ambition and transform him into an assertive and capable man have had little positive effect upon him, and she has, to some extent, given up on
him and recognized that the push for improvement in the
family's situation must come from herself. When asked to discuss the way he measures up to her ideal, she says, "You should
have asked me eleven years ago."

Despite the disappointment she feels over Mr. Littleton's lack
of occupational ambition, she praises his ability to provide for
the family. It is significant that, while she commends her husband for his economic support of the family, she regards her
own ability to manage finances as one of her weakest characteristics.

*I'd like them [the children] to have much better value of
money. It's hard for me to learn to live within a set income. I
am very extravagant, extremely so. I buy things for the children
that they could do without. I like to give gifts to people. In my
way of thinking it's right. According to finances, it's wrong.*

Mr. Littleton confirms his wife's economic mismanagement and
expresses the severest criticism that he shows for any member of
the family except himself. Thus one of Mr. Littleton's relative
strengths—his steadiness of economic support—is consciously
dissipated by his wife.

Mrs. Littleton's memory of a fatherless childhood, her own
dependency needs, and her resentment of her husband's emotional lethargy combine in another major discontent: Mr. Littleton neglects his wife and family. In her opinion he is undemon-

strative toward her and uninterested in the activities of the children.

Bobby is always affectionate and has always demanded it. His father doesn't show affection much. To him, to kiss at the door is just a formality. He doesn't feel it's necessary. With Bobby, it's important and it's very sincere.

Adult males have always been a disappointment to Karen Littleton. She sees her eight-year-old boy as a more satisfactory source of affection than her husband. In a sense, she has turned to the children, especially Bobby, for gratifications which adults have denied her. Her efforts to reconstruct the personalities and lives of her children represent, in part, the desire to create persons who will gratify some of her own needs.

Joe Littleton's lack of interest in the children and home is the emotional vacuum which, in Karen Littleton's opinion, no recreation or maternal compensation can substitute for or allay. She mentions this situation pointedly:

He has failed in the way that he doesn't take actual interest in the things the children do. The children bring things home. I ask them, "Did you tell Daddy?" I asked Betty that the other day. She said, "Oh, Daddy doesn't care." It isn't that he doesn't care. He is thoughtless. It may be that I've taken too much responsibility and have always done it.

Not only does Mr. Littleton lack interest, but, according to his wife, he is imperceptive in affairs that concern the children and insensitive to their psychological needs.

He forgot that he had two children besides Sally. He has changed since I've explained to him what it has done to Betty. She was an unhappy little girl. She lost her daddy. Betty must have been seven when I blew up but good. I could see that Betty hated Sally. She just hated her sister. It was done by her father pushing Betty aside. When they were little, Betty would ask her daddy to throw her up in the air after he had been throwing Sally. He would say, "Oh, you're too big." It did show finally.

Betty was pushing a lot of little girls around in school. I started finding a reason for it. I decided it had to have a reason and that was it. He admitted he had pushed her aside. Now he takes Betty on his lap and holds her and hugs her. A year ago, I saw Betty back to what she used to be. She likes everybody. She had started chewing her fingernails about three years ago.

The satisfactions and achievements Mrs. Littleton wants for herself and for her family are, at best, only partially fulfilled. The adaptive efforts at detachment and self-sufficiency she used as a girl to protect herself against the pain of unmet needs are maladaptive in a family situation, where gratification is a mutual function. She is vaguely aware that her tendency to compensate for the inadequacies of those around her by assuming their responsibilities not only has been unsatisfactory but has increased her family's dependence upon her. Her knowledge of this effect has increased her frustration and resentment. While she is partially resigned to her situation, she still engages in bitter arguments with Mr. Littleton about his work and their living conditions.

The perplexity Mr. and Mrs. Littleton have experienced in the effort to discover, define, and maintain objectives for themselves and for the family has been augmented in their children's efforts to regulate their own behavior by a rational and consistent code of expectations. The children are all intensely aware that parental love and attention are conditional upon conformity, but the expectations to which they should conform are vaguely defined.

The pressure these children feel toward conformity with an acceptable standard of behavior can be indicated by excerpts from the SCT responses of each child.

BETTY: *I am sorry when I / do something wrong.*
What gets me into trouble is / when I do something I know I'm not supposed to do.
Children / are often bad.
I don't like the sort of kids who / don't do the right thing.

SALLY: *I am sorry when I / do something wrong.*
What gets me into trouble is / things I shouldn't do.
Children / should be nice.
I don't like the sort of kids who / are mean to me.
The thing that really makes me mad is / when someone does something wrong.
What people like most about me is / that I am nice.
To make people like me / I will be nice.
BOBBY: *People think I am / bad.*
I am sorry when I / hurt others.
I hate / to fib.
I don't like the sort of kids who / hurt others.
The thing that really makes me mad is / people who do not help.
No one can make me / not help.

These responses indicate the intensity of the children's guilt and illustrate the diffuse nature of the behavioral code by which these children evaluate and punish themselves. It is a negatively defined code, consisting largely of taboos. Positive sanctions are even more diffusely conceived. One must, for example, "help others," "do the right thing," and otherwise behave in a moral fashion. The vagueness of the code is in part a function of the parents' uneven application of limits. We have mentioned Betty's awareness of the fact that fighting between the children is permitted to continue until Mrs. Littleton is sufficiently irritated to put a violent stop to it. Sally amplifies the inconsistency with which behavioral norms are applied:

Even if we fight and she finds out, she doesn't do anything. She yells at us, she tells us to quit. She doesn't do anything, but if we do it again she tells us to get out. If we lose something she tells us to look. If we don't find it, okay.

However, there are at least two areas of behavior in which the tolerance limits are quite narrow: talking back and lying. Mrs. Littleton's comments about Sally reveal the intensity of her feeling on both these points:

*In one respect I'm different [from other families]. I believe
that children have to mind anyone older without talking back.
They can think anything they want. They can think I'm crazy,
but they have to keep it to themselves.*

And later:

*Take Sally. They say it takes a long time to get over saying it's
someone else's fault. I tell her that if she's big enough and brave
enough to do something wrong, then she should be big enough
to admit it. What makes it terrible is that she denies it.*

In this context it is interesting to note Mrs. Littleton's recollection of her own childhood: "[My grandmother] was very old
and tiny. I'd argue with her. I had to have the last word. I must
have been mischievous."

The haphazard emotional organization that characterizes the
Littletons is reflected in the incongruity between the disciplinary
statement and the behavioral follow-through. Similarly, in areas
of family achievement and goals, words have lost their meaning.
Aspirations as an organizing principle in family functioning and
behavior have little effect because they cannot be realized, but
the statement of ideal behavior and unattainable goals cannot
be relinquished. The statement of cultural values and personal
desires provides a feeling of membership in the larger society
and protects the family members against the despair that would
follow complete and conscious resignation to reality. The discrepancy that exists cannot be completely repressed, however,
and the resentment and frustration aroused become channeled
toward other family members and transformed into self-blame.
The ideals must then be reaffirmed and deviations punished in
a ritual of expiation and renewal. But these rituals are conducted
and instigated primarily by Mrs. Littleton and thus do not substantially contribute to a feeling of group awareness and group
effort in meeting common problems and achieving group-related
objectives.

The Littleton family is scarcely in a position to organize time to serve the group's needs or to assist the family in its pursuit of overt individual or group objectives. The emotional separateness of the members is augmented by the daily routine that they have established for themselves. A summary of these routines is provided as each member describes the activities of an average day:

MR. LITTLETON: Work, work, work from five until two every day; five until three on Saturdays, home, bed, and up.

INTERVIEWER: Can you tell me generally what the family usually does on other days?

MR. LITTLETON: I couldn't tell you. I know what they do and where they go, but I don't know just when they have the activities. Now Bobby is beginning Cub Scouts.

The emotional tone, echoing fatigue and despair, with which Mr. Littleton speaks of his day reveals his distaste for his own routine and his uninterest in the family's daily schedule. His description shows a diffuse view of the day, anchored by the beginning and end points of his work schedule. He has little sense of being able to order his day, and he feels bound by a routine from which he sees no way of escape. Karen Littleton's report contrasts with her husband's in several ways:

I get up at seven-thirty. One of the children usually has my coffee made for me. I get the children's clothes ready because of the way we live. They're really old enough to get them ready themselves. I comb the girls' hair, and they go off to school. That goes on until eight-thirty. Then I straighten up around the house and make telephone calls. That manages to take until twelve, when they come home. I give them lunch. In this period I've had my bath so that I can be ready to go out. Either I have a meeting or I do shopping or visiting. I always want to be out. I come back in the afternoon. That means cooking supper and washing dishes. In the evening the children go to bed. They're all in bed at eight, at the very latest. I usually have sewing or visitors or I go out.

INTERVIEWER: How does your husband fit into this? I know he works nights.

MRS. LITTLETON: He doesn't fit in very well. He comes home at five in the morning. He goes to bed and gets up at one. He sees the children at three in the afternoon before he goes. Of course, now they're bigger and they go right to the Y. He doesn't approve, but he sees them on Sunday.

In contrast to her husband's impressions, Mrs. Littleton sees the events of the day in sharp detail. She feels some sense of command over the activities of all family members except those of her husband. His preferences about the children's activities are ignored, a fact that adds to his feeling of helplessness about the daily schedule. Mrs. Littleton emphasizes the obligatory nature of the day's demands; the occasions of interaction among family members are incidental. The children give vivid accounts of the typical day. Betty says:

Do I have to tell the truth? We wake up yelling and screaming at each other. The other kids are up, and I am still sleeping. When I get up, they are eating breakfast. I eat breakfast, then we get dressed and go to school, and after school is over at three I get my suitcase and I go swimming at the Y. And after swimming I wait a while and then I go swimming again. Then I come home and I eat supper and watch television, and after that I brush my teeth and get my pajamas on and go to bed at eight.

Betty's comments reveal her sense of discomfort over the quality of interpersonal relationships within the family. The day is hectic; emotionality is unordered and, to a degree, uncontrolled. Betty's view of the day omits her parents; she is primarily concerned with her own activities rather than with the family group or her part in it. Her outlook reveals detachment and self-containment. Her personal aims are not deeply interlocked with those of other family members. Sally's picture of the typical day shows a greater sense of involvement in the group:

My mother usually screams at us, and Tabby [the cat] is always hungry, and the television gets turned off. We usually do something bad, and we are always spending money, and we don't get to see our father because we go to the Y. After we come home we eat dinner, and then if we are good we get to watch television, and if we are bad our mother turns it off. Then we get our pajamas on and go to bed.

A note of despair marks Sally's account of a typical day. Events are described in terms of frustration or moral evaluation. Children are in danger of being unsatisfied or punished, and a sense of imminent deprivation is associated with the family's day-by-day events. Sally, more than the two other children, sees the family's activities as representing opposition between adults and children. Being a member of this family is, for her, a burden. Bobby is much more like Sally than he is like Betty. He outlines the day:

We get dressed. Sometimes Betty makes Mom annoyed—she doesn't get dressed. I get down first, and I get dressed first, and my mother wants me to go out and buy bread and milk. Every night she tells me to empty the garbage. We get to school at eight-thirty, and school starts at nine, and we come home at twelve, and we watch television. At twelve-thirty we go back to school. At three we come home. I usually go to the Y or Cub Scouts or to tap on Monday. Sally goes to tap with me. That's all I can think of.

Bobby, too, sees the relationship between adults and children as one of the prominent features of the family. Adults make demands—they can be annoyed by resistance and, presumably, pleased by compliance.

The most obvious aspect of these reports is that Joe Littleton is effectively separated from other family members. However, this fact is mentioned only by Sally. Even Mrs. Littleton failed to comment on her husband's schedule until prompted by the interviewer. The routines of Mrs. Littleton and the children keep them away from Mr. Littleton during the brief period that he is available to them in the afternoon. Mrs. Littleton makes a point of being out in the afternoon, and the children leave for the Y immediately after school. The separation among members of this family is mutually enforced.

The self-centeredness of the reports of daily activities suggests that the father is not selected as the sole target to be isolated by the rest of the group. Individual members of the family go their own ways with little thought of adopting schedules affording opportunity for family interaction. There is scant mention of group activities. Mr. Littleton speaks only of his own daily routine until asked specifically about the activities of other members. Even then, he reveals slight knowledge of the family's functioning while he is away. Mrs. Littleton details her own schedule, referring to other members of the family only when their activities make some specific demand upon her. She makes no reference to events in which, presumably, she and the children are together in an interactive situation. Dinner, for example, is for her a matter of "cooking supper and washing dishes." The high point of the day is the afternoon, when she feels free to go out, and she speaks of going out as an emotional necessity. The three children's reports similarly omit descriptions of group activities except to refer to themselves as "we" when speaking of activities the three of them are pursuing concurrently. Sally is the only exception in the group; she sees the routine as involving the three children. However, she also omits any reference to group interaction.

The weekend schedule offers an opportunity for family participation that is impossible during the week, but there seems to be little inclination to take advantage of the time thus provided. Mr. Littleton describes his weekend:

INTERVIEWER: *What kinds of activities do you and the family do together on Sundays?*

MR. LITTLETON: *None. I get up at noon. We watch television most of the afternoon. I'm a cook. It's Mom's day off. Once in a while we go out with the children. We have dinner. When it's nice weather, we go to the park. On Sunday evenings, when we* get a sitter, my wife and I go to the movies. We haven't been fortunate lately. Then she stays home, and I go to the movies. I don't see them on Saturdays. They're in the show.

Mrs. Littleton is in general agreement with the pattern of activities described by her husband:

On Saturdays we sleep until eight. Then breakfast. I get the girls off to dancing school. Bobby goes to the Y by nine-thirty. They all come back at noon. I do a lot of the big shopping on Saturday for the weekend. The children go to a show if there's a show that I approve of. If not, they play out, visit friends, watch TV. We have dinner, and then there are three heads to wash on Saturday night. That's about it. We don't go out on Saturday night. Naturally, my husband works. On Sunday we get up at eight. They hurry like mad to be in Sunday school by nine-forty-five. Because we're right around the corner, we have to hurry to get there on time. I'm secretary in the primary class, and I go to church at eleven from Sunday school, and the children go to choir. Then usually we go to the drugstore and have a soda or some sort of snack. It's up to them. Then we come home and cook dinner. We eat by four on Sunday. He gets up. If there are shows and plays that I want to see with the children, we go, and Dad stays home and cooks dinner. After dinner, I usually lay down and rest so we can go out Sunday night. We go to a show, or we have dinner for the children at home, and then we go out to dinner and the show. Some Sundays we all go out.

The Littletons see the day as a succession of unrelated events. Few family rituals help organize or integrate these events into a pattern with meaning for the group. Repeated activities are not accompanied by pleasure or group spirit and are not used ritualistically to promote a feeling of cohesion and intimacy among the family members. Life is met piece by piece, and the individual has little sense of purpose and integration into a design for living.

The separateness of the individuals in this family and their lack of periods of mutual participation and exchange obviously result in part from Mr. Littleton's unusual work schedule. However, the family's disinclination to seek opportunities for joint participation indicates that the family pattern is not merely an adjustment to an occupational inconvenience. There are two recurring situations in which the family could, if it chose, engage in group interests and exchange. The most frequent of these is Sunday afternoon, Mr. Littleton's day away from the job; the second is Mr. Littleton's annual vacation. The activities of a typical Sunday afternoon, as we have seen, are not enough to draw the family together. The three children report television viewing as their only activity on Sunday afternoon, and Mr. Littleton's comments confirm their recollections. This suggests that the other forms of recreation mentioned by the parents either occur rarely or are of little consequence to the children.

It is significant that each parent recalls the afternoon and evening as a time when they go to shows separately. However, Mrs. Littleton speaks only of her husband's staying home while she goes to the show; Mr. Littleton speaks only of his going to a show alone if a baby sitter is not available. Neither parent suggests that these divisive excursions are undesirable, and neither blames the partner for leaving the family group or extending the separateness enforced during the week by Mr. Littleton's schedule. Minimal group interaction is apparently accepted without serious complaint by the family. Of the three children, only Sally mentions Mr. Littleton as a participant in the Sunday afternoon activities. Similarly, Sally is the only one of the children to comment on her father's absence during the weekday activities. With this exception, the family shows little open discontent with its daily and weekend routines.

The use of vacations to continue separation confirms the view that this is a family which avoids occasions of mutual participation and intimate exchange. The Littletons do not take vacations together. The casualness with which this situation is accepted appears in Mrs. Littleton's comments:

INTERVIEWER: *What does the family do on vacations?*

MRS. LITTLETON: *My husband is from southern Illinois. Naturally, he goes there on vacations. He gets two weeks.*

INTERVIEWER: *Does anyone go with him?*

MRS. LITTLETON: *I have, a couple of times, and he has gone alone with the children. He takes one child alone occasionally.*

These remarks supplement other indications of this family's separateness. They also suggest something of the nature of the family boundaries. It is assumed that vacations are for the purpose of visiting relatives; wide areas of experience which might be accessible are apparently not considered in planning a vacation. The children, too, speak of vacation as a change in the frequency of recreational activities—more swimming, more shows, more play—rather than a time for new or unusual experiences.

The Littletons prefer a degree of sameness and repetition in their activities; possibly they take comfort and security from predictability. They are related to the past in a negative fashion through Mrs. Littleton's attempts toward reconstructing her early experiences in her children's lives. There is no contented continuity with the past, no feeling of inheriting a satisfactory and traditional way of behaving or of viewing and interacting with the outside world. Present acts are directed, in a sense, by the past, since they are designed to deny and change it. Mrs. Littleton claims that she lives for the present: "I've seen that tomorrow takes care of itself." Today's resources are expended, for the most part, to obtain immediate goals.

Mr. Littleton's early background offers little except dependable, though meager, economic resources. His own work career has been steady but not appreciably better than his father's, if a general rise in income and standard of living is taken into account. There are some indications that he sees himself as less successful than his father, particularly in his personal and family accomplishments. Even now, he occasionally suggests to Mrs. Littleton that they move to southern Illinois, although this suggestion usually provokes a bitter quarrel. Thus he brings to the group no sense of continuity with the life of his own parents; his wife interprets his attempts to establish a closer connection with his past as a show of weakness and a reluctance to assist her in her mission of securing a better life for the family.

Karen Littleton holds a deep, intense regret at losing her family as a child. She is aware of being alone in the world and would like strong ties with an acceptable past. However, she cannot assent to such ties with the tradition of her husband's family, and her own past is so painfully disappointing that she is unable to relate to it except as a circumstance which she is determined to overcome and from which she must spare her children. She recalls some aspects of her past with fondness and nostalgia:

I always liked to read because I was alone with adults. I was good in history and geography, and I very sincerely believed in God. It was a naïve feeling to believe in it the way I did then. It was through my grandma. She was very religious. I never got spanked. I wanted to learn to dance, which was a sin, according to her. I was good in skiing and running. I liked to go out in the fields. I really believed in fairies. Children who are alone a lot hold on to them.

But the fairies were not real, and the childish belief in a benevolent deity was torn by increasing awareness of the bitter reality of her own circumstances. Karen Littleton is attempting to deal with the past by avoiding intimate ties that might lead to a repetition of her early disappointments and by reliving the past through her children. Her intense desire to overcome her early deprivations is one of the primary sources of her drive to achieve a better social and economic position for her family.

IMPULSE, TABOO, AND ACCUSATION

Control of behavior within the family is sometimes regarded as comprising either or both of two family activities: the pattern of parental discipline and the socialization of the child. These concepts are important, but they do not in themselves differentiate sufficiently among the relatively homogeneous families of our study, nor do they describe the processes for mutual regulation that the nuclear family typically evolves. These processes cannot be understood apart from the nature of discipline, the psychological motivations that provide energy to enforce it, the psychological function for the individual of controlling or being controlled, and the emotional consequences of the affect or counteraffect aroused by the application of discipline and constraint.

In the Littleton family control is shared unequally by husband and wife. She is the more frequent disciplinarian with the children, and her disciplinary measures are more severe. Her relatively greater role is not, in itself, an unusual situation; most families see the mother as more frequently involved in disciplinary action with the children because of the larger proportion of time she spends with the family. However, many families of our group see the father as the ultimate and potentially more threatening of the parental authorities, with the mother holding a minor though more frequently exercised power. Mrs. Littleton has assumed control over the daily events of the family and over most of the major elements of family life. The only major area in which she has not been dominant is in her attempt to persuade Mr. Littleton to improve his occupational position. She is not inactive on this front, however, and it remains a source of chronic irritation between them.

Mr. Littleton's conception of his role in the family is strikingly similar to that he attributes to his own father. His comments about his parents reveal his mother as the disciplinarian of the home and his father as aloof and non-participating. Mr. Littleton's disciplining of the children on Sundays, the day he is "boss," helps him maintain the impression that he, too, is distant but respected and obeyed. He is apparently not jealous of his wife's dominance in the home.

I work nights all the time, so I don't see much of them. I don't participate. When they come home, I go to work. They're lacking a good deal in guidance as far as I'm concerned. Their mother does more than she should, not that she makes up for my lacks. They lean toward their mother. She does most of the handling of the children. I generally agree with her. I go along with what she says.

Mrs. Littleton has the desire, the initiative, and the ability to exercise authority in the family group. However, she shows some resentment over her husband's lack of participation, and she resents his leniency and indulgence with the children. On the SCT she says: "Children would be better off if their parents / co-operated," and "When father comes home / all rules are forgotten." She refers to him as more lenient than herself but asserts that he, too, would be more strict if he were around the children more often.

Mrs. Littleton is firmly convinced that the general standards of behavior she has established for the children are appropriate and correct, but she wishes for more self-control in her manner of enforcing taboos. She reports on the SCT: "I cannot understand what makes me / yell at my children." Recall, also, her statement that she yells at her children even though "I know [it] is the worst thing in the world to do with children."

The overt techniques that Mrs. Littleton employs are used in many families. She describes the methods in these terms:

I take their allowances away for [misconduct] checks on the report card. I'd rather they had F's and no checks. Before TV, they couldn't go to the show for a length of time. Since TV, I don't turn it on. It's controlled, anyway, in our house. They get put to bed. They still do. It hurts more now than when they were little. I've impressed them that I worry when they don't come home on time. If they're going somewhere, they leave a note on the table. At lunch, if they're twenty-five minutes late, there's no lunch. That has worked because my children like to eat.

INTERVIEWER: *What do you do when they fight with each other?*

MRS. LITTLETON: *Try to ignore it as long as I can, then yell. I listen so long and then I scream. They get a kick out of knowing* they've gotten my goat. If I had room, I'd shuffle them off, one to one room and one to another.

INTERVIEWER: *Do you ever lose your temper?*

MRS. LITTLETON: *Not too often. They've been spanked. It's not an everyday habit. When I get angry, I explain if I didn't care about them I wouldn't be angry.*

This excerpt reveals the unevenness with which discipline is applied. There is a rigid time limit on appearing for lunch, but fighting is ignored as long as possible. (We might suggest that Mrs. Littleton's own convenience is the governing consideration here; the children's being late to lunch is more inconveniencing than their fighting.) Discipline is often accompanied by a volatile verbal display and by explanations of how the mother's anger is an indication of love. Enforcement of behavioral standards is typically delayed so that misbehavior which is verbally discouraged is actually accepted. This covert acceptance of behavior which is incongruent with expressed standards permits aggression and insubordination to become integrated into the pattern of family exchange. As we have seen, the children perceive this discrepancy between the announced code and the actual limits. Mrs. Littleton's statement suggests that they are aware of the provocative effect their behavior has upon her and that her actions encourage the children to misbehave. It may also provide her with an excuse for directing aggression toward them and for the severity of the disciplinary measures she employs.

The nature of the discipline she uses is primarily deprivation of gratifications—withholding food, money, and recreation—though she also uses such directly punitive techniques as spanking. Withholding of affection is not only implied in the deprivation of food and pleasure but also used as a specific punishment:

Bobby's like me in the way he likes affection. That's the worst punishment for him, not to kiss him goodnight. He'll lie there until twelve o'clock until I do kiss him.

The three Littleton children hold in common a high sense of guilt over their impulses, although this is less pronounced in Betty than in the younger children. The feeling that they have done or are about to do something "bad" is one of the primary underlying tones of their relationship to their mother and to each other. Bobby has a tremendous amount of pent-up hostility, and repressing it is very costly in psychic resources. Much of his hostility is directed against his mother, but it is so intense that the issue of controlling or releasing aggression is his preoccupying concern. It is an unending struggle. Although he has some slight awareness of his feelings, they are entirely unacceptable to him. Being angry and wishing to hurt others are always bad and must be denied and counteracted at any cost. He is guilty over his hostility and obsessively tries to establish a reaction formation against it, as the previously quoted SCT responses show.

Twelve of Bobby's SCT responses are concerned with attempts or wishes to help others. However, his efforts do not really succeed, for he defines himself as bad. He feels that he does wrong things and has bad wishes, and he quickly blames himself for the punishments he receives. If he is punished, it must be his fault. But his fear of punishment contributes to a high degree of anxiety, and he is so intent upon expiating guilt that his emotional freedom is restricted. He devotes a great deal of energy to appeasing his mother, thus limiting what he has available for increasing his autonomy. An example of the manner in which these feelings are translated into behavior comes from an incident which Mrs. Littleton relates with obvious pride. It concerns a school meeting at which Bobby saw his principal, whom he didn't know personally. "He went right up to him and hugged him. He likes people and wants to show it. It's a nice feeling when you can be relaxed among people." It is almost superfluous to mention the relevance of Bobby's internal problems to his need for affection from his mother; the impact of his mother's refusal to kiss him goodnight has reverberations and consequences of which she is unaware. Mrs. Littleton's comments about Bobby's co-operation and conformity become more meaningful:

With Bobby, there's nothing that I can't handle with him. When others ask him to do things, he's stubborn. If you stop and explain why it's wrong, he listens to reasons. He co-operates with me, no matter what I tell him. . . . Bobby is always affectionate and has always demanded it. He may be spoiled. . . . He loves everybody so much. His teacher says she puts him in the corner and afterward he comes to her and says, "I love you, Miss T."

Bobby's view of the control processes in the family and of his place in the system is amplified by his comments about parental discipline:

INTERVIEWER: *What do your mother and father do to make the children mind?*

BOBBY: *My mother does it. Sometimes she has to say the words crossly. Sometimes she has to use my father's belt or shoe.*

INTERVIEWER: *When does she get cross?*

BOBBY: *When Betty brings five kids up to the house in one day, or else if we do something wrong.*

INTERVIEWER: *Like what?*

BOBBY: *Hurting smaller kids than us. Sometimes I bring out toys when I am not supposed to. She takes one up and throws it at me, and she tells me to put them away, so I do what she says.*

INTERVIEWER: *What does she do when the children fight?*

BOBBY: *She sends them both to bed.*

INTERVIEWER: *What does she do when you talk back?*

BOBBY: *She slaps us across the face.*

INTERVIEWER: *Does your father ever lose his temper?*

BOBBY: *When Mommy tells us to turn off the television, we don't do it, so he makes us do it.*

INTERVIEWER: *Do you ever lose your temper?*

BOBBY: *No.*

Bobby's TAT responses supplement even more dramatically the view he holds of himself and of the punitive controls within the family that have come to be a psychological necessity for him:

CARD 3BM: *The little boy is crying here. I don't know what he is crying about. There might be something wrong with him, or he has done something wrong and his mother had to punish him, and he might have to go to bed. Maybe he cracked a window.*

Sally's internal turbulence is not so great or so debilitating as Bobby's, but she reveals a similar tendency to punish herself. She, too, has a residue of deep anger, directed especially at her parents but aimed also at anyone viewed as a competitor for her desired love objects. There is some acceptance of her more superficial anger, but she attempts to dissociate the deeper hostility from herself. Overt expressions of anger tend to be limited to occasions of provocation; the bulk of her aggression is not outwardly expressed. Basically, she is an intrapunitive person. Guilt and anxiety are both moderately severe but alleviated by her intrapunitive tendencies. Her ego integration is fairly well maintained under aggressive arousal, but she sometimes suffers some mild impairment of ego effectiveness. Yet she feels herself to be a "bad girl," and she frequently tries to get out from under this burden either by acknowledging her guilt or by trying to justify herself and refute the insistent blame she heaps upon herself.

In the directly maternal aspects of their relationship, Sally also sees her mother as depriving. She is a harsh disciplinarian ("And sometimes if we are bad, she doesn't let us eat supper") and a shrill critic ("My mother usually screams at us, and Tabby is always hungry, and the television gets turned off"). Other aspects of the manifest role image include a forceful organizer of household routines, an omniscient detective of wrongdoing, and a helper when things go wrong. Compared to the mother, the father is clearly subordinate as a disciplinarian and authority and, at most, is seen as a supporter of his wife's standards. He seems to have few enforcement powers of his own.

Sally's comment in her tale of the daily activities ("We usually do something bad") is supplemented in these comments about her parents and their disciplinary behavior:

When we do something wrong, we always tell Mommy, because she finds out anyway. If she's really mad—if we do something wrong and don't tell her—she's really mad, and she yells at us.

INTERVIEWER: Does she do anything besides yell?

SALLY: Spanks, but she doesn't spank very much anymore. And sometimes if we are bad, she doesn't let us eat supper. When we come from the movie late—she tells us we shouldn't, but that is the time it's over—we don't get supper sometimes.

INTERVIEWER: What happens if you get bad marks?

SALLY: She turns off television for a month—even on Saturday and Sunday. And Sunday is Dad's day off. We can't watch. We get to watch because he likes to watch.

INTERVIEWER: What happens if you start fighting?

SALLY: We get a spanking. Even if we fight and she finds out, she doesn't do anything. She yells at us, she tells us to quit. She doesn't do anything, but if we do it again she tells us to get out.

INTERVIEWER: What happens if you talk back?

SALLY: She gives us a spanking or makes us apologize. My brother had to say "I'm sorry" to the teacher.

INTERVIEWER: Does your dad ever get very mad and lose his temper?

SALLY: No.

INTERVIEWER: Does he ever do anything to make you mind?

SALLY: He tells us over and over again, and he gets real mad, and he screams at us. Then he either hits us or turns the television off and we go to bed.

The wielding of authority in the family is frequently, for Sally as for the two other children, punitive and withholding.

The rewards for good behavior presumably lie in the temporary relief from corrective measures and from guilt and anxiety. An SCT response reveals Sally's awareness of the negative aspect of control and discipline and her wish that circumstances would be otherwise: "Children would be better off if their parents / would be nice to them."

Betty, too, has the pervasive sense of wrongdoing and badness that is evident in her brother and sister. The weight of guilt that she bears is revealed in her sentence completions ("Children / are often bad; I am sorry when I / do something wrong") and in her TAT responses. An excerpt from her story to Card 3BM is an example:

The little boy, he had woken up in the morning, and he was grouchy and didn't feel so good that evening, no that morning, he got put in the corner in school. He was a bad boy. . . . He went home real late and his mother scolded him, and he didn't get any supper because he was a bad boy, so he felt sorry for himself and started to cry and went in his room. So that night when he went to bed he said a prayer that he wanted God to help him be a good boy. The next day he was nice and decided to be nice all the time.

Although Betty's guilt provides an intense inner pressure toward conformity, her perceptiveness of the nature of discipline in the family has made her aware that conformity and "being nice" do not necessarily provide the rewards she wants or preclude accusations and punishments from her mother. She understands, or thinks she does, the motivation underlying rewards, and she is inclined to see these small favors as providing convenience and gratification for Mrs. Littleton rather than as benefits for the children. She responds with anxiety, as do the other children, to Mrs. Littleton's unusual concern over verbal truthfulness, but she accuses her mother of not believing her even when she does tell the truth.

Betty has a deep underlying resentment of both parents. She is aware of much of this feeling, though not able to admit its intensity. Her resentment is generalized to other adults and to the world in general. She describes the neighborhood as dirty and says the kids pick on her, but she is capable in such exchanges: "I know how to take care of them when they pick on me or my brother." Betty's resentment toward her parents, which derives from a basic feeling of emotional deprivation, is compounded by the fact that adult responsibilities and adult perspectives have been forced upon her. She resents having to get her own breakfast on Saturday morning, and she resents her mother's arbitrary discipline. She is obliged not only to protect her brother but to discipline him, and her considered hesitation in reporting to Mrs. Littleton indicates a tendency to make uncommonly mature decisions for a child of nine.

Betty is a girl who hopes for help from outside (". . . he wanted God to help him"), but she expects to rely on herself (". . . the next day he was nice and decided to be nice all the time"). In a vague and anxious manner, she assumes or feels a need to assume responsibility for the welfare of others, including her father. Her response to Card 8BM is an example:

This boy's father was getting sick and weak, and the boy asked the doctor to come over to see him, and the doctor said he needed a very expensive operation, and so the boy said he would help his father earn the money, and he got a job for $25 a week, and he said he would pay the doctor as soon as he could, so the doctor gave the operation and after a while he got well again, but he was shot with a rifle because of some bandits, so again the boy had to go to work. This time he didn't have enough money to pay for the operation so he went to a different job to earn $50 a week, but he had to work harder and harder. Finally he too became ill, but he got well again, and his father was saved.

This story discloses, of course, some of the ambivalence Betty feels toward her father, but its relevance here lies in her conception of a child's place and responsibilities in the family. She wants very much to be taken care of, but adults are weak and sick, and it requires effort on her part to maintain them. The status of a child is not clearly defined: she is compelled to know too much about adults' weaknesses and to see life from their viewpoint. Yet she is not trusted, is unjustly accused and frequently deprived of rewards that were presumably established as routine: "She takes our allowance away most of the time."

Betty also recognizes her mother's superior position in the family: "My mother argued about getting the blinds. He didn't want to. We got them. She always does." This observation coincides with her image of males, illustrated by her response to Card 2 (see p. 126). They are lacking in initiative and decisiveness and must be assisted and directed by females. The fact that she includes her own father in this conception creates a conflict of roles for her. As a female, she sees herself potentially more capable and assertive; as a child, she cannot easily exercise the superior prerogatives of her sex.

Throughout the interviews and SCT endings there appear references to two aspects of behavior that are of deep concern to Mrs. Littleton: deliberate verbal misrepresentation and face-to-face challenge of her authority. She insists on respect ("... children have to mind anyone older without talking back") and will not tolerate back talk. Her refusal to countenance the children's attempts to lie to her is accompanied by strong emotion, as in an exchange with Sally that she relates: "She'll stand there. I saw her do it. She'll cry and say it's not her fault. ... What makes it terrible is that she denies it."

The events that stir parents to expressions of anger toward their children are of obvious significance for an understanding of the parents as well as of the family's internal dynamics. We assume that these areas of overt irritation are not merely accidental or random but that they represent points of sensitivity and stress in the family's emotional interaction. The significance of these stress points may not be apparent in the overt behavior they induce. The aggressive nature of discipline in the family may be disguised by an array of rationalizations that conceal from parent and from child the underlying meaning of the disciplinary exchange. Mrs. Littleton's concern about her children's truthfulness and about a tendency to back talk recalls another statement she makes about children: "I've always said that I like children until they have a mind of their own. Then someone else could raise them." Mrs. Littleton freely admits her own stubbornness: "I'll do most anything to prove that I'm right." But she discourages this characteristic in her children: "I'd like them not to be quite as stubborn as I am." However, she recalls with no apparent regret her own stubbornness as a child.

The interview responses as well as the TAT fantasies reveal Karen Littleton's basic mistrust of intimate interpersonal relationships: "You're better off if you like everybody and are not too fond of anyone." These feelings derive from her memory of being deserted as a child by both father and mother. She wishes desperately to experience or recapture the love of her own parents: "I'm afraid you'll end up saying my heart belongs in Denmark, and I guess it does." But she forced herself to become independent, self-contained, and sufficient; and, in a manner that is being repeated in Betty, this became her pride, her pain, and her anger. She cannot escape her anger at her children, for they have parents, which she did not; they will develop minds of their own and will undoubtedly leave and reject her. She likes babies—they cannot question the relationship or refuse to love her. Thus the spoken word, conceived by an independent mind, takes on a symbolic significance: to lie is to reject the mutuality of mother-child and to reveal the infidelity that she believes to be inevitable in intimacy. She has been profoundly deceived and can never again rely on love that is not bound by some necessity —marriage, dependency, or enforced respect of a child for his parent. She refuses to give happy endings to her TAT stories, with one exception—the man who believes in God: "I know he'll be all right."

Mrs. Littleton is angry with her children before they misbehave because of her jealousy of them and because they, too, will withdraw from her. She accuses them in a multitude of irrelevant ways, taking minor childhood infractions as the vehicle and rationalization for her accusations. Her discipline necessarily assumes an erratic, impulsive, and arbitrary character and creates in the children a vast burden of guilt which is only vaguely related to the events that trigger the accusatory nagging voice. The children's anxiety is only partially socialized because parental discipline is lacking in social meaning. They retaliate by provoking her and by bringing down discipline upon themselves, to assist their control of their own unconscious anger toward her and to provide the temporary relief from chronic guilt that is afforded by overt punishment. The difference we have noted between the announced behavioral code and the enforcement of discipline thus serves psychological needs for parent and child: the child "gets a kick" out of aggressing against the parent and evoking punishment; the mother's anger finds justification and expression; and the entire incident affirms again her conviction that the children do not really love her. The children seek their individual adaptations to themselves and to their mother. They are dimly aware of her intense anger, and they recognize occasionally her motivations though they do not comprehend them. Betty is developing her mother's self-containment and sufficiency; Sally attempts to deny her guilt and transfer it to her siblings; Bobby attempts to transform his anger and fear into love, physical affection, and conformity.

Like his children, Mr. Littleton is vulnerable to control by accusation. His feeling of personal failure is intensified by his wife's charges that he has failed her by refusing to become occupationally mobile and that he has failed the family by refusing to devote more time to them. In response, he has withdrawn to his work, to television, and to vacations away from the family. When he cannot withdraw, he concedes by suppressing for the sake of the other children his preference for Sally and by doing housework on his day off (for the benefit of his wife). Mr. Littleton's control over the children is minimal, though of course he can discipline them because of his status and strength. His discipline, however, is primarily in support of his wife.

The avoidance of intimacy which characterizes the Littletons springs from a basic mistrust of the reciprocity and stability of affectional intimate exchange. It is also related, we believe, to an inadequately developed ability to communicate feelings of positive affect. The attempt to master affectional expressive techniques is vividly illustrated by Bobby's verbal and physical outburst of "love" toward his teacher, his school principal, and his mother. For him, and to a degree for other family members, physical contact is equated with affection. In a vague sense, Bobby recognizes the infantile nature of his wish to be mothered and held, and he is aware that physical contact is less acceptable to his father than to his mother. Speaking of the "things you like to do best with your family," Bobby says of his father: "Daddy usually lets us sit on his lap and watch television." Later, he adds:

> I think he likes me the best. I never bother him. That's why.
> INTERVIEWER: What bothers him?
> BOBBY: They always sit on his lap when he doesn't want them.

Thus Bobby believes he gains favor by renouncing his preferred mode of affective expression. He gains in intimacy, he believes, by accepting separateness. The importance of physical affection is also seen in Mrs. Littleton's description of her exchange with Mr. Littleton about his neglect of Betty: "Now he takes Betty on his lap and holds her and hugs her." Later, she criticizes his general lack of affection: "His [Bobby's] father doesn't show affection easily."

The most apparent affective gestures occur within two sets of paired relationships: Mrs. Littleton and Bobby, and Mr. Littleton and Sally. Mr. Littleton's preference for his second daughter is evident from his wife's remarks about her sympathy for Betty, who "lost her daddy" to her sister. Mr. Littleton's comments about Sally confirm these conclusions:

Sally is more like her mother than the others. She is blond. In appearance she looks more like her mother. She is more like her mother than the others. She's a likeable child, I'd say. She got more cards at Valentine's Day than the others. That might be proof. She has girl friends, and even boy friends, who are interested in her and come here. Her mother is handy in sewing. Sally takes an interest in that. She'll probably be more of a homemaker, maybe more than her mother. She likes children, babies. She will have sixteen when she grows up. She's a very feminine girl. She likes dolls. Of course, she does play marbles. She's strictly all girl, though. She is almost a carbon copy of my wife. I get along better with Sally than with Betty or Bobby. I wouldn't say she's my favorite. Probably my wife says she is. Maybe I do, too, unconsciously. She's the one, when I'm sitting down, who climbs up on my lap.

It is relevant here to introduce a consideration of Mr. Littleton's image of adult females and his psychological approach to them. From his interview we learned that he believes relating to women has been a problem for him since boyhood. In describing his son, Mr. Littleton says: "He and I both have trouble with girls, our sisters. I used to, not any more. My mother disapproved of the children fighting. . . ." He offers these responses on the SCT:

Most women / I like and admire.
Most men / are braggers.
Compared to men, women are / more thoughtful.
Compared to women, men are / every bit as good though they don't often show it.

In his TAT responses, the woman appears as stronger, more able, and more assertive than the male. In contact with maternal figures, others become fearful and ashamed. The maternal figures attempt to be helpful or instructive but do not offer emotional support. His responses to the following TAT cards illustrate this.

CARD 6BM: *This has several possibilities. Maybe this man here is bringing sad news to this woman. Maybe a tragedy, the son or father has been killed. He is about to or has broken the bad news and she has turned away in grief. It could be that he is this woman's son, and he has done something wrong and something not in accord with his mother. She's grief-stricken and is turning away from him. He feels very remorseful. He hangs his head. It could be any number of things. He may have lost his job. She feels very bad about it. He might have done some dishonest thing. I think that covers it pretty thoroughly.*

CARD 7GF: *This looks like a mother trying to explain something to her daughter. She has a book in her hand. It looks like it may be. The daughter is about the age where she should know something about sex. That's probably what the mother is trying to put across to her, some facts of the sex life. The daughter is hoping in shame and half in fear that she will not do something wrong. She turned her head away. The mother is trying to tell her that there's nothing wrong, that it's all the way you approach the subject. The daughter still plays with dolls, but she's old enough to wonder about certain things. The child is old enough to read herself, so the mother wouldn't be reading a story out of a book to a child her age. She could read her own story if she wishes.*

Mr. Littleton sees his wife as the disciplinarian in the family, impatient and harassed with the children:

She yells at the kids. I don't know whether she has told you different. It's not her fault. She is cooped up with them underfoot. When she was ill, it was too much to take. It only aggravates her when the kids are too full of life, when there's too much racket.

Later, he compares Mrs. Littleton with his mother:

My mother was more the old-fashioned type, home type. She created more of a home as far as cooking meals and things of

The Dynamics of Disconnectedness

163

that sort. My wife does, too. She doesn't neglect the children as far as food goes.

In his interview Joe Littleton suggests that his wife may have misrepresented the situation in her interview comments. He is one of the very few husbands of our group of families to criticize or question their wives openly to the research staff member. This, together with Mrs. Littleton's open criticism of him and her reports of bitter quarrels between the two, indicates the chronic conflict that characterizes their relationship. His most forceful criticism of her involves her carelessness with the family budget. His primary positive contribution to the family welfare and the most obvious support for his self-regard is his ability to earn sufficient money for the family's needs. Her failure to recognize its value is a serious insult. He attempts to temper his criticism with excuses, but these only faintly disguise his feeling of ambivalence.

Mr. Littleton finds in Sally a duplicate of his wife, without the threat that adult females hold for him. He has displaced onto his daughter some of the affection and physical contact that he no longer displays to Mrs. Littleton. To kiss his wife at the door is an unnecessary formality; yet his affection for Sally was so obvious that Mrs. Littleton felt compelled to obtain a more equal distribution of his attention. Mr. Littleton's preference for Sally increased competition and complicated the relationship between the two girls. Jealousy between the two is intense. Betty is particularly vocal in her objections to Sally's attempts to tag along when one of Betty's boy friends walks her to school.

Mr. Littleton's devotion to Sally provides considerable support for her at the expense of Betty, who experiences a constant fear of desertion. Their stories to TAT Card 4 illustrate Betty's fear and Sally's optimism about the outcome of interpersonal relationships:

BETTY: *This lady and man were in Mexico. They believe in all different kinds of things, and so one night he had to go on the* important job and she didn't want him to go because she thought that he would get killed, and she said, "What do you think you are?" And he said, "I think I am like a little jug. It holds water, and that's what it's made for, and I am made for this job. I'm a little jug." He said to her, "I am going whether you like it or not." She held on to him, and he pulled away from her, and when he pulled away the little jug fell down and broke, and she was crying and she picked up the pieces, and when he went out the door she screamed because she thought he was going to get killed like the little jug had broken.

SALLY: I think that she did something to him, and he's still mad, and after a few days she'll try to tell him that she's sorry and he still doesn't care. He's still mad at her. He's thinking that he won't forgive her but he will, and she loves him a lot and she's a pretty lady, and I think she has maybe a little girl. I think they're married already too, and I think that they live happily and I don't think that they ever got mad at each other before, and I don't think they're very poor or very rich.

Mr. Littleton chose between his two girls in selecting one of his children for an object of special affection, and it is significant that he picked the one who most closely resembled his wife. It is significant, too, that Mrs. Littleton settled upon Bobby as the particular object of her affection. Bobby is a duplicate of his father in appearance, but in the crucial characteristics—affective expression and self-confidence—his mother believes they are opposites. She wanted Betty to be a boy but is proud of her acceptance of Betty in spite of her sex. "I wanted a black-haired boy, but I did not push Betty aside." Mrs. Littleton openly prefers male children:

He [Bobby] co-operates with me. It's partly me. I prefer boys even to work with. I can always find an excuse for a boy. With girls, I think they should just behave.

Mrs. Littleton is determined that Bobby will not grow up to be like his father. When Bobby showed signs of timidity, she initiated a program designed to force him to independent and self-confident action. She has insisted upon an open, physical demonstration of affection from him to the extent that Bobby has seized upon this type of behavior as a mechanism for appeasing adults. She feels that Bobby's need for affection is an accomplishment of which she can be proud. When she describes his refusal, or inability, to go to sleep until he has received the goodnight kiss from her, she ignores the terror that underlies Bobby's need for symbolic physical contact.

Bobby provides Mrs. Littleton with an opportunity to punish and attempt to alter behavior which she rejects in her husband but which she has been unable to change. Her resentment against Mr. Littleton is displaced onto his son, and one of the psychological functions served by the boy is that he provides a male object for the release of her resentment. Bobby's attempt to appease her by becoming more affectionate affords her an additional substitute gratification. Bobby is attached to his mother and uses desperate measures in his attempt to please her, but he is also competing with her and with his sisters for affection from Mr. Littleton. However, Mrs. Littleton's possession of him, together with Mr. Littleton's attachment to Sally, have effectively pre-empted Bobby's bid for a satisfactory relationship with his father. Mrs. Littleton sees her husband's fondness for Sally as a threat to Betty, but she believes that Bobby was untouched:

It didn't have any effect on Bobby. Whether he was satisfied with my love I don't know. He didn't need his father. This is often true of little boys. It didn't do anything to him. He never took Bobby anywhere. When he went to the park, he took Sally to the park; he takes him [Bobby] now. To Bobby it's the biggest thrill to follow his Daddy.

However, Bobby's story to TAT Card 4 presents feelings that his mother seems quite unaware of. Bobby's longing for his father and his wish that he be a full-time protector are underscored in the conclusion to this story:

*I think the lady is liking the man, and the man doesn't want
to marry her, only she wants to marry him. She wants to get engaged to him. She thinks he looks pretty to her. He doesn't like
her at all. I think the man is going to go away from town. Then
she won't be able to see him. She thinks he looks pretty. The
man probably works and that's why he doesn't want to get married. He has to do hard work. I think he teaches children. Maybe
he has some children of his own. That's why he doesn't want
to get married. He has to keep care of his children.*

Bobby's response to Card 7GF repeats his concern about the
father. In his story, the girl is worrying "because the father
didn't come home for a couple of days." And his association to
7BM shows his wish for closer contact with father-like figures:

*The old man and his son, I think they're riding on a train.
The old man is talking to his son and the son, he's worried, and
the father has a blue tie and a white shirt, and he seems proud
of himself and his son. The son is proud of going places, and
this old man, he likes to go places, and he tries to get enough
money to go wherever he wants to. Both are sitting together.
They seem to like each other. I think the father is looking at the
son very closely.*

On infrequent occasions Bobby is permitted to visit the restaurant while his father is working. Bobby describes these visits
as among "the things I like to do best" and volunteers that he
would like to work in a restaurant like his father. Altogether,
Bobby has constructed for himself a more positive image of his
father than has any other member of the family.

Mr. Littleton's first comment about Bobby is that he talks
back more than the other children. He sees him as a boy with
many personal problems and believes that Bobby's lack of male
peers is responsible for his difficulties:

*He is the little one with the most problems. He is slow in his
education in school. He is not as bright as the other two. He
tries hard. He is trying to get into the first part of the class. I
think he'll make it. He is slow in reading. His spelling and arith-*

metic are good. *It's not his eyes. We had that checked. He is a boy thrown in constant contact with two girls. There are not many boys in the building. He is hard to handle. This stems from too much contact with the girls. I had some trouble like that. We were evenly matched, three boys and three girls. I had trouble with the girls. He has a pretty good temper. He flies off the handle easily. He talks back once in a while.*

INTERVIEWER: *How does he get along with his mother?*

MR. LITTLETON: *Same as with me. He has had more checks on his cards than the other two. He is hard to handle for some teachers. He is a little difficult. If he doesn't grasp something right away and the teacher is harsh, I don't know whether he'd sulk or cry. I think he's trying. The teacher doesn't realize. He thinks she picks on him. . . . He has been good lately with the teacher. He has improved a lot. I think his mother helps him quite a bit.*

INTERVIEWER: *In what ways do you think Bobby is like you?*

MR. LITTLETON: *He looks like me quite a bit. His mother said he looks exactly like me.*

INTERVIEWER: *How would you like Bobby to be like you?*

MR. LITTLETON: *I have no outstanding characteristics that I'd care to pass on to him. As long as he is himself and turns out all right—I don't see any outstanding characteristics. I want him to be a good, honest boy.*

Later in the interview, he compares Bobby with Sally:

Bobby is smaller than Sally. He is left-handed. She is right-handed. She has been the more favored one, as far as we're concerned and in school. He probably resented it. He's overcoming it. He wore corrective shoes because he was knock-kneed. He just stopped lately. Sally is healthier and huskier. He is inclined to have a sensitive stomach. There are certain foods that don't agree with him. I wouldn't say he was delicate. There is nothing radically wrong with him.

Mr. Littleton recognizes that his son is something of a problem to the family as well as to himself, but he feels unable to assist Bobby toward a solution. His own sense of inadequacy is intensified by the demands for an identification model that Bobby places upon him. Unlike his wife, he is unable to attempt substitute reconstruction of his own life through Bobby. Possibly he sees the attempts that Mrs. Littleton is making toward molding Bobby into a non–Joe Littleton and feels that she is more capable than he in teaching the boy to become a man.

The affectional ties among the Littleton children are, in general, summarized by Betty:

Maybe you would want to know how we three get along. We're O.K. towards each other. If anybody else is in trouble, we stick up for them. We might have quarrels, but that's all.

In discussing daily routine, for example, the children frequently use "we" and "she" in referring to their interaction with Mrs. Littleton. We have already noted Betty's tendency to protect, as well as discipline, Bobby. She appears to be fond of him and grateful for the fact that he doesn't interfere with her.

What I like about my brother is that he usually plays by himself and doesn't bother me. What I like about my sister is if she is in a good mood, she'll play with you and be friends. . . . Bobby is softhearted like my daddy. He'll give in to anything you want. Sally is stubborn . . . like my mother. I'm not as stubborn as she, and I don't want to go around with everybody's girl friend like she does.

INTERVIEWER: *Who do you think your mother gets along best with?*

BETTY: *Bobby. He'll be the first one to jump up and do anything for her.*

Betty's bitter fights, according to Mrs. Littleton, are with Sally. Other material confirms that the sibling rivalries in the family lie between Sally and the other two. Mrs. Littleton, too, is in obvious conflict with the second girl. She praises Betty and Bobby but has no compliments for Sally, other than a comment about her "lovely voice." Mrs. Littleton makes the following remarks about Sally, at various times throughout the interview:

She's just a very average youngster where Betty has been different. . . . So far I can't see anything specific that's encouraging. . . . I took her to a doctor. I thought she was talking too much.

With Bobby, there's nothing I can't handle. Right now, Betty is at an age where she knows more than I. By telling her, "Now that's enough," she stops. Sally has a bad temper. She cries when she loses her temper like me. I can't fight. I cry. In that respect, I see myself in her. She flies off easily.

Betty likes to give away almost more than to receive, and I like to give things. Sally is like me with her crying and temper. I've learned to control it now, but I was like her when I was little. She is not much like me as far as looks.

INNTERVIEWER: *In what ways do you think she is not like you?*

MRS. LITTLETON: *She's very, very selfish. She'll cry her heart out because she had to give a present. I've done so much talking on that, trying to make her see she can't keep everything for herself. I threw some papers of hers out. There was no room. She cried. Bobby gives in to her. He went in and asked her if she wanted dessert. She gets herself in good with teachers, but she doesn't get along so well with children. Everything for Sally. It's always got to be in her favor.*

The children fight and argue and pick on each other, but let someone else try it and they'll stick by each other. I was worried about Betty. I wondered if she would really hurt Sally if she had a chance.

INTERVIEWER: *You didn't tell me before about the ways in which you think Sally is like your husband.*

MRS. LITTLETON: *She isn't very affectionate. You get a kiss from her and it's really a compliment. And she has a pretty voice and her father has a very lovely voice. I can think of other people in his family who she is like, but not him. He has one sister. "I'm for me and the rest of the world can go jump in the lake." That sister always prided herself that she never needed anything from anyone. At present her husband is working for my husband. That's a darn nice feeling.*

The aspects of her younger daughter that Mrs. Littleton censures most strongly are characteristics that she admits have been problems for herself. Sally's greatest sin, however, is that she holds the favored position with Mr. Littleton. It is this alignment that makes her the target of attack from her mother and her siblings. Thus Sally's relationship with her father, whom she sees only on Sundays, costs her daily conflict with the other family members.

The affective relationships within the Littleton family display the fragmentation characteristic of the family's mode of life. Paired relationships are developed at the expense of other family members and to the detriment of family cohesion and harmony. Affection is not generally available; it must be bargained for and bought at great psychological cost. The need each family member has for affection is so great that in a sense each member is for himself, and none is sufficiently secure to meet the emotional demands that are placed upon him.

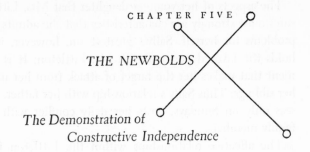

CHAPTER FIVE

THE NEWBOLDS

The Demonstration of
Constructive Independence

The Newbolds live at a brisk pace, with an energy that seems to demand activity. The members of this family have a high sense of themselves as persons and a purposefulness about which they are readily articulate. Determined to make their own lives, they assume responsibilities and carry them out in their own way. With established self-command, they enter into affairs, assured that they can mold their circumstances. They communicate a sense of driving forward against challenge as though to multiply strength and independence. Even at home they seem intent on doing and constructing, and their life together has something of the character of a consciously created product. Nothing significant is left to chance—neither the day-to-day activities nor the long-range career plans of the family's junior members.

Theirs is not a life in which significant feelings and ties are confined to their own family circle. The Newbolds are accustomed to being needed by others, and they take for granted that they can exercise the leadership which is asked of them. Though not always of a mind to accept, none finds it easy to decline these opportunities. On the whole, they find it natural that they should be in positions to guide the activities of others, and they do not readily acquiesce to constraints exerted by other people. They expect much from themselves; coupled with this is a touchiness at any hint of interference with their freedom of choice.

172   THE NEWBOLDS

The standards to which they adhere emphasize firmness and staying power and a disdain for "keeping up to date" for its own sake. The excitement in their lives is not located in shiny new possessions. They take a "sensible" attitude toward the modern conveniences, believing that it is reasonable to reduce physical drudgery but finding no further gratification in the devices which make this possible. With their readiness to take on new experience is joined a belief that the past, in its impersonal aspect, provides a certain amount of solidity. The Newbold home, in which the family has lived for twenty years, is in an old upper middle class suburb of Chicago. During the war, when her husband was away, Margaret Newbold insisted on remaining in this house because she felt that the continuity of residence would help her sons through that fatherless period.

The home, though modest in most respects, speaks of an effort to accumulate visible tradition. Although it includes a heterogeneous collection of bric-a-brac and all the contemporary kitchen gadgetry—dishwasher, freezer, etc.—these are incidental to the beautiful antiques and family heirlooms that are obtrusively placed and eagerly described by Mrs. Newbold. Aside from the antiques, the prominent show of fine art is a group of oil portraits of the family members and a number of paintings by contemporary naturalistic artists.

The backgrounds of both Mr. and Mrs. Newbold contribute to the emerging family heritage. Frank Newbold's father was a successful professional; Margaret Newbold's father was an enterprising businessman. Both parents' backgrounds included a financially secure, well-traveled, and educated ancestry and, as the Newbolds tell it, a self-confident, stubborn hardheadedness in business and personal affairs.

The emphasis on family tradition suggests the Newbolds' strong sense of family pride, even self-satisfaction. Without exception, each member of the family mentions certain characteristics of the group or of other family members that he believes to be superior to or more desirable than those of other middle class families. The Newbolds like themselves and their way of life. The significant critics are within the family, not in a generalized and impersonal public.

Nowhere is the family pride more evident than in the three males' admiration for Mrs. Newbold. She is an articulate, intelligent, forceful, energetic leader among the civic-minded upper middle class women of her community. She easily and quickly rises to the top in various civic and cultural organizations and holds office in at least a dozen major civic groups. In fact, she apparently maintains close contact with a group only so long as her energies and talents are useful in some executive role. In more than one instance she has formed a new group, directed it through its initial stages, and departed when she felt that the group was sufficiently autonomous to carry on without her assistance. Mrs. Newbold compares herself with her husband in these terms:

We both handle people the same; we expect top work from employees. We have pretty high standards, but we're fair. It's all stated clearly, few words minced, and that's how it's going to be and we stay with it.

Her boys take vicarious pleasure in her ability to out-maneuver rivals and factions within the organizations of which she is a member.

Mrs. Newbold's appearance and manner are attractive, unpretentious, generally pleasant, casual, and comfortable. Characteristically, she assumed control of the situation at the first interview, asked about the research until she was satisfied that the project was legitimate and of some significance, then permitted herself to be interviewed. She was eager to talk about her family and her own childhood, and she extended the interview much longer than requested by the staff member.

Her expressions of family pride were unmistakably contrasted with her recollections of her own childhood. Mrs. Newbold says of her mother:

She never quite knew how to be a mother. Too tense, too reserved, too tight. We kids managed without her. Her relation-

ship to us kids was entirely different from mine. We are very free here. Hers was never that way and still isn't. . . . There just wasn't enough freedom of choice and time, and she tried to do our thinking for us. But I don't think she had too much success in most respects.

While she excuses her mother in part because of the lack of educational opportunities available to her, she is critical and unforgiving of the restriction and lack of consideration she remembers in childhood. Mrs. Newbold feels that her own children are proud of her and free of the unreasonable restraint she associates with her own mother. However, in spite of her criticism she is clearly proud of her parents' social place, their good taste, exacting demands, capabilities, and insistence upon controlling and shaping their environment. She feels that she has selected the best of these qualities and added rationality and warmth to them.

Frank Newbold is a tall, solidly built man with a hearty manner. Though he sees himself as a hardheaded realist, he occasionally confesses to underlying sentimental and romantic feelings. While he denies that there is any display of affection within the family ("I wouldn't fit into the cooing and billing very well—we're isolationists"), he admits to an attraction for the displays of natural beauty. "I will get up bright and early to look at a sunrise."

Mr. Newbold is the second child of a professional family. His older sister is married to a Philadelphia lawyer. By profession, Frank Newbold is an architect who has organized other architects into a group under his direction. He has chosen to shift his activities toward administration, and he plans to take on an associate to handle individual clients and provide more time for administrative work and promotion of the organization.

Frank Newbold participates only minimally in his wife's civic functions and activities. He encourages her participation and occasionally acts as her adviser, but his daily professional schedule leaves him with little time for her civic interests. He works a six-day week and usually spends part of the weekday evenings at the office with a client or working on one of his organization's projects.

The adolescent sons are dissimilar to each other both in their personalities and in their relationships to Mr. and Mrs. Newbold. Ted, at fifteen, is a duplicate of his father's overt characteristics—strong, candid, confident, and prominent in his peer group. He has his parents' contempt for weakness, either in himself or in others, and his parents' ready acceptance of open competition. This is illustrated by his comment that he is no longer interested in swimming because "I can swim faster than anyone else." Ted is outspoken in his disdain for small towns where "no one's doing anything—you can't even get in trouble." He boasts of his plans to become an architect, not only because it will extend the family tradition another generation but because "it's something not everyone can do." Leadership falls upon him naturally and rightly, he says, because of his superior organizational ability. He is proud of his family and identifies openly with both parents.

If the family is proud of Ted, it is fond of Curt. Three years younger than Ted, he is a tall, blond, slightly awkward boy. He is less outgoing than the rest of the family but seems comfortable, though reserved, in his response to strangers. He is an excellent student and a discriminating reader. Mrs. Newbold describes him as modest, popular, and generous—a boy who likes but doesn't need people. Curt has puzzled and possibly disappointed his parents by wanting to become a farmer. The overt parental reaction to this un-Newbold-like choice has been one of reserved support, though there are suggestions that the family assumes that Curt will change his mind as he moves into his late teens and is forced to make a commitment. There are times when Curt seems to share this assumption. He used the following words to describe his ideal person:

The person I want to be like when I grow up is a farmer in the northern part of Wisconsin. Owning his own farm at the age of twenty-eight. Having many sports, skiing in winter, bicycle riding. Happy. He is imaginary.

Curt's feeling that such a person is imaginary is probably entirely correct. Mr. Newbold realizes that Curt at present doesn't want to go to college. He makes this comment about his son's ambitions:

It makes no difference to me what he turns out to be. That is for each one to decide for himself. Little Curt, he comments on his desires to be a farmer. It's very commendable—he becomes an independent individual. His success will depend on his ability. His feeling is that a farmer doesn't have to go to school. However, he'll have to decide very hard that he doesn't want to go to school before we'll accept that.

Mr. and Mrs. Newbold are pleased that he was asked to take over the safety patrol of a difficult street corner but a little disappointed that he waited until he was asked. In a family of eager volunteers, Curt's reserve is not easily understood. Mrs. Newbold describes the two boys:

Ted is much more extroverted. Absolutely no qualms about saying or doing anything. Likes to be, matter of fact, has to be the leader. Curt is much different. He is very co-operative in groups. Curt is a good student, as a matter of fact, superior. Ted is, oh well, he hates to think about things he's not interested in. Take spelling—there's nothing worse. They have an awful lot of characteristics that are a lot alike. Ted needs people, though. He has to be in the center—lets people know he's around. But they are both bored at certain social functions. If they are really not interesting they come home. They have the same standards of cleanliness. Good taste, appreciation of nice things and home. Curt is much more generous than Ted. Curt is always making things for someone and giving them away. Ted is likely to be late with that sort of thing. I certainly think there is the same close relationship with both boys. I don't think we like one more than the other. No, I'm sure.

Curt is aware of his father's reservations about his occupational choice:

I haven't asked my father—he'd like it, I guess. So would Mom. What my father thinks is if I'd go through college he'd rather put money into a place where the guy knew what he is doing.

Although his parents try to assure him of a secure place in the family, his brother's success in meeting the family standards has created some resentment in Curt. He does not find it easy to compete with his older brother, but he has not given up trying, despite some of the non-competitive solutions he works with in fantasy. Curt has selected the more sensitive and, in some aspects, independent characteristics of his father. In doing this, he has provided an external stage for one of Mr. Newbold's inner conflicts: the struggle between his desire for form and order and his resistance to conformity and repetition.

SELF-SUFFICIENCY AND THE MASTERY OF EXPERIENCE

Paramount in the Newbold outlook is the belief that each is the master of his own fate. This view gives rise to some complications in family living, particularly since family membership is also valued. But the more urgently felt requirement is to be an individual, with all that it implies. The Newbolds are highly articulate about the several meanings bound up in this conception.

Most highly prized is each person's determination to remain the locus of control. This means not only a high value on self-control and individual responsibility but, more importantly, a refusal to cede control of a situation to another. The Newbolds stress taking a stand, choosing a direction for oneself, and sticking one's ground against any outside deflecting forces. All of them feel that one should change course only upon individual and well-considered decision. These are the terms in which they appraise themselves and one another. Frank Newbold says of himself as a father: "I'm satisfied. If I felt there was something

I ought to change, I would. If it were really worthwhile." And his wife says of him in this same regard: "He has high standards for the boys. . . . He never quibbles. He is just firm and knows what he wants." She observes that "sometimes he's rough and blunt, but it's always right."

His values are evident also in the brief paragraph he wrote concerning what he would like a child of his to be like:

A healthy, moderately good-looking, intelligent being, of sufficient conscience not to harm his fellow man, nor of so much conscience that he is unable to enjoy himself or his work. Seems that if the above is true, life itself should be pleasant and full.

His statement views the good life as largely self-contained. It testifies to the need for internal controls but also reveals concern that such control is potentially inhibiting. One's own powers are what count—health, adequate appearance, intelligence, and the right balance of control to realize one's own satisfactions.

We have noted that Mrs. Newbold is of a similar mind. She, too, prizes individual powers, the development of capacities so as to be ready for anything, and setting a course free from outside interference. In her essay she writes clearly and decisively:

As a mother, I want for my children a life with purpose and direction—a real sense of values, and the wide experience of an educated, traveled, and capable man. I want that they can face everything that comes their way with good judgment and that theirs will not be a life lived on regrets. Certainly I shall want them to have enough money so that life isn't just a struggle for existence; not that money will be their god.

Also, I shall hope that they will always be good friends and that their own lives and families will give them what they even by now know they want.

Where her husband focuses on keeping sufficiently distant from others in order to have one's own kind of life, Mrs. Newbold adds a more affirmative notion of what should go into that life. She begins and ends with the idea of purpose, while also express-

ing a need to cope with whatever untoward events may inter-
vene. Her conception of interpersonal relations is softer than her
husband's, though still cool. Certainly neither sees the major
satisfactions of life as issuing from ties to others. A person's
primary responsibility is to himself, to develop his capacities and
to know what he wants. With good fortune, those closest to
him will contribute to his aims.

The importance of personal strength for Margaret Newbold
is quickly apparent in these responses to incomplete sentences:

I despise / neurotic people.

I don't like the sort of person who / is frustrated and insecure.

*A good mother always / leads her children on to independ-
ence and responsibility.*

*I don't like the sort of kids who / are spoiled, pampered, and
act like brats.*

Materialistic indulgence has little place in this orientation
toward the world, though the primary gratifications are centered
in the self rather than in others. Yet, while self-centered, the
desired life is lived through action in and contact with an external reality rather than primarily through inner experience,
such as contemplation or faith or feeling loved. When the interviewer asked Mrs. Newbold, "How would you change your life
if you could?" she answered:

*I'd make very few changes. I don't like a life of regrets. We
try to face things as they are. As far as achieving what I wanted
to, it could have been better, but I certainly am not ambitious
for any more than I have. We aren't measuring success by dol-
lars and cents. Our values are higher, and I think the kids have,
too—travel, more education, good interesting living.*

Liveliness and a sense of doing something with one's own executive faculties—these are the preferred qualities of experience.
Intelligence, judgment, broad knowledge, the ability to establish
goals and to make choices, the ability to surmount defeat—these
are the executive characteristics that make such living possible.

The value of rationality in living is described in the following way by Mr. Newbold, in reply to a question how his family differs from others:

You have family units that are compatible and some that aren't. Ours is compatible. Compatibility is lack of argument. In place of argument there is discussion. My wife is alert and sufficiently well educated and sufficiently intelligent to keep ahead of them. She is exacting and demanding, which is not to their detriment because it calls forth participation on their part. The children hold her in esteem, I'm happy to say. Kids often like to think of a battle as just my ma against their ma. My ma'll take 'em.

Alertness and intelligence are valuable because they help to control combativeness and also to keep ahead of others. Frank Newbold likes his wife's capacity in this regard, as well as her ability to be tough and demand much from their children.

Another resource with which they endeavor to live is related to alertness—candor. The Newbolds pride themselves on being able to see the truth without veneer, and they believe that plain speaking, whatever its immediate discomforts, minimizes difficulty in the long run. In this way they strive to be honest with themselves and with others. Of this characteristic, Ted says: "Mom and Dad are really quite frank. They don't beat around the bush. I like that." Everything we have seen so far points up the family's belief that it is more constructive to be realistic than pleasant.

Neither parent believes in being soft toward children or toward others. Good performance is what counts. Implicit in this view is the slant that childhood does not really count for itself; its primary importance is as a preparation for adulthood. Partly, this is because rationality is seen as not really possible in children. It is also because children are in many ways still vulnerable; adulthood enables full personal control. In Mr. Newbold's own words:

In these years, their formative years, their primary objective is preparation for their mature years—whether it be formal learning or their social background, ethics, knife and fork . . . that is the major job of the child. Because as he learns the ethics he is taught in the home and church, he will learn the niceties that make him a pleasure to have around, and as they go to school they will learn to make their way in life, and they learn the social graces so they won't be uncouth bumpkins as they come in contact with their fellow men.

An additional note is struck in these remarks: the value of good form as a means of being a tolerable person. This is in keeping with what we have seen earlier: the problem of living is how to make one's own way without being too bruising to others. There is no generalized exhortation to be helpful or to be well liked. Nor does Mr. Newbold anticipate pleasure from experiencing other people. He is saying that it is important to be competent in one's social relations, to be able to handle oneself. It is important to be effective. Only adults are really effective; children have too much yet to learn.

The ideal of being strong, effective, and completely in control of oneself dominated Ted's essay on the kind of person he would like to be. Though it has a tone of adolescent overstatement, it differs little from what his parents feel:

The person I think would be the nicest to pattern your life after would be one who did everything and was good in each. He would be a person who would work and make it seem fun. I think he should be able to lead and able to take orders. He should have a feeling of duty and responsibility.

When I said he should be able to do anything I meant he should have outside interests from his chosen vocation, which may be school or earning a living.

My ideal person would be strong physically and mentally. I think he should be able to stand just about anything good or bad that comes his way.

The emphasis throughout his statement is on individual capacity for living and on not being subordinated by circumstance.

Make your work seem like fun; don't let it get you down. Don't let anything else get you down. Even in his reference to taking orders, Ted does not suggest that he wants to be obedient or that obedience is a virtue. What he says is that he wants to be able to take orders, because he knows obedience is sometimes a necessity. His reference is again to the inner capacity.

Being in control of oneself and one's own life means living energetically and forming individual interests. Asked how his family differs from others, Ted answers:

We probably do things more than other families. We all have our special interests. Curt likes to fish, Dad likes golf, Mom likes to read. I don't think there are too many families where the kids do so much housework. We have more responsibility than most other kids do. Anybody in our family could be at home in any kind of group. Have as much brains. Wouldn't classify ourselves as one group as such.

The family as an interacting unit is de-emphasized; Ted values responsibility for its own sake and only secondarily as evidence of a contribution to the family's common life. He tells us:

Responsibility is good. Gives you a feeling of self-confidence. Like at church, this guy tries to make me commit myself to speak on something I did this summer. One thing I've learned is never to commit myself unless I can do a good job. Another thing—it teaches a sense of possession. Our bikes are old but in real good shape. Other kids have things given to them. No responsibility. They get a new bike, and in six months it's just a piece of junk.

Responsibility, then, is much more a commitment to oneself and one's own standards than it is an inner pressure to help out, to do one's share, or to be nice.

This is not to say that joint activity has no place but simply that identification with a group—the family or any other unit— is a secondary motive for Ted and the others in his family. Ted says of his family:

It's a fairly close group. We stick together pretty much on the things we can. Mother has to go out. Dad has to go out. But like on Sundays and Saturday nights we do things together. When we go on a trip we go as a group. Most everything we do, we do as a group. Go to the show as a group. That's the big thing; we're together as much as we can be. Dad tries to stretch his time at home. Everything is teamwork. Like painting the basement this summer. One guy'd be on the ladder, one guy'd hand the paint brush.

In this answer to the interviewer's opening question regarding the important things about his family, Ted describes the occasions of joint activity and, especially, the efforts to achieve such activity from a base of individuality that is taken for granted.

Curt's essay, presented in the introductory section, suggests less direct assertiveness in comparison with his brother and his parents. Yet the ideal of independence and individual mastery finds expression not only in the fantasy of owning a farm but also in his choice of sports (skiing and bicycle riding) that depend solely on personal, rather than team, skills. While his essay may signify a wish for an idyllic, non-competitive, productive life free from authority, it also suggests the same need to be master of his own fate that the other members of his family have. That he, too, strives for and enjoys noteworthy success is apparent in his account of activities.

Ted and me both like swimming. We're leaders. We instruct kids at the village community center. We have lifesaving medals. . . . We're in the Leader Club. The Leader Club is something special. You gotta work for it. You get voted in. There's a year where you get to pass your tests and then you're in. If you don't go to take care of the kids—just not go and say you have something else—you can be voted out after you miss a certain number. The younger kids in the pool are between eight and thirteen. And in the club I'm almost thirteen and the oldest is fifteen or sixteen.

He, too, takes pride in being able to meet difficult tests and in strengthening himself through responsibility. His desire for accomplishment also expresses a wish to be constructive. Describing a typical day, Curt tells us that after school:

Sometimes work around the house or maybe go riding with a friend. Sometimes work in the basement. Got quite a bit of tools and stuff. You make tables and benches. . . .

His use of the pronoun "you" instead of "I" suggests some problem in his feeling of mastery, but his wish to engage in constructive activity is clear. His father describes him as "a little more of a dreamer. Capable of doing things with his hands."

This same interest in building something useful is evident when Frank Newbold talks about his firm and its success: "Whenever a thing is developing and flourishing, a man is happy and things are happening. I'm happy. As happy as one can anticipate." As we have also seen in the way Mrs. Newbold functions with an organization, the members of this family wish to work upon a raw material and convert it into a demonstrably useful product. Ideas, things, and human associations are all approached with this kind of aim.

The Newbold ideology is basically derived from the upper middle class cultural values. However, it has selected certain aspects of the cultural ideology for emphasis and has virtually ignored or taken for granted other elements. There is no mention of morality, for example. This is not through any lack of moral behavior on the part of the Newbolds but because morality, as such, is not an issue in this group. Their insistence upon self-command and reasonableness in behavior precludes the necessity for emphasizing morality as an individual virtue. The Newbolds judge their own behavior by internalized standards rather than by conformity to an external code of actions that are in themselves right or wrong.

Mastery, rationality, personal responsibility, self-discipline, and productive, useful activity are the cultural values to which the Newbolds most energetically subscribe. On these elements the group has achieved tacit consensus. To these the family adds a more idiosyncratic tone: the need for zest and enthusiasm in competitive challenge. It is not sufficient that the individual be prepared to meet and master the variety of social, vocational, and intellectual difficulties that are presented to him; he should seek them out with eagerness and confidence. Exciting activities, especially if the element of competition is involved, provide a nucleus of communication among family members. The locus of these activities, when they involve competition with others, is in the extra-familial world. As illustrations of adherence to the family image, they provide a social bridge between the values of the family and of the culture. Family ideology is seen as realistic and effective in contacts with members and institutions of the society. It is apparent from the interviews that the family conversation frequently deals with the conquests of individual family members in their various areas of action. In this and other ways the family reinforces the values of conquest and mastery over oneself, one's fellows, and the environment.

PATTERN FOR AN ACTIVE LIFE

The Newbolds are people of considerable energy. In their very manner of recounting what life is like from day to day they communicate a sense of vigorous intensity and impressive stamina. The day begins at different times for various family members; the interests of the family separate them before breakfast. Frank Newbold often plays a few holes of golf at a nearby country club before the morning meal. Breakfast is not a family affair; each person eats as his own schedule dictates. It is coincidence if two or more members are at the breakfast table together.

The pace and pressure of the family routine are illustrated by the parents' description of a "typical day." Mr. Newbold says:

Weekdays I get up at six-fifteen, play golf until seven-thirty, have breakfast. Shower and dress and take off about nine. I visit various projects and stop at the office. Lunch, then back to the office. Dash in for dinner at six. Very rare that I don't get home for dinner. At seven I leave again and work at the office until nine-thirty or so. Go home, have a highball, go to bed. Saturday I work until about six.

This kind of day bespeaks a man who makes heavy demands on himself. Golf before breakfast indicates something of his intention to live according to a highly self-disciplined regimen. His account suggests that his is a day without waste motion; every part of it counts. Assertive vigor is evident not only in specific early morning athletics but as part of his general style of living; this can be seen by comparing the verbs he uses with those used by Mr. Lanson. Donald Lanson's quiet steadiness is evident: "We start . . . we prepare . . . I am ready . . . I leave . . . the rest of the day is work." Frank Newbold is in action: "Get up . . . play golf . . . have breakfast . . . shower, dress, take off . . . visit . . . stop . . . dash. . . ."

Some of the same characteristics are apparent in his wife. Her considerable energy resources are effectively channeled into a variety of action modalities—supervising her boys, cleaning house, responding to demands for action that come in by phone, entertaining visitors in midafternoon, active social participation away from home, and sedentary work at a desk late at night. The heavy demands of her day require self-discipline, as well as energy. Her ability to keep many things going at the same time is evident in her account:

We get up. That hour before the older boy goes to school is one spit. Getting everything done, getting breakfast, checking on books, being sure they have warm enough clothing, seeing to it that they change their shirts. Then straighten up the kitchen and leave the house about ten for some civic job. I never leave without the house being in good order—beds made. Also the phone has rung at least five times in that hour. Some of the messages will have to be cared for right away.

I try to get home for lunch with Curt. Afternoon it's either civic responsibilities or something here: ordinary housework, serving, marketing, or cooking. There's always somebody dropping in for coffee. Then it's three and the children come home. They talk constantly about their day. Then the boys go to the club or something. They all have their club responsibilities. Then it's dinner. Everybody assembles at six. Dinner at home is very pleasant; everybody has something to say. Always something interesting. I sometimes wish there weren't so many things going on. Father goes back to the office. Boys straighten up the kitchen and then do homework and then bed.

After the house is quiet and everybody's in bed I do some desk work and wait for Mr. Newbold to come home. I never go to bed until he comes home. There are nights when I have to go out to dinner—dinner meetings, mostly. On those days I plan to have things in the oven, and the boys can handle it from there on.

While Mrs. Newbold describes the early morning in terms of her responsibility, seeing that everything is well under control, the boys talk about the beginning of the day in terms of their separateness. Ted observes: "I usually get up quite early. Don't see anybody. By eight o'clock Curt and Mom are up and Curt's breakfast is made." And Curt says: "You get up about six-thirty. You make your own breakfast and then Mother comes down." Thus, all the members seem to be saying that from the beginning of the day each is in control of his own routine.

The weekend offers little time for the entire family to be together. On Saturday Mr. Newbold usually works until late afternoon, then putters about the yard and house, polishing the car, maintaining the house, etc. The boys think of Saturday as a day for individual rather than family activities. They work around the house in the morning, go to their club in the afternoon, and on occasion go out with the family after dinner. Their work about the house includes painting, washing floors, cleaning rugs, and other household chores. The weekend routine is best described by Mrs. Newbold:

Weekend starts Saturday night. Saturday is not a family day because of Mr. Newbold's office commitments. We have adult commitments sometimes—either going out or having friends in. If we go to a movie the boys go along. They love to go, want to go, and of course we like to have them. Then on Sunday, Curt and Mr. Newbold go fishing. Ted and I sleep. Then they come popping in about nine. Curt gets into Sunday school clothes and runs off to Sunday school. Ted and I have been getting and having breakfast. If it's weather like last year, Mr. Newbold and Curt go skiing instead of fishing in winter. I go to church most of the time. In the afternoon it's a family thing. If we stay home we all stay home. We may take a drive. Sometimes we go into town and visit foreign neighborhoods. The boys know the city as well as any kids their age. We often go to museums, but not the common ones. We go out of town quite often. It's a long drive to Michigan, but it's worth it. Sunday evenings we quite often go out to dinner.

Although Mrs. Newbold is out of the home a great deal with her several civic activities, she keeps in close touch with other family members and organizes her routine by them. She comes home for Curt's lunch although she has only fifteen minutes with him; she is available to her boys for an hour after they return from school; she has dinner prepared when the family assembles at six; and she waits for her husband to return from the office at night. Her schedule is frequently interrupted by outside demands, but even then the home schedule continues by pre-arrangement.

There are specified times and occasions in the day when the family members are responsible to one another in a fashion not dictated by the demands of any one individual. That is to say, the family assembles at six because dinner time is an important family occasion. Despite the demands of busy individual daily schedules, there are times when the family members can count on one another and anticipate group interaction. Being together is felt worthwhile and is planned for. While it is taken for granted that most of the time the family members will be engaged in their individual activities, in accordance with their own interests and with the external demands for which they hold responsibility, times are set aside and designated for interaction.

The management of time is used by the parents as a training ground for responsibility. Instead of instructing the boys to be in at certain hours, they expect their sons to assume a commitment which they should honor. In describing the boys, Mrs. Newbold says,

I've had a very open understanding with them. Even now, we say, "When can we expect you from a movie?" And they set a time and stick with it.

The boys confirm their mother's insistence upon meeting time commitments. They feel they can never be even a few minutes late without being subjected to questioning from Mrs. Newbold. It is not unusual for Mrs. Newbold to restrict the boys' out-of-home freedom as punishment for failure to reach home by the prearranged time.

Toward the larger sweep of time that refers backward to the past and forward to the future, there are certain attitudes implicit in what has already been said. The past is split into two parts. One consists of all that was unpleasant, that one had no control over. The stance adopted toward this part is that one should face up to it and know it for what it was but not allow one's later life to suffer for it. This attitude is revealed in Mrs. Newbold's effort to be factual about her mother's shortcomings, her feeling that she has developed beyond the point where these have any contemporary relevance, and her assertion that she does not live a life of regrets. Frank Newbold, in military service when his children were very young, feels that from a present-day perspective his absence was no reason for concern:

It's very fortunate my wife maintained my image in front of them. I also feel the first four or five years were not the years— all the years are formative, but I as a figure was not entirely essential. That care was very well handled by my wife, and my addition was not too important. And she recognized these things.

Side by side with this handling of the unpleasant past—putting it aside and regarding it in a detached way—is a less clearly formed but evident interest in temporal continuity. For all their concern with individuality, the Newbolds show positive interest in the past, or a part of it which is seen to have a conserving value. We have already mentioned that the parents—mostly Mrs. Newbold—collect antiques. Frank Newbold has followed in his father's profession and wants his older son to do the same; Ted expects to do so.

The Newbolds do not usually regard those activities closest to the center of their lives as engaged in because they are sanctioned by the past. Yet they seem to invest some energy in looking for the value that can be found from the past. Closer to their central notions about themselves is the push toward new experience, venturing into new areas, insisting on being able to feel at home in any setting. Mrs. Newbold expresses it:

Vacations always have to be a contrast. We never take a cottage and sit on a lake all summer. That would kill Mr. Newbold and Ted. Curt and I like the country. We see the country and the big cities in our trips. We have motored all over the United States. We know the Civil War from seeing the South and the North thoroughly and studying it. We took a trip west and saw all the old sites—Leadville, Central City, and many others. And we stayed on a ranch. We always take our vacation after the boys get home from camp. Mr. Newbold's a wonderful father. He's taught the boys a great deal on these trips. For example, on the trip west we all slept out up in the mountains and everything.

There appear to be several functions served by the Newbold travels: excitement, education, family interaction, and conquest of new experience. In this area of family life, Curt outshines Ted. Ted is committed to a more urban style of life and apparently is not particularly jealous of his brother's reputation in the family as an outdoorsman. Mrs. Newbold speaks of the difference between them:

The older one is most like his father. He has the same kind of mind. Likes the same things. He likes the big city. The younger one likes farms and hates the big city. He doesn't like the rush, the traffic, and the noise. Curt wants nothing more than to finish school and get out in the country on a farm. He loves all the natural things and animals and so on. It's the real contrast between the two. Ted loves the city and all the things in the city, and Curt is the outdoor boy. They are both good campers, but Ted doesn't have the zest that Curt does.

We can suggest that Mrs. Newbold is here presenting a selective picture of family structure and alignment. Notably, it ignores the fact that Curt and his father go fishing and skiing together—activities in which Ted does not participate. Despite this, she asserts the similarity of Ted and his father, construing Curt's individual ways as an idiosyncratic, though acceptable, version of masculinity. Its key feature is that he likes to be in the country with animals; he doesn't need people as much as does his brother. But Frank Newbold is a man who takes a week's vacation by himself away from the family. Further, the TAT picture he selects as the one he likes best is Card 19, a picture without people in it and to which he tells a story about remote mining camps. Here, then, is one sign—and we shall present several more—that Curt is defined in his family as being like no other member. He is assigned a special role—a process in which he co-operates—and becomes a figure of special concern, liberating the other three members from anxiety about each other's intentions.

There exist among the family differences in attitude toward travel that Mrs. Newbold indicates only casually. Mr. Newbold states them openly:

We've traveled together and taken trips, but the interests aren't entirely compatible. The boys enjoyed Yellowstone Park very much, but I question whether Mrs. Newbold likes sitting while we went riding. On the trip east, it is questionable whether Curt enjoyed himself. I take two weeks' vacation in the winter, one week with the family. We may go up to visit the in-laws. Something very genteel. One week by myself, which may be a trip to New York for skiing. I take two weeks in the summertime. Sometimes we take the children, sometimes not. We took a trip to Vancouver two years ago. This summer we drove to Philadelphia.

There are indications that vacations and trips serve an important psychological function for Mr. Newbold that is incompletely shared by the family. On the Sentence Completion form he mentions vacations twice: "It's fun to daydream about / vacations. If I had my way / I'd take longer vacations." He responds to Card 19 on the TAT as follows:

This reminds me of the figures and snow one sees in the Rocky Mountains in the middle of winter. There are a lot of little mining camps. The houses have few windows.

He reminisces of the pleasant hours he spent in places called to recollection by the picture.

Vacations thus appear to meet a need for relief from professional and family routines and pressures to an extent that is not true for his wife. In view of all that we have come to understand about him, it is not surprising that he should select as his favorite this card with no people depicted. Interpersonal relations are less significant for him than his sense of hardiness, an experience more easily had when one is on one's own. It is probably not accidental that he, and not his wife, informed us of his week's solitary vacation. It seems also reasonable to suppose that she is more accepting of it than many women would be. The family image not only allows but insists on individuality and separate activity, so that in pursuing their own goals the family members are promoting group unity by demonstrating adherence to common family values.

Another perspective is also relevant here: the intellectual organization of space. For the Newbolds, the whole world is a legitimate province. Their view of where it is meaningful to go is not circumscribed. Any place that is interesting is worth going to. Both parents have been overseas. Their travels in this continent have been from coast to coast and from Canada to the deep South. And Mrs. Newbold has said: "We're so darn travel-minded. We can hardly wait to go to the Orient . . . and we can't wait for the kids to go to Europe alone."

Not only is their horizon broader than that of any of the other families portrayed in this book, but they have the capacity to organize large spaces in meaningful ways. Their travels within the country have included a study of the Civil War. The North and the South for them are clearly delineated realities, organized into a conception which they have related to their own lives. Their trip west similarly was not aimless but organized in terms of comprehending a large segment of this country's history and geography. The sweep of their gaze takes in a complex social reality that extends far beyond the limits of neighborhood and the residence of extended family. Their style of life takes for granted a worldly outlook; a significant part of self-definition in this family is to be not provincial.

THE REGULATION OF INTERPERSONAL EXCHANGE

One obvious fact of family living is the differential in power and authority that exists between generations. Physically, psychologically, and socially, adults have an unquestionable advantage over their children. What the adults of a family make of this fact has important consequences for family interaction, since the characteristic pattern of handling generational distance is determined initially by the adult members. The Newbolds have dealt with this problem in straightforward fashion: differences are too obvious to be denied, are a desirable aspect of family living, and should be utilized for the good of the child and the smooth operation of the family group.

Frank Newbold is an authoritative father. He believes that parental demands should be clear and inflexible. Children's respect for their parents is an essential principle of family life. He says:

I hope that I am still considered as a father in terms perhaps like the Germans consider a father. When a father says something, it's law. Certainly I hope they have respect for me and I have their companionship. Did I ever spank my kids? I did. That was ten years ago. We are after all like animals, though more intelligent. Children recognize what they can get away with. If your demands are simple and strict you have no arguments. You can't demand all the time. You get nowhere. They know where I stand and I know where I stand. That's good.

Mr. Newbold's authority position is rarely questioned by his adolescent boys, so that very little overt disciplining is required. The quality of the discipline is quiet—his sanction has sufficient reinforcement value that he rarely has to implement it with any additional disciplinary measures. Corporal punishment was the order of the day earlier; even then it was not from loss of temper but from a considered plan for establishing appropriate family relationships.

The boys agree about the effectiveness of their father's discipline. Ted says:

When Dad gets angry—just stand back. He doesn't yell or get coarse. You just stand away and leave him alone. Last week there was something I'd done. He didn't like it and said so, and I told him why I did it. That was that. We just didn't speak for a couple of days, sort of mutual. It's a sort of a freeze—cold shoulder—something like that. I can sense it in his movements. He's very quiet, and his voice is steady, quiet, no deviation.

Curt's comments supplement his brother's:

He doesn't get angry too quickly, but in a way he makes you do what he wants. There are no arguments. You can't argue. There's something about his eyes. You can't do nothing. He stares at you. When he tells you to do something, you know when to do it. When Ted and me get into a fight, if Dad comes in everything settles down.

At the infrequent times when Mr. Newbold finds it necessary to reaffirm his status advantage in the interests of socialization, he uses moderate techniques.

If they don't do as they are supposed to, they are reminded that it hasn't been done. Everything ceases until it is done. If that isn't sufficient, they are restricted or curtailed from a privilege. They are too old to be taken over the knee. They are of an age where reasoning is of more value.

Mr. Newbold recognizes that when he loses his temper he is "nasty, domineering, oppressive," and prides himself that he rarely loses control. He is careful to limit discipline to those behaviors which violate a few well-defined rules—rules which he believes support the ideology of the family.

The firmness of law that Frank Newbold wants his word to have sometimes outweighs, in the eyes of his children, his desire for reasonableness. They admire his perseverance but find that it often turns into inflexibility. Ted says of his father, "When he sets out to do something, it's done." In a later interview, he amplifies this:

I'd like it if Dad wouldn't go off on these spot ideas. He gets an idea and wants to carry it out without thinking it out, sometimes a little unreasonable. We'll be sitting around loafing, not wanting to do anything. He'll decide we're going to a show. Or he'll come home some afternoon and say "I think I'll dust off the car" and makes a whole job of Simonize and everything.

And Curt says of his father: "Sometimes he does things you know darn well are wrong. You tell him so, and he just keeps on doing it. He says, 'So what?' "

Despite his insistence on the finality of his word, no member of the family, including Frank Newbold, wants to feel that paternal law is the principal incentive in regulating household activities. It is to be invoked only when necessary, and willing co-operation is considered a more desirable motive.

However, co-operative privilege has its qualifications. It is a privilege to be earned not by virtue of being a member of the family but by living up to the family standards of behavior and achievement. Mr. Newbold feels that small children should not have a significant voice in family decisions or their own activities. Co-operation is primarily one-sided—that is, children co-operate with the adults—until the values of the family are sufficiently internalized in the children to allow for reciprocity. Mr. Newbold says: "This ideal co-operative proposition varies with their stages. In these years—their formative ones—their primary objective is preparation for their mature years."

The foremost application of the co-operative ideal in the Newbold home is the boys' responsibility for household chores. Their assignment is not simply to get work done. It is intended to promote their participation in activities about the home and to provide them with supervised indoctrination in the virtues of responsibility and achievement. The boys both describe their areas of responsibility with pride and see them as occasions for family interaction and unity.

The delegation of responsibility at a relatively early age has, in common with discipline, two aims: early internalization of family norms and the emergence of ability to act independently and responsibly outside the family group. The boys both feel that they have earned freedom and privilege in activities outside the home by demonstrating their abilities under the supervising parental eye. Self-control and responsibility in the basic social behaviors must first be demonstrated at home. In the Newbold home the capable discharge of responsibility, as well as the children's conformity to rules, acts to decrease the authority differential between parents and children by securing for the child greater influence and negotiating strength in the family group. It is thus one principle of the Newbold ideology that status differences in the family should be used to achieve status equality.

Mrs. Newbold's relationship to her husband is partly based on the co-operative ideal of which he speaks. Her admiration for him is unmistakable, and her description of him as fair, loyal, bright, independent, and honorable is not essentially contradicted in any of her responses. She sees herself as very much like him in a number of ways, and she supports easily and naturally his authority with the boys—she held up his image to the boys while he was away during the war. No important differences in disciplinary expectations or methods are reported by either parent or by the children.

When the children were young I never bothered about eating; they took it or not, as they liked. As for sleeping, they knew right away that they went to bed and stayed and that was all. They never ran away—they stayed outside all the time. I was with them a great deal. When I worked, I took them with me in the kitchen. Curt played in the kitchen. I've had a very open understanding with them. I never holler at them much. They know what's expected of them and they do it. If they don't hold to their word, they forfeit a pleasure, but they scarcely need discipline at all.

It is important to note here that the parents not only expect the boys to obey but press them to internalize the injunction and make it their own. Unlike Mrs. Littleton, Mrs. Newbold is not content with external conformity in her presence; she is concerned to develop in her sons the capacity for making and honoring commitments.

Mrs. Newbold's disciplinary techniques command respect and obedience from the boys. Ted describes it:

If we go to the show and come home fifteen minutes late, it's "Where were you?" If we stay out a few minutes longer bike riding than we should we can't go riding for a month or two. So I get along without for a while, that's all. You never question it. If I knew I was late all the time I won't be so angry, but when I feel justified I'll get extremely mad. But when Mom loses her temper, just shut up and let her blow her lid and not say anything—that's the best way. She yells, but it doesn't get high-pitched. She hasn't lost her temper very much. We've found out that when she gets really mad is when Curt and I start fighting. She and Dad never get angry with each other that we know of.

Curt chimes in:

When you have to do things she kinda orders us around the way we don't like and that's one thing I don't like. I like it that she doesn't complain very quickly. If Ted and me wanta do something or not do something she won't interfere quickly.

Mrs. Newbold's status and prestige in the home are inseparable from her position in the community, and both derive in part from her unusual ability to control and organize groups. The congruence between her home and community roles and the compatibility between these roles and Mr. Newbold's professional and home activities are illustrated by his comments about her.

The Newbold parents appear to be unconcerned about the rivalry between their boys. They recognize the open arguments and fights that occasionally break out between the boys, but they describe these as normal. However, it is obvious that Ted is the preferred son. He appears to be aware of this, though his cockiness makes his feelings about it a bit difficult to determine. He says:

Mom and Dad and I are alike in that we're all leaders and Curt isn't so much the leader. That's the big difference. He's off on a limb by himself.

The fights that he and Curt engage in are kept from the parents, if possible. The boys have apparently, by Ted's own descriptions, evolved a technique for fighting silently. Ted, at least, believes that this method is effective.

Curt tells of a typical episode:

This is what happens when Ted and me get into a fight. Let's say I'm sitting in a chair and I'm in the way of Ted, but he can get by, but he moves my chair anyway. I get mad, and then it starts. Sometimes we kid each other a lot, and sometimes the kidding goes to extremes. We used to have fights. We were about the same size, but then he grew and it ain't the fairest thing with my size now. He takes advantage of his size—he's dirty—and I get kind of irked. Let's say I'm down and grab his toe, and if I get really irked I'll grab his fingers, and then he gets really mad, and that's the end.

Though the parents are not particularly concerned about the competition between the boys and actually believe that they are not really competitive because their interests are so different, there is reason to think that competition not only exists but has significant consequences. Though Curt has told us that Ted usually starts the fights, his brother and father both indicate the reverse. However, the correct assignment of "blame" is not what is most significant here. Rather, it is the indication that Curt unconsciously invites defeat in contests with his brother. Their father describes the situation in this way:

Once in a while they fight. Curt kinda tends to nag. See how much he can get away with. Tantalize. He knows he can't lick his big brother and he tries to, and then he gets what he's been sort of teasing for.

When Ted was asked in what ways he might like to be different from the way he is now, his comments tend to confirm the picture his father has given:

I probably wouldn't be quite as temperamental. Every so often I'll get mad. Thing is, I'll usually tell someone I'm going to get mad. They don't believe me. I'm not the one that gets hurt. It's their tough luck. That's especially with my brother. . . . He shouldn't be so wacky about things. He'll sit and sort of tease. Even Mom gets angry. It's like "I'll dare you to beat me up." . . . I don't think you can get him to change. The umpteenth time I've beat him up; he hasn't changed.

Curt almost seems to be trying to experience over and over again his secondary status.

His father's view of Curt is also evident in more explicit ways. Mr. Newbold says of his family: "My wife is very much above par. My older son is above par. My younger son is—such—more of an artistic temperament." At another point, he compares the boys:

Ted has always done well. Curt has always done well enough. I don't know why, I guess I don't give him enough credit. I sometimes think he feels annoyed at Ted.

Curt cannot compete successfully in those areas that make the parents proud of Ted—leadership, assertiveness, extroversion, audacity, and masculine skills. Curt has developed other virtues and talents. The qualities he presents to the family—responsibility, sensitivity, reserve, modesty, academic skill, thoroughness—are valued as fitting the middle class cultural ethic. However, they rank less prominently in the Newbold ideology. The Newbold males should become masculine, realistic, hardheaded professional men, preferably men who design, plan, and control; Curt would be a farmer.

His wish to be a farmer when his family expects him to be a professional may perhaps be construed as a desire to leave the competitive world, while at the same time it is a fantasy of passive aggression against his parents. Yet the wish to leave is in no sense a final commitment of himself. His Sunday morning excursions with his father surely represent a wish to be close to his father, to identify with him, to acquire the kind of skills and outlook that the father values. From the father's point of view, these activities may express his wish to make up to his younger son what he has withheld in esteem of him. That Curt hopes to be successful, despite his self-doubt, is brought out in the following exchange with the interviewer:

INTERVIEWER: How are you like your dad?
CURT: I like him because we have a lot of fun.
INTERVIEWER: How are you like him?
CURT: We have the same color eyes and everything else like that. We like to do the same sort of sports.
INTERVIEWER: Do you have any characteristics like him?
CURT: I don't know—ask somebody else.
INTERVIEWER: Are you something like him?

CURT: *I don't know. You'll have to ask somebody else. I never thought of it that way.*

INTERVIEWER: *Who do you think you take after?*

CURT: *I hope I take after my dad.*

INTERVIEWER: *Why?*

CURT: *Oh, he's a lot of fun . . . I don't know.*

INTERVIEWER: *Are you anything like your mom?*

CURT: *Gosh, I don't know.*

INTERVIEWER: *Take after her?*

CURT: *Probably.*

One further pair of comments is revealing in this context. Ted characterizes both his parents and himself as "leaders." Of Curt he says, "Every so often he pops up with a good idea, but usually he is more or less passive." But Curt says of his brother:

Ted agrees with too many people. He will go around with lots of different kinds of people. He goes and does too many things other kids wanta do. Maybe a guy wants to go this way—he'll follow 'em.

INTERVIEWER: *Why?*

CURT: *Maybe he wants to stay with them. . . . I kinda take a friend on equal basis. I wouldn't do all the things a friend of mine would want to do.*

Implicit in Curt's comment is his acceptance of the family's expectation that one should be a leader and not a follower. He is also saying that one should go one's own way regardless of what it costs in the way of attachment to others. Hence, he is asserting, he is the one who is true to the family expectations, and not Ted. We may take this to signify that he is a long way from renouncing completely the competitive struggle to gain an esteemed place, however much he may play with the edges of resignation. And, as we have seen, a portion of the family's energies will continue to be drawn into the issue of the boys' relative standing. They will try to head off Curt's idiosyncratic direction, while they continue to regard him as slightly wayward. But as they endeavor to nudge him back into proper channels, they will also be trying to strengthen capacities in him—e.g., self-assertion —that may enable him to go his own way more decisively. The outcome of this complex interplay of forces cannot be predicted at this date.

The tensions that arise in a household and the methods the family has evolved for dealing with them can best be evaluated in perspective with other facets of interaction, particularly the affectionate interchange among the group. Affection among family members is generally regarded as a privilege and a duty inherent in the nature of family life. As one of the characteristic modes of family communication, the expression of affection may be primarily symbolic—like obligatory kissing among relatives— or so intimately exchanged that subtle physical and verbal gestures of affection replace in part, more obvious physical contact. The display of affection is, of course, differentiated by sex; in addition, great differences appear in variations adopted by individuals. This is particularly true for fathers, since the cultural definition of the appropriate affectional role for the father is at worst ambivalent and at best ambiguous.

Like many American fathers, Mr. Newbold takes considerable care to defend and reassert his masculinity. Softness and physical affection are qualities which he has not managed to integrate into his life style, though he has strong romantic and affectionate strains in his personality. Suppressed tenderness gives him an underlying attachment for his artistic and sensitive younger son, and he is easy game when Curt wants a fishing partner, sometimes getting up at five in the morning to share this experience with his second child. Curt, too, recognizes this bond between them and mentions it as the only significant resemblance he has to his dad. It is this subtle, affective attachment between the two that bolsters Curt's self-regard and alleviates some of the painfulness of his inferior status in the family. The alignment between them also acts as a socializing lever upon the boy, repeatedly renewing the pressure and the desire for conformity to family norms.

Mr. Newbold's affection for his older son is phrased in masculine terms which they share and in which there is no discomfort. He admires Ted as his product and as his own emerging image. They understand each other, and Mr. Newbold is sufficiently secure to feel unthreatened by the growing assertive virility of his adolescent son. Ted thinks his father is a "great guy" and adds that "we get along well and are good friends." This friendship is that of two colleagues, and it suggests a future for Ted as junior partner in his father's firm. Ted's identification with his father is wholehearted. He says that he wants his children to be like his parents. While this does not prevent him from criticizing what he regards as his father's foibles, there is no substantial conflict in his desire to emulate his father in occupation, personality, and life style. Ted's relationships to his mother and to his peers carry the same casual acceptance and good nature that are shown in his interaction with his father.

Mrs. Newbold speaks proudly and affectionately of all members of the family and believes that she more than adequately fulfils her maternal and wifely roles. She says that she never goes to bed until Mr. Newbold has come home. Before bed they have a nightcap; this brief period of communication is apparently highly meaningful to both. She is the only family member to acknowledge a significant similarity to the younger son. "Ted is like his father and Curt like me. Curt and I enjoy much of the same things. I suppose we are the same in temperament. Then Curt does an awful lot that is creative."

Ted's affectional relationship to his mother is very similar to that he displays toward his father. He disavows physical affection and calls his mother "a good friend in all things." Though he talks of her affection for his father, he describes her otherwise in non-feminine terms. "She is the smartest woman I know," he asserts, and adds that she is "frank, forward, talks well, reasons things out quickly, thinks straight all the time, and gets a job done." The masculine style of interaction between Ted and his mother is encouraged by Mrs. Newbold's slight awkwardness and difficulty in showing tenderness and affection for her boys. In part, her greater success in expressing affection toward Curt comes from his approachability and the fact that he has maintained some aspects of being the baby of the family. Mrs. Newbold's unconscious desire to create dependency in her sons complicates her affectional expressivity. She refuses to accept this inclination, however, and she modifies it into maternal protectiveness, particularly in the areas of time and schedule commitments. The inflexibility in the boys' commitment to be home at a given time was mentioned earlier. To fail to return to the family circle at the appointed hour, to assert independence of the maternal schedule deserves severe reprimand. It is perhaps relevant that Mrs. Newbold recalls her own childhood as one in which the children managed without the mother and one in which there was little show of affection and little feeling of warmth. Certainly her own children do not see her in this light. Though they may feel that she is sometimes too restricting, their affection and attachment for her are quite genuine.

THE SOURCES, MANAGEMENT, AND RESOLUTION OF STRESS

A family generates stress. The hierarchical nature of the family system is itself potentially aggression-producing; the effort to achieve a satisfactory congruence of images is likely to involve attempts at manipulation and resistance of these attempts. These and many other circumstances, internal and external, create conflict or tension among family members. However, it is not so much the presence or even the intensity of stress that differentiates the families of our study but the amount and character of open and underlying conflict and the nature and effectiveness of the techniques developed by the family for coping with both covert and overt tension.

Our consideration of stress in the Newbold family ignores for the most part the effects of external situations; it focuses upon tensions that arise within the family and that potentially threaten the smooth operation of the family unit. Within the Newbold family, the nature and strength of parental authority is at once a source of stress and of strength for the group. There is, in addition, tension arising from the disparity between Curt's behavior and the criteria set by the desired family image, a problem related to the conflict that occurs between the family ideals of group unity and consensus and the pressure toward active mastery and participation in the outside world.

The presumption that individual members' personalities create stress for the family group does not necessarily imply malignant personality characteristics. The issue here is one of efforts toward achieving compatibilty in self and family images among a group of individuated and dissimilar personalities. Aspects of personality that potentially produce stress in family interaction vary from person to person, creating almost infinite variety in the emotional organization that evolves when several personalities become interconnected in the complexities and intimacies of family life.

Mr. Newbold demonstrated one of his weaknesses and one of his strengths by quietly resisting the interviewer in her data gathering. He required her to meet him at his office on one occasion—a technique that a number of fathers used. He opened the session with the comment: "Here's where I feel I have the advantage. The things I don't care to tell people, I still don't care to tell." On a sentence completion he responded: "I don't know what makes me / answer all these forms."

This reluctance to reveal himself is by no means unusual, but it is not typical of all respondents, and it offers a useful clue to Mr. Newbold's attitudes toward himself and his approach to others. As these and other clues indicate, Mr. Newbold is quick to see interpersonal situations as a competitive struggle and feels secure only when he can detach himself or assume command. His competitive approach as well as his self-confidence are again revealed by his response: "When others do better / I do better." It is an almost necessary corollary that he is concerned about the loss or destruction of his strength: "My greatest fear is / being incapacitated." Mr. Newbold's success in asserting and maintaining control and power in life situations is reflected in his ready acceptance of the supervisory role: "People under me are / given their jobs to do." Mr. Newbold feels that consistency is his strongest characteristic but admits that "Fathers sometimes / lose their tempers." However, though he permits himself an occasional lapse, he is generally intolerant of weakness and ineptness and may use such characteristics in others in his attempts to manipulate them.

Although—or perhaps because—he desires to control others, he is unusually sensitive to anyone's attempt to exercise control over him. "When told to keep my place I / feel as though I'm back in service."

Frank Newbold objects to interference and obstruction. He reveals a stubbornness, competitiveness, and intense desire to control others that introduce elements of friction into the family interaction. As we have seen, these qualities of personality are customarily controlled and their derivative energy diverted toward productive and orderly activities. They are partly responsible for the strict adherence to family ideology demanded of the Newbold boys and for the orderliness that helps maintain the family's effective functioning.

Mrs. Newbold shares her husband's tendency to want control of situations. Like her husband, she does this in what she believes to be the best interests of the group. Her competitiveness appears in the response to Card 2, which she sees as a family group of two sisters and one brother: ". . . one sister is devoted to the soil; one is going to get some learning. The gal who's going to stay on the soil is sure feeling superior." In 9GF the young woman in the picture is running away because ". . . her sister married the man she wanted to marry."

In other TAT responses Mrs. Newbold shows considerable tension over family and other intimate relationships. In 7BM the two men are consoling each other upon the death of the wife and mother. She tells this story casually and flippantly: ". . . jokes from the New Yorker." In 8BM the boy

. . . hates his father. He has a rifle and is thinking about getting rid of his father. . . . The father has been dominant and the child has been subservient to him. He may be the center of attention once his father is out of the way.

Despite her picture of the ideal mother leading her children to responsibility and independence, Mrs. Newbold may have difficulty in relinquishing control of her boys. Her ambivalence between her contempt for dependent males and her inclination to induce dependency in her own children is apparent in her response to Card 6BM:

Oh, dear. Here's a son who's tied to his ma's apron strings. He's telling her he wants to get married. She tells him it isn't the thing to do. He isn't man enough to lead his own life. She knows she'll win, and he will stay home and take care of her.

An excerpt from her interview is relevant here:

Our two sons are most certainly developing along the lines we are pleased to see. . . . It's interesting to note that they enjoy and want to be in the company of their parents and often choose to be with us instead of being with their own friends.

We have noted earlier Mrs. Newbold's open criticism of her parents' performance. Her responses to the TAT indicate strong underlying feelings of resentment. Self-control and her conscious commitment to a pattern of family living and maternal role minimize the effect of her feelings upon family relationships and interaction; however, a residue remains to create stress in the family emotional organization.

The potential sources of family stress that derive from the parents' personality characteristics are exemplified and in part mediated through the status and control structure of the Newbold family. The stern enforcement of parental rules, the insistence upon the boys' participation in household chores, the expectation of conformity with family ideology, and the parents' overpowering control arouse conscious resentment and underlying hostility in the two boys. However, Mr. Newbold's patriarchal view of his role stimulates relatively little resentment in his wife. Mrs. Newbold's interview comments give no substantial clue of resentment, and her TAT responses involving hostility to father-like figures may reasonably be seen as directed toward her own parent.

Curt's inability to live up to the family ideals instigates an ideological conflict for the parents and an emotional conflict for himself. This circumstance represents a failure in the family scheme that not only arouses disappointment and chagrin in Mr. and Mrs. Newbold but jars the major interactional systems of the family as well. Curt's immaturity and lack of the prized Newbold assertive characteristics force an alignment among the three other family members that none of them desires, with the possible exception of Ted. The alignment of three and one requires each family member to relate to Curt in an individual fashion and, to a degree, on Curt's terms. The parents respond to his sensitivity by behaving in a more affectionate and tender manner than they display to Ted; Ted is concerned about Curt's immaturity and occasionally offers his support, but he is too ambivalent toward him to be of much help. Ted is even more puzzled by Curt than are the parents, and admits that he can not understand him.

The family alignment which isolates Curt, or by which he has isolated himself, alters the authority and control system which Mr. Newbold is committed to enforce. Mr. Newbold's view assumes incipient masculinity in his sons, and his stern discipline and inflexible achievement standards are calculated to strengthen character, to develop toughness and assertiveness. The patriarchal system was not designed for sensitive sons. Mr. and Mrs. Newbold's relationships with Curt recognize Curt's sensitivity and are often expressed in modes of fondness rather than in the casual exchange that characterizes the interaction among Ted and his parents.

The Newbolds' conscious adherence to family ideology puts Curt in a difficult position. As we have seen, Mr. and Mrs. Newbold have great personal involvement in an enthusiastic, active mastery in approach to the outside world. They demonstrate this belief in their own acts and reward such behavior in Ted. They also consciously support the values of autonomy and self-determination. When these values coincide, as in Ted, their personal satisfaction is maximized. By not meeting the image of enthusiastic assertiveness, Curt brings into sharp conflict in the parents the values of assertive mastery and the right of autonomy. They cannot deny the merits of autonomy, but neither can they relinquish their image of the Newbold male as dominant, tough, assertive, and capable. They try to deny the conflict and the intensity of their feelings over Curt's farmer aspirations and his non-assertive social behavior. Faced with commitments to two values that must conflict if they do not coincide, they attempt to make the best of the situation by supporting autonomy in Curt while continuing to hold before him the standard of zestful, active mastery.

Curt does not accept the necessity for social testing of Newbold family values. He prefers the family as his arena for validation, and he realizes that he has the family's affection and, to a limited degree, its backing. These are important and useful supports for a boy in early adolescence, and without them Curt's difficult situation might become desperate. However, they carry with them restrictions that narrow Curt's freedom to develop alternative solutions. Unable to meet the requirements that would make him a complete member of the group, he can only continue to seek partial gratification and dream about escape to the presumably happy release of rural freedom.

The fourth major source of stress raises difficulties experienced primarily by the boys. As we have seen, family participation, closeness, and unity are experiences highly valued by the group. However, the nature and extent of the physical activities and commitments of family members present the family with a dilemma. The zestful, active participation in extra-family experiences encroaches upon the opportunity for mutual interaction and family cohesion. Curt's remarks about his father reveal that resentment and feelings of being neglected are aroused in the boys. Ted's comments are even more direct:

We don't see him [Mr. Newbold] *as much as other kids. On Saturday, the so-called day off, he has an early morning confer-*

ence, visits his projects after lunch, then plays golf or goes to the club. In the evening he may have dinner here or go out with Mom. Mom does quite a bit of outside work. We see her less than other kids, I imagine, although we see her quite a bit. One problem in the family is getting together as a group—the four of us seeing more of each other.

Since Ted's opening comment about the family emphasized the closeness of the family group, the inconsistency between his remarks was apparent to him, and he explained to the interviewer that his was a busy family and basically a happy one.

Mrs. Newbold shares the discontent with the demands of outside activities. Although she is the one member of the family who is best in a position to decrease outside responsibilities, she feels unable to do so. Her conflict over this situation is revealed by the following Sentence Completion responses:

It's fun to daydream about / *having all the time and energy you need to do all you want.*
My greatest fear is / *that I'll not get to all the things I want to accomplish for myself and family.*
I often think of myself as / *running around in circles.*
Sometimes I feel like / *I'm on a merry-go-round.*
What gets me into trouble is / *suggesting work that is always accepted and then also giving me more jobs.*

While these responses reflect internal tensions in Mrs. Newbold's personality, they also become elaborated in the conflict between family and non-family responsibilities. Mrs. Newbold believes, with her sons, that Mr. Newbold spends too little of his time at home. However, she appears to be convinced that he, too, would like to join more frequently in family activities. Mr. Newbold is the member of the family who is untroubled by the heavy demands for home and outside participation. At no time does he indicate that he feels he should spend more time with the family. He enjoys the family—probably in a more intense fashion than he admits in the interview. His use of the words "pleasant," "compatible," and "co-operative" in speaking of the group and his consistency of participation and willingness to extend himself for the benefit of family members indicate that he obtains personal satisfactions from the family. He is aware that his schedule limits family interaction time, but he feels that the allocation of his time is appropriate.

A family's capacity to tolerate stress is both a matter of individual members' frustration or stress tolerance level and of safeguards and checks built into the family social system for coping with external and internal strain. The Newbold family is well defended on both points. A high level of conscious control over impulses is characteristic of all family members. The relevant effect of such control is to minimize the expression of tension and resentment toward other members of the group. Individual control operates to keep tension and strain covert and to prevent open disruption of family functioning.

This family has several devices for minimizing stress and for coping with it when it arises: Mr. Newbold's authoritative control over the behavior of family members, the group's emotional commitment to family ideology and tradition, the insistence upon the individual's responsibility to common family interests and routines, and the displacement and dissipation of individual competitiveness and aggression in extra-family arenas.

The nature of the control administered by Mr. Newbold and its effectiveness in suppressing overt expression of conflict can be observed in his own statement about his behavior when the boys are slow to perform as they have been instructed: "They are reminded that it hasn't been done, and everything ceases until it is done." His discipline permits no lapse; he intensifies the pressure toward conformity and dramatically enforces the taboo on disruption of family order and routine. His very presence is usually sufficient to quell the minor conflicts between the two boys. We recall an already quoted comment by Curt: "When Ted and me get into a fight . . . and then Dad comes in and everything settles down."

One of the features of Mr. Newbold's command of emotional

expression in the family is his tendency to suppress conflict immediately—before the exchange of hostility can become a recognized and accepted part of family interaction. This is in sharp contrast to some families in which open conflict is verbally prohibited but permitted to continue within broad limits. In such families the open exchange of aggression becomes a part of family communication and self-concept. Thus the immediacy as well as the strength of discipline in the Newbold family enforces self-restraint and maintains consistency in family interchange. Mrs. Newbold's discipinary techniques are almost as effective as her husband's, so that an evenness of control prevails. Mrs. Newbold does not find it necessary to discipline the boys with threats of punishment to be administered when Mr. Newbold comes home; she wields authority herself in an effective fashion.

The continuity of the Newbold family ideology is maintained by explicit verbal instructions and through concrete behavioral situations. There is sufficient sense of tradition and agreement about essentials in the family to create in the boys a sense of Newbold-appropriate behavior. They realize that their family has insisted for at least two or three generations upon high standards of achievement, self-direction and control, mastery over the environment, and a contempt for weakness, self-indulgence, and inactivity. The elements of the ideology operate both as ego ideals for the boys and as criteria by which they measure their acceptability to their parents. The image of the family is explicit; Mr. and Mrs. Newbold make policy on grounds that they are prepared to state. Ideology and sternness of family discipline interact to help internalize in the boys the positive and negative sanctions that tend toward discussion rather than argument, restraint rather than impulse expression, compatibility rather than competition, and responsibility to the family as a unit.

Ted and Curt see the authoritative nature of their father's discipline as natural, right, and largely for their own good. They accept the household duties assigned to them and regard them as character building; they view their own conformity with family norms as signs of internal fortitude and family superiority. The out-of-home responsibilities of the parents are seen as fulfilling the ideal of active mastery rather than as parental neglect. The family rituals such as the dinner hour are invested with significance and are used by all family members to affirm and reinforce the positive aspects of the family image. The individuals' responsibility to these family gatherings is more than an indication of socialized conformity—it is an active and necessary affirmation of the ideal of family compatibility and cohesion, and it is a denial of the threat to family unity that might be presented by individual involvement in non-family affairs. Conflict between family responsibility and individual independence is blunted by integration into a coherent family self-image.

While the family ideology involves Curt in conflict, it also offers emotional support and comfort for the conflict thus created. His failure to live up to the assertive, tough, dominant ideal is indeed a source of painful stress for him and a disappointment for the other family members. However, elements of secondary importance in the ideology come to his aid. The sense of family compatibility and closeness affords a feeling of acceptance as a member of the group and gives him sufficient freedom to assert himself in family decisions and to initiate family activities. This is a privilege that is in part delegated to him by other family members. Mr. and Mrs. Newbold's active efforts to encourage assertiveness and participation on Curt's part are illustrated by the group TAT. During this session the parents together directed twenty-five comments to the boys which requested or encouraged participation. Of these, sixteen were directed toward Curt. Another indication of the parents' sensitivity and consideration is that although they together made eleven remarks in the group TAT that might be considered deflating or mildly aggressive, none of these was directed toward the younger boy. Considerate acts of this nature and other attempts to make Curt a more equal member of the group are not lost upon him. While they do not materially improve his concept of himself, they make open expression of his resentment difficult.

Curt's dilemma reveals the vulnerability and logical fault of a system such as the Newbolds have developed. They are essentially without adequate means for coping with an ideological misfit; homogeneity is a prerequisite for effective functioning and optimum personality growth of the individual. It is in such a fashion that family strengths are family weaknesses.

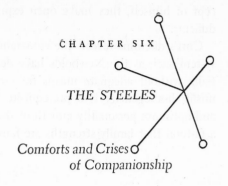

CHAPTER SIX

THE STEELES

Comforts and Crises
of Companionship

Achieving a desirable degree of closeness and separateness is an issue inherent in the structure of the nuclear American family and must be met in some fashion by every family group. The Steeles have dealt with this issue by making family cohesion and companionship the focal point of group effort as a source of self-regard for the group. This is a family that "does things together" in the best American tradition. It is also a family that believes in action—overt, obvious action. Companionship is defined as activity jointly shared. Co-operative effort of this sort is purpose-ful—one of the outcomes of consistent discipline and persistent conformity to the Steele family image. This interactional mode was developed as a response to inner needs of Mr. and Mrs. Steele, each of whom relates to it in somewhat different ways.

John Steele is a man of tough outer strength. His mettle was tested early; his father died while John was still getting used to the strange new feeling of adolescent growth. John accepted the economic responsibility of the family by necessity but apparent-ly without rancor. Sturdy and stubborn, he met successfully the initial test of forced maturity and physical stamina. He would not wish it for his own son, but in retrospect he believes that hard experience made a man of him. It was from this back-ground that John Steele determined to introduce into the family the theme of strength and freedom through discipline.

Mr. Steele lives by the skill and strength of his calloused

hands. To his boy he is an "engineer," a man to be copied and respected. His practical skills in repairing and maintaining the house receive the admiration of the entire family. John Steele knows no weekend. A carpenter by trade, his job is continued at home with little time taken off for personal relaxation and variety. However, between self-assigned jobs around the house he is able to enjoy outings with his family, and he enters into the spirit of park and picnic with hearty enthusiasm. Mr. Steele enjoys physical activity; he relates to the physical world through manipulation of tools and materials and, to a great extent, relates to his family through physical contact and proximity. Throughout these activities there is an underlying emphasis on being able to "handle things" and to perform with competence. In the SCT he says, "What people like most about me is / I can do things." For this man, physical activity is a preferred way of dealing with inner tensions.

At the age of fifty-two, John Steele is a tall, husky man, with a voice and manner that give the impression of power, sureness, and control. These are tempered by a readiness to smile and a relaxed sense of humor. He has a deep respect for the usefulness and rightness of authority and obedience, and he believes that there are "certain rules that can't be broken without punishment." He recalls his own family as a close group in a home where "all things were compulsory." It was a large family and poor. John recalls that the children accepted without resentment the economic difficulties and the strict discipline of his father. "We had a happy life," he says, "with no real conflicts." His disinclination to complain about his circumstances is one example of his refusal to give in to feelings of self-pity or self-indulgence. In his view of life, weakness, failure, and dependency are states of mind to be avoided by direct attack on the problem at hand. These responses on the SCT illustrate his determination to avoid self-doubt and incompetence:

The fact that I failed / I don't think I have.
My greatest fear is / I have no great fear.

What gets me into trouble is / I don't get into trouble.
I get down in the dumps when / I don't get there.

John Steele defines courage and strength as the ability to face
one's problems and conquer them. While fantasies of despair
and hopelessness show through in his stories to TAT cards, his
interview and SCT responses reveal strong efforts to prevent
such feelings from becoming part of his conscious mental activity.

Phyllis Steele is an intelligent, verbal woman with considerable spontaneity and ease in her manner. She is proud of her
husband and her family and gives the appearance of being generally satisfied with life and with herself. Her view of herself is
that of a happy, practical, down-to-earth person and enlight-
ened mother. Though believing herself to be strict, she also feels
that she is reasonable and basically sympathetic.

Mrs. Steele comes from a small family, which she recalls as
much less interested in family life than it was in religious activities. Phyllis herself attended a denominational college for some
time and was involved in social welfare work with a religious
group before her marriage to John. Her parents were both born
in this country, in the Midwest, but spent some time doing
religious work in Mexico. The family was not one to take life
lightly, and Phyllis remembers with some wistfulness that her
parents never played with her. "People were serious and older
faster in that generation," she says. "My parents were old before
I knew them." Her solemn view of the family and its lack of
buoyancy and spirit is possibly related to the fact that her father
was a minister. However, the religious devotion of her father is
only part of her more general view of the group as detached
from the immediate, realistic, and human concerns of living.
"Everything was from the academic point of view."

Phyllis Steele's parents held personal standards and goals
which she does not accept. Her readiness openly to oppose her
parents and to do so successfully gives her a sense of emanci-
pation, but her effort at achieving independence was not without

218   THE STEELES

conflict. It appears likely that Phyllis Steele emphasizes the differences between the emotional atmosphere of her parents' home and her own as a way of reassuring herself that she chose the best path and that her children will be better off because of it.

I think there are a lot of false ideas about education. My father was a great man for education. When John and I got married, my mother objected violently. My father said that you can go through college and get a degree, but you can stay out of college and be willing to learn and still be an educated person. But it bothered my mother that I did not have a degree. But I'm not sorry. I think that basic adjustment to life is what's important.

The rift between Phyllis and her mother was apparently a fundamental one that cut much deeper than a passing independence of adolescent disillusionment and individuality. She grew away from efforts to emulate and identify with her mother and chose a different, though related, profession.

I did nursing at a hospital in Pittsburgh, near a slum area. I liked it, but I don't think I was terribly good at it. I was young. I had wanted to become a social worker because that's what my mother was, and I thought my mother was wonderful. I became disillusioned though, or she became different. She lived through other people. If she was caring for a person, that was her life. She would do anything for them. It was almost an obsession. Unless my mother was directing someone else, her life was not happy.

One of Mrs. Steele's discontents with her parents arose when they gave up their own home and went to live with relatives. She felt that this arrangement was a fortunate one for them, especially for her father, but she could not deny the feeling that she had been deserted. "I resented the fact that I had my own adjustment to make. Not having a home to go to and having to help my parents whom I had depended upon to make their own adjustment." All this is in the past for Phyllis Steele, however, and although disappointment is echoed in her recollections, she is bolstered by the sense of her own maternal adequacy.

Like her husband, Mrs. Steele struggles against tendencies toward emotional inactivity and dependency, and also like him, her methods of coping with such feelings are sufficiently adequate to keep her in command of herself and most of her life situations. These, together with some persisting resentment toward her own parents, create conflicts that drain away some of her emotional spontaneity. She is often not able to act in accordance with her feelings—in fact, she often attempts to act in exactly the opposite manner because of what she believes she should do as a decent person, wife, and mother. She gives a great deal of thought to her behavior as mother to her three children, and, on occasion, she involves her husband in discussions on disciplinary methods and other attitudes and behaviors affecting the children.

Three children comprise the younger generation in the Steele household. Susan is twelve, Bill is ten, and Nancy is seven. Susan is an alert girl, brisk and bright, with a sharp, crisp sense of humor. Tall and straight, she thinks some of her father's physical features have been passed on to her. Susan's closest friend is her brother, and she likes the rough-and-tumble activities and outdoor sports that he prefers. However, she likes to read, and in telling us of her daily routine, she says that after dinner "we sometimes read or go into the basement and play ball or watch my father." Later on she says: "We tussle. We both like building things and stuff." The interest in books comes up again on the SCT when she comments, "If I had my way / I'd have all the books I wanted." Outside the family, Susan's interests center in school. She mentions choir practice and confirmation class only in the context of school and "after-school" activities. There are indications of a growing interest in boys, but these initial attempts at social contacts are also carried on at school.

Susan has a frank, straightforward quality which comes in part from the fact that she is preadolescent and in part from more directly personal characteristics. She volunteers that she "doesn't get along so well" with Nancy and adds that her own temper is partially responsible for this situation. Susan comments quite directly on her place in her father's affection: "I'm not exactly my father's favorite, but he was determined that I be a girl long before I was born. Nancy is my father's sweetheart; I am my father's girl." Susan self-consciously evaluates her share and tries to come to terms with her father's image of her.

Bill is a chunky, good-looking boy who, when he laughs or smiles, bears a remarkable resemblance to Santa Claus. There is a sparkle about him that echoes his mother's spontaneity and Susan's alert manner. Bill was less comfortable in the interview situation than his sisters and seemed to show, in his attitude toward the tasks, a marked concern about the acceptability of his performance. He has a friend who lives in the next block, but he spends most of his free time at home, watching his father work around the house, playing ball with Susan, "fooling around" in the basement or in his room. He is clearly identified with his father and his manual skills: "I like making things out of clay and I like to tinker around in the basement." Bill plays with other children in the neighborhood, but this is usually on occasions when they join him and Susan in the family back yard.

Although Bill tries to pattern himself after his father's strength and skill, his mother believes that he bears a strong resemblance to her. "He tends physically to be like me. He is short—small hands and feet." She is proud of his ability to help her in small chores about the house: "He is very handy. He is helpful in the kitchen where Susan mostly gets in the way."

The family views Bill as the cause for some concern. In the group TAT responses any suggestion that one of the children of the pictures might have gotten into trouble was turned toward Bill, although this was apparently done with a spirit of good-natured teasing. Whatever the intent, Bill was aware of being identified as having problems, and he reacted with embarrassment and chagrin.

Nancy is short and pretty. She is bright and talkative, with her mother's sparkle and spontaneity. The tasks requested by our staff member she approached eagerly and as if they presented an opportunity for her to display her imagination. She seemed to feel that she had to do things better and longer than the others. We learned from Susan that Nancy is her father's favorite. However, although Nancy is happy to be a special object of her father's affection, she is more centrally concerned with the fact that Susan and Bill's close friendship shuts her out and leaves her feeling alone in the group. Nancy responds to this feeling by asserting herself into the family activities with eager enthusiasm, showing no reluctance to offer opinions and ideas in the group TAT session, and exerting herself to develop skills in the sports that Bill and Susan appear to enjoy so thoroughly.

Mrs. Steele draws clear distinctions among the early childhood behavior of the three children and their response to her. She recalls Susan as a serious, solemn baby who would smile for no one but John Steele. "She never paid any attention to me until after she was two." Bill was a baby with a cheerful, affectionate disposition: "Bill was one of those cuddly babies. He couldn't get close enough to you." Nancy was left more to herself. Like Bill, she had a "sunny" disposition and caused her mother no trouble. "I never had to tell her not to do things. She was just a happy child." Mr. Steele sees the children in different terms. To him, Susan is a competent girl who enjoys herself and is easy to please. He recalls her as a "sullen-faced" baby who would respond only to his attentions. He spent a great deal of time with her when she was an infant, and he believes that he has helped her develop into a warm, friendly person. His view of Bill is concerned with Bill's developing interest in working with his hands and with Bill's lack of psychological strength and stamina. Mr. Steele recognizes the difficulty Nancy has in finding a place in the family. His image of her, however, is less clear than his image of the two older children. "I think she'll get

along all right. She doesn't seem to have developed characteristics that are outstanding yet."

THE THINGS A FAMILY SHOULD BE

Mr. and Mrs. Steele are aspiring, for themselves and for their
children, to a level of personal and family life that they have
never quite reached. They see themselves as en route, in process
of transforming certain dimensions of the family's world. Mr.
Steele has an urge to constantly improve the family's circumstances and resists the thought that he might not be doing as
much for the family as he should. The focuses of greatest concern are the cohesion of the family as a group and the personality development of the children. Both John and Phyllis have
invested heavily in these objectives, although they have different
reasons for doing so. There is a constant, self-conscious awareness of family processes and of the relation of individual members to the family. This is a family that is turned toward itself.

John and Phyllis Steele have a clear image of the family atmosphere that they wish to provide for their children. Many of
their standards of family behavior are explicitly stated and openly discussed. Self-conscious awareness of family values is in itself
a family objective.

The central chord of the Steele family ideology is the importance of companionability and sharing. Mrs. Steele expresses it
in this way:

Our basic attitude is that we are a family, and we all share
alike. It is whoever needs something [that really matters]. John
and I are the center of the family, and together we have the
children. They are not my children or my husband's children.
This is not often the case with other families.

Susan evaluates both parents in terms of spending time with the
family. Mr. Steele, she says, takes them on picnics, while other
fathers that she knows do not. Mrs. Steele goes along on these
trips for the sake of the family, according to Susan, even when
she would rather do other things. Bill and Nancy also bring up

the family group activities as the things about the family that they like most. The Steeles' emphasis on co-operation is illustrated by these responses on Susan's SCT: "To get along with people, I / try to be considerate and helpful. A good mother always / tries to be helpful."

This desire to share appears to be associated with a sensitivity and awareness toward other family members' activities and feelings. Mr. Steele, for example, is much more familiar with the daily routine of all family members than are most of the fathers of the study. Not only does he know what they are doing while he is away at work, but he has a conception of the emotional tone of the home during his absence. "Bill and Susan come home from school happy and hungry." The feelings and experiences of each member are in a common family domain.

This emotional democracy which Mr. and Mrs. Steele attempt to achieve for the group has definite limits. Sharing and companionability occur within the structure of a firm enforcement of status differential. "A man and a woman have their first loyalty to each other. Children are the next high priorities," says Mrs. Steele.

In this family the generational difference is accentuated, the distinction between expectations for adults and for children clearly maintained.

INTERVIEWER: *In what ways do you think your family is different from other families that you know?*

MR. STEELE: *Our children have a little more respect for other people than many others. In our associations with other adults, they reply as persons rather than as children, without being brash.*

INTERVIEWER: *Do you have any ideas about why this is so?*

MR. STEELE: *We did spend time and thought with them when they were small. Maybe it was rough for them at times. They do not seem to resent it.*

INTERVIEWER: *What do you mean when you say you took time?*

MR. STEELE: They definitely were a part of the family. When people came they were always allowed to stay up and be introduced and then went to bed. That gave them the feeling of being a part. Perhaps some of it is due to insistence on most things.

INTERVIEWER: What kinds of things?

MR. STEELE: Certain rules that can't be broken without punishment, a distinct infraction of a well-known rule like not letting us know they did something when they should have told us. In the beginning we never made a promise but that we carried it out—both good and punishment.

Freedom within firm limits is the philosophy of child rearing that Mr. and Mrs. Steele tried to adopt. They see the lines of exchange between children and parents in emphatic terms. This view is illustrated by the following comments from Mr. Steele:

INTERVIEWER: What would you like to have them do when they've grown up?

MR. STEELE: I do not intend to influence them. I will counsel them if I can. I'd like to be sure that they do what they want to do and what they are good at, to point out their particular capacities. I would put my foot down if they did things I don't think they should, like certain forms of entertainment for a livelihood. A year ago Susan got interested in ballet dancing. I perhaps openly discouraged it.

The Steeles see the status of both parent and child as imposing reciprocal obligations. Parents are under obligation to demand respect and to enforce their standards upon the child. Though this is expressed as a problem of obedience on the part of the child, it assumes a parental duty for teaching prescribed behavior to the child. Fulfilling these obligations is a prerequisite to the rights to family interaction and intimacy. Speaking of Bill's temper, Mrs. Steele says, "He's made to get by himself and work it out—to go to his room until he's ready to be a decent human being." Bill says of an ideal mother, "When you're in trouble, a good mother should help out if it's bad trouble that you can't get out of yourself." In another context Mrs. Steele justifies the inflexibility of discipline with these comments:

We believe that children who behave themselves have more fun than children who don't. When we take them out, there is no roughhousing or snooping around, so as a result they are asked out.

Thus the Steeles' image of an ideal family is one in which mutual obligations properly discharged are requirements for satisfactory interaction within the family and for acceptance in the outside world. This is the formula for dealing with the issue of individual autonomy; it has to be earned by attention to established limits.

The children agree that the family rules are strictly enforced, but they only partially accept the rationale for this that their parents offer. While Mrs. Steele professes to be confident that the children will eventually agree that strict discipline was for their benefit ("When they grow up they will like me better"), at this point the children see discipline as restrictive and confining. Susan's comment on the SCT is illustrative: "Children would be better off if their parents / let them do what they wanted once and a while." In spite of these feelings, the children appear to regard the orderliness of their family as a source of family pride. Bill speaks of the "envy" with which the Steeles are regarded by their neighbors and cites his own parents' strictness as one of the reasons why his family is better than others in the neighborhood.

The high value which the Steeles assign to companionability is expressed in the area of work as an emphasis upon co-operation and individual responsibility. Closely related to the co-operation theme is the value placed upon the children's learning to do things for themselves. They are given tasks about the home and are expected to carry them out as part of the daily or weekly routine. Even the youngest has a part in the house cleaning, according to Mrs. Steele: "Nancy is supposed to clean the pow-

226   THE STEELES

der room after dinner." On Saturday morning Bill and Susan are expected to clean their rooms. Mr. Steele's work around the house is seen as a part of the attempt to maintain a co-operative atmosphere. When he is unusually pressed for time or working on a major project, the other family members are expected to take over part of his share of routine chores around the home. With Bill, helping his father in his do-it-yourself tasks is a privilege and a boost to Bill's self-esteem. In turn, Bill expects an ideal father to "help kids in doing things . . . help kids learn about different things." In this family the process of basic socialization is seen in the context of co-operative effort.

The Steeles view males and females as displaying qualities which promote group unity in different ways. Men are stronger and more decisive in everyday affairs, but women have the right to express opinion and influence group action. Males are expected to be particularly competent in providing direction and in making and doing things; women are more helpful and more self-sacrificing. Phyllis Steele sees males as more practical but less introspective and insightful than women. However, men are inclined, in her view, to be stubborn and unreasonable and to pay too little heed to women's wishes. On the other hand, she sees women as having difficulty in exercising maternal control and care without being overly motherly or bossy. John Steele regards women as quite different from men but hard to understand—he is not quite clear about the dimensions, other than physical, along which the sexes are distinguished. Men are inclined to indulge their impulses, and women are often too weak to deal effectively with the problems that men pose for them. But women, in his view, would like to control men and would assume command if men were not careful to assert themselves. Both parents agree, however, that it is appropriate for a man to exercise authority in family affairs and for a woman to share in this authority but exercise it by counsel toward her husband and helpfulness toward the children.

The stress that the Steeles place upon co-operation is expressed also as a sanction against non-co-operative activities.

Susan expresses part of this view on the SCT: "I don't like the sort of person who / won't play the games they don't know how to and sit back and smirk." Mrs. Steele reprimands herself for not being sufficiently considerate when the children are caught in minor infractions. Control of tempers is a necessary corollary of the Steele ideology, an attitude illustrated by the fact that Bill's temper and irritability are a cause for general family concern. After the interview session with Bill, Mrs. Steele inquired of the staff member whether Bill had "co-operated."

The emphasis in this family upon individual responsibility is one facet of a secondary family theme which may be stated as the wish to avoid dependency and inability by developing personal adequacy. This issue derives from a concern which both parents share. They have emphasized the avoidance of weakness and self-pity as an end in itself. While this is translated in behavior as a demand for performance, it is more closely related to a wish for self-sufficiency than to accomplishment or achievement in the competitive sense.

The Steeles have an image of family life, and the role of the individual member in maintaining this picture commands their serious effort and concern. They invest heavily in trying to live up to this image; furthermore, they use it as a standard by which to measure their own behavior and to evaluate that of other families. Their emphasis on co-operation, companionability, and responsibility affects both overt and underlying emotional interaction among the group. It is to this ideology that the individual family member must give testimony.

THE ARENA OF VALIDATION

One dimension of family living is the demonstration and validation of the family ideology and the cultural values which the family emphasizes. For the individual family member, such reaffirmation displays to himself and to the group his adherence to the values on which there is consensus and his right to respect and affection in group interaction. For the family, reaffirmation enforces the family ideology and emphasizes, by contrast, behavior which is in disharmony with shared values. Although testimony of this sort is expected to apply to only a part of family or individual behavior, it is particularly important because of its relevance to the continuation of specific elements of the family image. Each family develops its own methods for demonstrating adherence to the family code and defines the proper audience to which testimony should be offered.

In contrast with the wider community toward which the Newbolds are oriented, the Steele family's audience is more narrowly defined. For them, testimony is directed primarily toward the family circle. This tendency appears in the way they construe and organize a "typical day."

The Steeles show relatively high consensus in their descriptions of daily activities and in the emphasis on group or joint activity as significant points of the daily routine. In response to the question, "Will you tell me about an average day?" the Steeles' initial answers were:

MR. STEELE: *Phyllis and I get up and have breakfast together.*
. . .

MRS. STEELE: *John and I get up first and start breakfast. . . .*
SUSAN: *We get up in the morning early and eat with my father. . . .*
BILL: *The kids go to school. . . .*
NANCY: *My father gets up real early. My mother goes and fixes breakfast. He helps and they have breakfast together. . . .*

Thus all family members with the exception of Bill see the day as starting with interaction—most frequently with co-operative activity. Even Bill, while not emphasizing interaction, speaks of a joint activity. This emphasis on the "together" aspect of breakfast is unusual in comparison to most families of the study. A considerable number of the families see breakfast as a serial event with "every man for himself" in the before-school and before-work rush. Those who do eat breakfast at the same time rarely see it as an occasion for mutual exchanges.

The remainder of the Steeles' day is certainly not statistically unusual. The two older children come home for lunch; Nancy plays until about eleven o'clock, then goes to school; the children come home from school and play about the house or in the yard. Their bedtime is about eight-thirty. Mrs. Steele tends the home, goes shopping two or three times a week, and occasionally has a few hours out with friends for lunch.

Mr. Steele comes home, reads the paper until dinner, works around the house "a few hours." Mrs. Steele sums up the chronology and spirit of the day in her description:

John and I get up first and start breakfast. I get dressed a few minutes later. I usually make his lunch then. By that time it's seven-ten and he goes off to work. The children get up at seven-thirty. Sometimes they eat first, sometimes they get dressed. It's not unusual for me to wash and iron something for them to wear. They get off at eight-thirty. Then it depends on what I have to do that day, washing, sewing, or clearing the mess made the day before. I have until eleven to do that. I wash twice a week. There are always phone calls, etc. Usually I don't pay any attention to the kitchen until after Nancy has lunch. I'm not a persnickety housekeeper. After lunch the children go off to school at twelve-thirty. We usually discuss what happened at school during lunch. After lunch I get terribly sleepy. Often I take a short nap. Usually after that I sew or iron. The children come home at three-thirty. They're in and out. There's a lot of confusion. When they go out, I begin to think about dinner. If John's working that night we don't expect him until six-thirty. Now Susan and Bill do the dishes. They do them separately because they spent so much time playing when they did it together. Nancy is supposed to clean the powder room after dinner. Then they do homework or Bill invents something. Nancy reads to us sometimes. John reads the paper or does something on the house. When he works on the ceilings, it's a convenient time for me to do mending because I can sit and watch him work. Eventually I get tired. I go to bed about ten-thirty. John has half of his breakfast before going to bed.

Other family members emphasize, more than does Mrs. Steele, the importance of the family dinner. Mr. Steele comments that "the whole family has dinner together every evening." It is, however, only a part of the total pattern of home-centered activities. In the afternoons, the children usually play in the back yard. This is in sharp contrast to the Clark and Newbold families, in which the group is scattered after school and gathers again at dinner. Bill and Susan are close friends, and, although they mention other children with whom they play or go to school, they have no close friendships outside the family. The two of them may occasionally wander about the neighborhood, visiting the park; Mrs. Steele assumes that they will usually be together. The house and yard define the world to a greater extent than is true of most of the families of the study. Companionability may be a feature of the activity of the entire family, or it may apply to pairs, as at breakfast with Mr. and Mrs. Steele or in the after-school activities of the children.

Mr. and Mrs. Steele rarely entertain in their home and go out together in the evening only infrequently. Mr. Steele provided the information that, on Saturday evenings, "a good bit of the time is taken up with baths and getting ready for bed. We go out very little." An evening out is a "party of some sort or dinner given by the couples' club connected with our church, to a rare concert, or occasional movie." Nor does the family often take vacations away from home. Mr. Steele says: "We haven't taken a vacation in several years. We did usually go to a cottage where there was water and a boat and loaf and enjoy the rest." Mrs. Steele confirms her husband's report:

John and I go together to the movies. When we do go, we pick very carefully since we don't go often. Our social life is not extensive but it's satisfying because we enjoy each other's company. We don't have vacations. When John doesn't work he doesn't get paid. . . . Last summer my sister took the children for a week, and so John and I took a weekend. We had a vacation here. It was wonderful. Years ago when we had a vacation, we went to a lake.

When the Steele family does leave the small world bounded by the property lines around their lot, they go to a park or forest preserve for a family picnic. While she offers no objection to these family excursions, it is Mr. Steele and the children who revel in outdoor jaunts. Mr. Steele describes them:

INTERVIEWER: *What do you like to do best with your family?*
MR. STEELE: *Playing games. If we go on a picnic, I like to play ball and take long walks—the deeper the woods the better. They get the feeling of adventure. They like to climb trees, and they like nothing better than when I climb with them. We go on picnics often.*

His wife emphasizes his enthusiasm by reporting: " 'Go higher,' he tells them." Bill, when asked what it is about his father that he likes most, mentions only his father's taking them on picnics.

Because the demands of work and school are relaxed for the weekend, Saturdays and Sundays offer a useful picture of the family's preferred activities and of their attitudes toward spending time with each other. Mrs. Steele offers the most detailed account of the family weekends:

That's when things happen. We don't get up as early. It's just miscellany all morning. If John has something special to do, I go to the bank and shop by myself. There's always some project going on. Once in a while he goes over to the church to make some repairs there. We don't eat dinner on Saturday until seven. It consists of bacon and waffles. John and I go out once in a while.

On Sunday, once in a long while John goes to church. The children go to Sunday school. If there's something that John is going to work on that day that I can help with, I do. We always make a point of going to church when there's good music. We all like music. We have our big meal at noon. In the afternoon something is always going on. Before we started working so much on the house, we used to do things together more. We miss some of those things. We still do some. We're very picnicky.

Sunday is more or less a family day. We don't encourage the children to go other places.

The Steeles are a family highly aware of themselves as a close-ly knit, interacting group. They structure their daily and week-end activities to emphasize and to achieve their desire for family intimacy and exchange. Repeatedly they return in their inter-views to statements of mutual participation and the pleasure they obtain from being together and doing things together. In-teraction is centered about work as well as play; in fact, the distinction between these two forms of activity is not as signifi-cant to the Steeles as the distinction between being together and being apart. With the exception of school, where no alter-native is available, the activities which they see as meaningful are carried out as a family or by pairs of family members. They are a centripetal family, drawn together, constantly sensitive to the reassurance of mutual activities. The arena in which they demonstrate behavior valued by the family and by the wider culture is a relatively narrow one, both emotionally and geo-graphically. They take picnic trips together but do not range far in pursuit of recreation. Home is never far away; the family atmosphere is always about them.

As the home, yard, and park are physical boundaries of the family universe, the audience to which they play is limited to the family. In most families, the family unit is the central and most significant audience; for the Steeles it is virtually the only group from which important evaluation of individual accom-plishment is expected. However, the most distinguishing feature of this family is that the behavior with which family members affirm their possession of valued characteristics is itself expected to take place in family interaction and in a family context. This is in sharp contrast to the Newbolds, where family dinner is an occasion for relating experiences each member has had on his own during the day and where individual achievements in the extra-family world provide much of the validating evidence of congruence with family ideology.

The open encouragement of a close friendship between Bill and Susan and the lack of encouragement toward attachments outside the family group are other aspects of this family theme. Mrs. Steele says:

I don't think Susan or Bill have any close friends. With Susan it's a problem of finding a girl as active as she. Most girls are too sissy for her. She has never had a bosom friend, and she has never gotten along. Maybe they find enough satisfaction in each other. I don't know whether that's good or bad. I have seen cases where bosom friends were so terribly important in children's lives. We are rather critical about their friends.

INTERVIEWER: *What do you mean?*

MRS. STEELE: *The way children behave. We discuss people quite freely. We discuss the way we do things and the way we feel about it. A family down the block has a completely different outlook.*

The Steeles are not a family concerned with their children's popularity in a peer group. They assume that their own standards of behavior are as good as their neighbors', and perhaps better. A suggestion of exclusiveness appears from time to time in their observations about themselves in relation to outsiders. Susan has difficulty finding a friend who can match her level of activity and assertiveness; other families are less strict with their children (and by implication, less responsible); other families are less reasonable than the Steeles in regulating family affairs. The family tends to emphasize characteristics which differentiate it from other families rather than characteristics which affirm similarity and communality with others. Father is more strict; he takes the children to the park more often; he teaches the children outdoor skills; the family goes on more picnics than other families. To this family there is significance in the fact of differentiation itself.

In line with one of the Steele family themes, individual members are expected to demonstrate self-sufficiency and ability to perform adequately in various areas of behavior. The concern on this point is focused upon the ability to perform adequately rather than achievement in specific tasks. Nancy complains that her mother expects her to do more than she is able. "Sometimes they put us to bed or spank us. That is what my mother did yesterday because I couldn't open the door and it's easy. Everybody said I could, but I couldn't, so she spanked me." She brings up the same incident again later in the interview: "She said I am a baby because my brother and sister had to open the door for me." Bill, in speaking of a good mother, says she should help only if children are unable to take care of their own difficulties. John Steele, too, stresses the need to overcome weakness and assumes that this can be accomplished by a show of will power.

As failure to show competence is punished, demonstration of adequacy is praised. The parents speak of Susan's ability—as a teacher's assistant in Sunday school—to inspire confidence in adults. John Steele is proud of his son's inclination to "do things with his hands" and to take an interest in mechanical things. The children's poise around adults and their ability to carry on conversations with them is also a point of pride for Mr. and Mrs. Steele.

Acceptable testimony is thus the demonstration of self-sufficiency and overcoming of weakness. Evidence of ability is welcomed in any area of behavior, but it is most highly valued in areas in which the parents feel themselves weak. Bill's problems are sharp reminders to Mr. Steele of his own childhood inadequacies. He wants these corrected—"eradicated" is his term—in his son. The child's behavior must demonstrate not only his own capability but the parents' success in dealing with their own problems. This burden of double proof is especially heavy upon Bill. Both parents' concern is displaced upon him, and he does not have at this age the stamina to deal with it effectively.

It is relevant to speak in this connection of the major and most effective disciplinary method the parents employ. It is generally agreed in this family that the most powerful punishment is putting the children to bed. This may occur at any hour of the day. Psychologically, this punishment is the opposite of the family emphasis upon adequate performance. It represents enforced immobility and dependency; the child is stripped of clothes, the symbol of protection and cover, and reduced to a condition of relative vulnerability and regression. The struggle against feelings of inability is heightened, and the value of competence as a condition for growing up is reinforced.

The testimony expected in the Steele family is predominantly an incident of observable physical activity. That is, the emphasis is upon what the children do or do not do rather than upon what they feel. Actions rather than feelings are important. Judgments are made intellectually and are based upon what people should do rather than upon how they feel or how they may react internally. John Steele forced himself to learn to talk to strangers in spite of his shyness, and he believes that children can be taught to do the things they should no matter what the inner cost. He is not unaware of some of his children's feelings; he is convinced, however, that to give in to feelings of inadequacy and weakness is to invite despair. His TAT responses are concerned with the threat of inner catastrophe and overwhelming dependency. In his own life he has fought back the doubts that threaten him and by stubborn, sometimes bullheaded, determination he is getting from life the things that he feels he wants most. But this very attack upon his inner conflicts requires a repression of feeling and an increased value upon performance, which is, to John Steele, a tangible and permanent assurance that personal worth has been validated.

"THEY TAKE YES AND NO FOR ANSWERS": THE NATURE OF FAMILY REGULATION

John Steele runs a taut ship. The lines of control, both emotional and overtly punitive, are unyielding and inflexible. His preferred image of a family—companionship and co-operation—begins with the premise that the family is shaped into the desired image by the external application of discipline. Mr. Steele has strong feelings about conformity on the part of the children to the rules established for both positive and negative expectations.

John Steele dominates the home as well as the children. His wife is dependent upon him for many major household decisions. He apparently makes for the family such long-range decisions as the purchase of a home. The surface harmony between the two parents that Mrs. Steele talks about is maintained in great part through her flexibility and adaptability and her willingness to submerge her own preference in favor of those of her husband and children. The children believe that she has done a good job—they all agree that there are no fights between the parents. Bill denies that they have any disagreements: "No, they are quite happy." Susan concurs: "They always agree. They never have fights. Sometimes they disagree, but they don't raise their tempers against each other. My mother says it's a good marriage." From Nancy the interviewer's question calls forth a congruent, though more dramatic, response:

INTERVIEWER: *Do your mother and father ever have argu-ments?*

NANCY: *No. My mother says "I don't think it could be this way." He says, "Yes." Then they settle down. Once in a while my father says, "It's up to you."*

In his dealing with the children, Mr. Steele relies upon the principle of inevitability of consequences and following through on verbal commitments. He expresses some regret that his busy schedule has recently led to some disciplinary negligence: "We have become more lax than in the beginning, I guess, because of having too much work and because we felt that the beginning was more important." In general, however, his consistency in discipline has fostered an impersonal quality—the children feel that they are required to adhere to a system of rules and that punishment is a just consequence rather than Mr. Steele's personal vindictiveness.

It is thus the inevitability rather than the physical severity of discipline that makes it effective. Mr. Steele believes that if discipline is consistent, it need not be physically harsh. He gives a general picture of the system in these comments:

Punishment didn't run to spanking. Just their fingers were slapped when they were small and you couldn't reason with them. After they were older, it was restriction on activities. This is a perfect illustration. They had been told about not going into the street. They knew it was wrong. One day I drove by and saw my two out in the street between two parked cars, stopping traffic. I said, "You know what this means. March right home and crawl into bed." They know that infractions of that sort meant taking off their clothes and climbing into bed. When something is said, it's done and finished. They take no and yes for answers. I think that is basically the best answer.

INTERVIEWER: *What happens when they don't come home when they are supposed to?*

MR. STEELE: *Restrictions of activities. They can't go out and play. Even now bed is a form of punishment. It's not necessary to do much of that. We know that they're going through periods, and they can't always be the perfect angels that they were when they were smaller.*

INTERVIEWER: *What happens if they talk back?*

MR. STEELE: *Immediate retraction. They have to say they're sorry. If that doesn't work, restriction of activities for a while. We sound like we're tough on them, but mostly it's done without anger. They know well that it's going to be done and that there's no question.*

John Steele's stance toward the overt formal aspects of regulation emphasizes the generational distance in the family. Children are essentially without negotiating power. Their strongest and most effective position is gained primarily by conformity to the family ideal—the demonstration that they are "decent" persons, thus qualifying for the rewards that the family has to offer. John Steele does not intend to establish a "democratic" family; parents know what is best for children and are morally obliged to enforce behavioral standards. His attitude is a duplication of that of his own parents, as he recalls it:

We lived in a strict home where church was compulsory and all things were compulsory. It may be that I'm considered as strict as my father then. No infractions were tolerated. We had a happy life.

The association between strict discipline and "a happy life" is not accidental. The entire family subscribes to some degree to the tenet that happiness is achieved through restraint and discipline. Mrs. Steele's remark that children are happier and more welcome in the outside world when they are well behaved is obviously relevant to the point. The three children also share this view, although with some ambivalence. They mention, as we have seen, Mr. Steele's strictness as one of the advantages their family has over other families that they know. This attitude is illustrated by Bill's comments:

A family down the street envies us. We go on picnics and they don't. We don't like to be envied. My mother is a lot different from her. She's always getting stuff for the kids—my mother doesn't except for birthdays or Christmas or when we need something. The father is different. My father is an engineer type. He's a salesman; they are very opposite.

INTERVIEWER: In what ways do your parents treat you differently from the way those parents treat their children?

BILL: Our parents are more strict than theirs. When the kids do something wrong, she [the neighbor] puts on punishment. Then she feels sorry and doesn't do it.

INTERVIEWER: How is that different from your family?

BILL: Ours don't put on punishment as bad, but they make us do it. When I hit Nancy once, my father made me go to bed. If she [the neighbor] made her child go to bed, then she would let him get up early because she was sorry.

Bill adds to this picture later in the interview when he asserts that a good father should "be strict when needed."

Mr. Steele's account of his disciplinary techniques is confirmed by the children. Susan comments that being sent to bed is the most effective punishment used by her parents. She also agrees with her parents' report that she gets into trouble most frequently over displays of temper or minor fights with Nancy. Bill, however, not only has difficulty with his temper but recalls a range of activities for which he is punished:

If it [misbehavior] is pretty bad, he makes us go to bed for a few hours. When we were younger he used to give us a spanking —he has a hard hand.

INTERVIEWER: *What do you do that he disapproves of?*

BILL: *When my big sister and I start bothering Nancy she bawls, and he punishes us for that. When we take sugar at the table. And once there was an old woman down the street who nobody liked, and we were playing near her house, and he punished us for bothering her. When I knocked the lamp down, I got a spanking.*

Mr. Steele also speaks of Bill's lack of responsibility as raising occasions for discipline. This is consistent with his concern over developing co-operation in his children; Bill's concern is primarily around the issue of punishment for expressing impulses.

Nancy's account of the disciplinary methods is in essential agreement with her brother's and sister's. Like Susan, she gets into trouble over sibling quarrels ("My father stops the fight and we go to bed"). However, she seems to believe that Susan and Bill are more frequently than she the object of discipline.

The group sees Mrs. Steele in a minor disciplinary role. Because of the greater amount of time she spends with the children, this is almost certainly not true in terms of total number of occasions. However, Mr. Steele is seen as the more severe, ultimate authority. He says in response to a question about relative responsibility for disciplining the children:

It's pretty close, evenly divided. Slightly more on my side. On the more important ones it has been with both of us, not just Phyllis.

Mrs. Steele appears to agree:

They [the children] think their dad is more the disciplinarian than I am. They are freer with me. I am here more. The children think their dad is very strict. He brooks no nonsense. If he says, "Go do it," they're expected to do it.

Mrs. Steele's methods of handling the children differ occasionally from those of her husband, but she attempts to maintain a consistently united front with him vis-à-vis the children: "John and I never contradict each other. John's main criticism of me is that I make threats and I don't carry them out." She is generally positive in her evaluation of his performance as a father:

I think he is a wonderful father. John has a tendency of not taking into consideration the stage that the children are in. I have often wondered whether it would be easy for the children in adolescence. He has been on his own since he was fourteen. I don't think he will have patience with adolescent indecision, but he has so much interest in what they do and has great affection for them. He will do most anything with them. He gets provoked, but he doesn't lose his temper at any time. He has a world of patience. He doesn't see the sense to losing his temper —you can't gain.

Lots of times I feel terribly deficient. It seems to me we ought to be able to do more things together. The mechanics of living get in the way. I get provoked at that. When they dig in the dirt with their best jackets—it's minor and I should be able to take it better. I could do more good if I had more of sense of humor about more things. I am more likely to comment, whereas a funny twist would be much better. I get provoked too often.

INTERVIEWER: Do you ever lose your temper or get mad?

MRS. STEELE: When the children do things, like the other night Bill got ink all over his hands. It never entered his head to wash his hands, so it got all over his shirt. This aggravates me. They dawdle so much, like when they clean their rooms. . . . We are really having a time with the children now. Nothing Nancy does is okay with them.

INTERVIEWER: How do you handle it?

MRS. STEELE: I just paddle them, which isn't good. Sometimes I separate them. That is the usual way. . . . Their friends, when they are here, are expected to do the same things they are. It doesn't bother me a particle to send a child home. The other day Bill had a friend over and they were playing. They began tussling. This doesn't go. I asked the boy to go home, and I told Bill to go to bed. That is worse than paddling—taking their clothes off and getting into bed.

Mrs. Steele is clearly more dissatisfied with her role performance in this area than is her husband. She is concerned about her motives and her inability to control impatience and irritation. The comparisons she makes between herself and her husband are not reassuring to her. She wants to be effective with the children but is distressed by her impulses toward rejecting them when they misbehave. Mrs. Steele believes that she is more competent with Nancy than with the other two children:

She [Nancy] has always had a sunny disposition. As a small child she was no trouble at all. I never tried to tell her not to do things. She was just a happy child. The reason I guess is that she was the third child and I knew how to handle her.

Like many contemporary mothers, Mrs. Steele tends to blame herself for emotional or behavioral problems which the children encounter. Susan is too demanding of affection, she believes, because there has been some deficiency on the part of the parents. Mrs. Steele's ambivalence over acceptance of the children and her role as a mother arouses a good deal of guilt on occasions when she believes her children to be experiencing internal strain or open difficulty. She is particularly worried about Bill's inability to control his temper and his anxiety.

When Bill gets upset, he looks like he is going to cry. We never mention it to him because we never want him to have an excuse for it. He probably gets teased by his friends about it, and

242   THE STEELES

that may be why he fights. When he loses his temper he has a regular tantrum, but he is so much better than he used to be about it. He doesn't like to be disturbed. . . . Bill gets lots of checks [at school]. John talks about it, but there isn't much we can do. On parents' night we wanted to see his teacher. He had been called in for fighting. He has been going through a phase at home too like this. We have tried to tell Bill not to start fighting, but I'm not sure he doesn't.

The children agree that their father is the principal disciplinarian; their mother takes over when he is absent.

SUSAN: It depends upon who's home. If it's at night, my father. If he's not home, she does. Then she tells my father at dinner. We discuss family matters at dinner.

Bill's opinion is illustrated by this exchange:

INTERVIEWER: Who does most, your mother or father, to make you mind?

BILL: My father. . . .

INTERVIEWER: What does your mother do to try and make you mind?

BILL: She always yells at us.

INTERVIEWER: What kind of things does she yell about?

BILL: When we talk back. She doesn't punish us for big things. She lets Dad do that.

In a sense, the firmness of the boundaries that define the Steele universe is suggested by the clarity and severity of disciplinary control. Things are never permitted to get out of hand. One of the central aims of discipline is to circumscribe behavior. Initiative and the pursuit of individual goals are discouraged. The Steele children are taught responsibility for assigned tasks, but autonomy is permitted only within narrow limits.

THE STRAIN OF INTIMACY AND THE FEAR OF SEPARATENESS

In a closely interwoven family, both emotionally and physically, one's attention is drawn to the psychological purpose served for each member of the family by the imperative toward companionability, the individual member's emotional reactions to an ideology of intimacy, and the resultant interaction. For the Steeles, family closeness is of central importance. Since there appears to be no basis for this desire in the external social conditions with which the family lives, no apparent discrimination against them, no feeling that social or ethnic barriers force them to turn to each other, we conclude that the desire for intimacy represents a stance developed over a period of years which most nearly meets the way the family members wish to relate to each other and to the outside world.

Mr. Steele, as we observed earlier, recalls his parents' home as a happy, close one. Part of his conception of his own role is that of a competent father who acts to promote and maintain family solidarity by being a helpful adult, an effective disciplinarian, and by displaying a willingness to make personal sacrifices for the good of the group. He makes these responses on the SCT:

Fathers sometimes / give up too easily.
A good mother always / should have the help of a good father.
When Father comes home / things should be better.
Children would be better off if their parents / lived with them and for them.

The theme of doing for others emerges in the TAT. In response to Card 1 he says, in part:

Perhaps he's thinking of what the instrument can do for people for whom he plays rather than what it can do for him. . . . His thoughts are of doing for people rather than for himself if he's a true genius, rather than of taking advantage of circumstances.

And on Card 2:

. . . I see nothing but strength and willingness to work or go ahead with what's put before him for the man.

Mr. Steele says that he is "just average" in achieving the role of father which he sees as ideal. There is some evidence that he is being modest in this appraisal of himself. On the SCT there are several responses indicating that he feels he has succeeded in his role and that he feels considerable confidence in himself. He is obviously proud of his family and of the fact that the children admire and like to be with him. They share a common enthusiasm for minor outdoor adventures and for manual skills.

There appears to be very little friction between John Steele and his wife. They maintain the appearance of consensus in dealing with the children; differences of opinion or technique are discussed when the two of them are alone. Mrs. Steele says that there have been no significant quarrels during their married life. ("We've been married thirteen years and never had a fight.") The children's reports appear to support her claim. The unity that the two of them have reached on family matters is a meaningful component of their relationship. When queried about their attitudes or opinions in the interview, they characteristically respond in terms of what "we" do or think or feel. The value they place upon mutual respect in their dealings with the children is applied in their own relationship.

John Steele's responses to the TAT cards and in the interview, however, show a concern about interpersonal relationships. He admits in the interview that as a boy and adolescent he was not at ease in social situations:

> We have stressed the fact that each one [of his children] is an individual, that they don't have to be like anyone else, that it's easiest to be themselves. We do that to overcome these inferiority complexes that can become almost an affliction, as in me when I was young. I was very timid.

In overcoming this "affliction" John Steele concentrated on developing individual skills and personal strength and a stubborn adherence to his own point of view rather than on developing a capacity for easy interpersonal exchange. He emphasized the advantages of being able to do things for people, to use his strength and perseverance in order to earn respect from himself and others. In commenting upon his emergence from adolescence with an "inferiority complex" to an assertive adult status, he says, "After that . . . I was capable of talking to most anyone." The perception of social ability as assertive, unilateral action and the concern about personal capability rather than emotional exchange are characteristic of his family relationships.

The threat of disruption of personal relationships by hostility, withdrawal, or weakness is a prominent feature in Mr. Steele's responses to the set of TAT cards presented him. His repeated comment that there were no serious conflicts in the home when he was a child and his statements indicating that very little disagreement or irritation arises in his relationships to his wife and children suggest that he attempts to handle this problem by denying or minimizing both the threat of disruptive conflict and the significance of overt disharmony.

Relating to others is a basic problem for John Steele. This is confirmed by his reluctance to enter into social exchange outside the family. He attends church even more rarely than other members of the family; he agrees to an evening out occasionally because he enjoys his wife's company; he belongs to no clubs or social groups other than a couples' club at the church. Within the family his interaction is characteristically mediated through doing things—working on a project with Bill or with Mrs. Steele, climbing trees or hiking with the children. Both the activities and the fact that he is doing them with members of his family are important to him. (He liked Card 14 because of "the fact that a man can get enjoyment from such simple things as the outdoors.") One of his preferred situations is to have his family with him in the woods. Being near the others is more important to him than verbal communication.

Mrs. Steele says that she and her husband never contradict each other.

Even if I knew he was too strict, I don't say so in front of the children.

INTERVIEWER: *Do you and your husband ever have disagreements?*

MRS. STEELE: *Not really. We don't always agree perfectly, especially about certain things on psychology. He thinks it is foolish. But he gets to the same place by different means.*

In other ways she confirms the general picture of Mr. Steele's social and family relationships, and she adds this significant comment: "Her [Susan's] love of children is like John's. When he sees a baby he just has to pick it up. She has the same patience with small children that he has."

Mrs. Steele would prefer to interact more freely and frequently with adults outside the family. She is quite active at the church:

I like people. I enjoy group activities. I belong to a mothers' club at the church. It's a very active group. I like to teach Sunday school. I like teaching older children.

Mrs. Steele believes that she and her husband are happier than most couples. Her respect for him is expressed both directly and indirectly; she is especially pleased with his practical, sensible approach to life. His lack of an education bothers both of them, but they share the feeling that his accomplishments have been all the more remarkable. She gives special praise to his performance on the job:

He likes it. He is given a lot of responsibility. He enjoys being with people and working. He enjoys change, not always working in the same place. It irritates him that the boss does not always plan to have the materials there. They send him places where they want to make a good impression. He is an asset to the company because he is so practical. The men like to work with him. He enjoys thinking of short cuts.

Mrs. Steele's responses on the TAT also show concern about interpersonal ties. However, her fantasies display considerably more exchange among people pictured on the cards. Card 2 she immediately identifies as a family scene, but one without harmony:

. . . neither the daughter nor the parents understand each other. The daughter will either run away or if she's made to stay will feel frustrated or bound all the rest of her life. I think, though, she'll probably run away.

She selects this card as one of the two she likes best, commenting: "It has something to say and says it well. You can feel the emotion involved and it seems like a natural emotion, both on the parents' and on the girl's part."

Her open admiration for her husband conceals a moderate fear of emotional dependency on him: "My greatest fear is / that something might happen to my husband (I don't sit around worrying!)."

At times the confining closeness of the family's world oppresses her; she would welcome expansion of the family limits and an opportunity to get away from the children. "Sometimes I feel like / running away for a few days with my husband to get a better perspective," she says on the SCT. Of the things she would like to do that she cannot now, she says, "Travel. Do things together away from the house. Take vacations." Her feeling that the family's demands are excessive is illustrated by these comments in the interview:

She [Susan] is very affectionate—sometimes too much so—annoyingly so. She'll stop me with a pot of hot gravy in my hand to kiss me. We worried about it for a while. She is more demanding than she should be. Must be some lack or it would not be that way.

Mrs. Steele is primarily responsible for the position, expressed by her husband also, that the parents are the center of the home, with children taking a secondary place. In a sense, she is in competition with the children for a place with Mr. Steele. He and the children enjoy picnics more than she. One of the children sees her as a reluctant participant in these outings: "Even if she doesn't want to go on picnics, she goes anyway. She has her say so, but she wants us to have fun, so she'll go."

The children and her home are exceedingly important to her

as evidence that she is providing more for them than her parents gave her when she was a child. "If only my father had / taken time to play with me," she says on the SCT. Her disappointment at the time her parents sold their home has already been noted. Unconsciously she still defines herself as a daughter vis-à-vis her parents, misunderstood and unappreciated. Her contemporary roles are carried out with a feeling of strain.

The family intimacy and companionship differ in their significance for Mr. and Mrs. Steele. To him, the feelings of paternal responsibility and family closeness provide relationships and attachments which meet his affiliative demands and offer the only stage for significant social exchange available to him; to Mrs. Steele, the family closeness is testimony of her competence as a mother, but she is not as prepared as her husband to accept the emotional demands made by the children. She feels a need to evade them for a time in order to reaffirm her relationship to her husband. The group is too close for her comfort; yet dissent would violate her image of maternal competence and threaten her relationship to her husband. Both Mr. and Mrs. Steele deal with these underlying issues by maximizing the importance of the family and by drawing a tight circle about their little island. Since the family so obviously comes first, Mr. Steele can ignore his wishes for lateral social exchange outside the family and Mrs. Steele can indulge her wish to escape as an impossible fantasy. For Mrs. Steele, the group's tight, close intimacy supplies delayed satiation for her need for emotional warmth, which she feels her own family did not offer. The Steeles' defenses are strong, and the gratifications that they obtain from the family and from each other are deeply significant. This combination of effects provides a smoothness and stability to their emotional life.

The Steele parents have differing affective ties to the children. As a baby, Susan was her father's favorite, and she has responded more easily and warmly to him than to Mrs. Steele. John Steele wanted a baby girl before Susan was born. His preference for the girls rather than Bill is so apparent from his interview and from the comments of the other family members that it may be openly recognized. For her part, Mrs. Steele says that Susan "was not the cuddly type."

She was self-sufficient. She never paid any attention to me until after she was two. When she was eighteen months old, Bill was born. Bill was one of those cuddly babies. He couldn't get close enough to you. It wasn't until after Susan saw how much affection Bill got because he was cuddly that she started to demand it, although we always showed affection to Susan—but Bill always liked it.

Susan has responded with obvious preference for her father.

He's nice. When we play ball, he helps us, and he always helps us with our contraptions. He's real considerate. He's the kind that doesn't complain very often.

INTERVIEWER: *How does he compare with other fathers?*

SUSAN: *He's strict. Next door the father is not ever home. They never go on picnics. My father takes us places, more than other kids. Last summer he let the kids in the neighborhood come over and play on the scaffold. They loved it. He let us have a big bonfire. That was fun. But he does make us have special jobs. . . . He loses his temper, but he doesn't yell. He told my mother not to yell so much.*

Susan's image of her father is of a restraining disciplinarian, a strong, self-controlled yet often indulgent authority, approachable and helpful. She is fond of him and proud of her place in his affection. Unlike her mother, she says, he doesn't take sides. The implication is that he likes all the children and is available to the entire family. At one point in the interview, Susan complains that Nancy tries to corner the market: "She likes to pull my father up to the dinner table. She runs up and almost takes him out of our hands."

Susan's image of her mother is less vivid. She comments on similarities between herself and Mrs. Steele:

We both get cold . . . I don't know.

INTERVIEWER: *In what ways would you like to be like her?*

SUSAN: *I'd like to sew like her. I'm starting, but I'm not so good.*

INTERVIEWER: *Any other ways?*

SUSAN: *I don't think so.*

She seems pleased, or perhaps reassured, that her mother goes along with the family on picnics, even when she has other preferences. Susan recognizes in Mrs. Steele a strong loyalty to the family and a readiness to help. However, she feels some reserve in her commitment to her mother. "My mother / is handy to have around at times," she says on the Sentence Completion instrument.

From Mrs. Steele's account, it appears that Susan as a baby rejected her mother. Mrs. Steele relates, after a dozen years and without questioning or encouragement by the interviewer, that Susan would not respond to her as a baby. It is probably a lingering resentment of this fact that leads her to complain about Susan's "annoying" attempt at affectionate exchange. From early indifference, Susan has now come to expect and demand too much from her mother. For her part, Susan would like her mother to be more available and more helpful. In her TAT responses she frequently sees adult females as harried, critical, and sad.

Susan is ambivalent about the enforced intimacy of the home. She says on the SCT that sometimes both fathers and mothers are "mean." Although Mr. Steele's arrival at home after work is presumably an exciting time of day, Susan says on the SCT: "When Father comes home / we have to turn down the radio and let him sit in his chair." She thinks that the family is a "fairly happy one," but "brothers and sisters / get on your nerves quite often." She denies the companionship theme ("When the family is together / we usually do different things") in contradiction to comments in the interview. She feels that the family is too confining and restrictive.

Susan is feeling some inner pressures toward greater individuality and separation from the group and its demands.

I'd like to have a new bedroom set and a room of my own. I absolutely want a room of my own. I think things would work out better if we had privacy.

Her response to TAT Card 14 is related to this theme:

He looks as if he was going out or looking out the window or maybe going in through a window. Maybe he's a thief. It looks like it's probably in the summer because he has his sleeves rolled up. That's about all.

The most obvious disharmony in the interpersonal relationships among family members is between Susan and Nancy. Although Susan was initially enthusiastic about the idea of a younger sister, she soon became disillusioned:

When I was little, I wanted a little sister. But then I had to take her out, and I didn't want to. I wanted to go out and play. As Nancy got older, she got a little spoiled. Since she's the youngest, she tries to be like us. . . .

And again:

Nancy and I don't get along so well. She comes over to my side of the room . . . she starts singing the same thing over and over. After a while I get mad. When I get mad at Nancy, I get bawled out. My mother is more often on Nancy's side because both of us are against Nancy, and Nancy is such an innocent age. If you ask her to promise not to tell my father and mother something, she promises; then she tells. I can't touch her or she tells.

Bill is Susan's closest friend. Around the home or on jaunts to the nearby park they are frequent and close companions. Mrs. Steele comments:

Susan and Bill are very good friends. They have tiffs, but they have great fun together. It is too bad that Nancy never gets in on these things. Their longs walks together are John's idea. They wander all over the community. As long as the two are together you don't worry. They take care of each other.

Like Susan, Bill has difficulty with Nancy: "What gets me into trouble is / bothering my little sister."

Bill is his mother's favorite. She says, comparing Bill and Susan:

> Susan is much more like me—like I was when I was growing up. Yet I don't feel close to her as to Bill; I'm not sure why. . . . Bill is lots of fun to be with because he shows his pleasure. He gets a big kick out of things. He likes any activity. I am very pleased that he is that kind of a person. It's too bad that he is short and Susan is tall. As far as personality trends, he doesn't follow the family.

In infancy the two older children were each assigned to one of the parents. Mr. Steele made no attempt to hide his preference for Susan. He felt Mrs. Steele should properly show unusually intense interest in Bill. Mrs. Steele describes the situation:

> I have told you that Susan was her father's girl from the beginning. When Bill arrived, he insisted that Bill be my boy, and that's the way it turned out. Before Nancy came to the table to eat, Bill insisted on sitting near me, and Susan insisted on sitting near her father. We felt that this was not good. At about five, we decided that they should rotate. Now there is not a great deal of preference for either one.

Although Bill was the least communicative of the three children, his remarks suggest that he feels somewhat neglected by his father. He boasts of the times he was permitted to join his father on the job. "He let me help and watch. I like the job." This is a more familiar scene about the home: "When my father comes home he starts to work on the house, so usually I watch or help." When asked to talk about the family vacations, he says, "My father mostly works on the house. . . ."

Some distance between the two males in the family is suggested by Mr. Steele's comments. He describes Bill as having a good sense of humor but not the ability to be a good loser or to finish things that he has begun. He speaks of Bill's problems:

Temper and lack of emotional stability in Bill. That's what I want eradicated. He'll stamp his feet even though he knows he will immediately be sent to his room. If there is a snowball fight and he thinks he has been wrongfully treated, he really boils over.

In the group TAT, after the family had discussed one of the cards, Mr. Steele urged Bill to summarize the ideas of the group. This led to the following exchange:

MR. STEELE: *You tell Mrs. B. [the interviewer] the salient points, Bill. Speak your piece. The time is now.*

BILL: *I've forgotten part of Mommy's story.*

MRS. STEELE: *He came home, and they had an argument about some part of his work, and he's going to do as he pleases, no matter what she says.*

MR. STEELE: *You told that fine, Bill.*

BILL (appears flushed and uncomfortable): *Should I tell her [Mrs. B.] now? She already knows.*

MR. STEELE: *Yes, let's see how you put it. Perhaps looking at the picture would help.*

SUSAN (to Mrs. Steele): *You just told it to her.*

MR. STEELE (to Bill): *Look at the picture.*

BILL: *The man is discussing with his wife.*

MRS. STEELE: *About?*

BILL: *About his job.*

MR. STEELE: *That's another step toward the end.*

MRS. STEELE: *What is he going to do about it?*

BILL: *As he pleases.*

MR. STEELE: *Your teeth came out easier than that.*

(Everyone laughs. Bill is very flushed. Mr. Steele, although he smiles, is certainly not amused by the situation.)

MR. STEELE (to Bill): *Better listen.*

Bill feels that his place in the family is by no means secure. A deep sense of guilt and anxiety is apparent in his responses and in his behavior during the interviewing sessions. He refused to complete more than half the items on the SCT. He also feels that the home is confining and restraining, and he seeks, in fantasy, various routes of avoidance or escape. He likes the house because:

There's a nice attic to play in, a lot of cubbyholes to sneak around in. I like the neighborhood because when we play hide and seek there are lots of places to get through so you can get away easy.

In response to a question about the things he would like to do that he hasn't been able to do, he says:

I'd like to do more horseback riding. I'd like to go on a long vacation trip by plane or train. I'd like to live on a farm because I like animals. I can't have any pets because it makes my mother sneeze. That's why I'd like to live on a farm. There are big places to play on a farm.

His discontent with the home is presumably in part a matter of physical confinement. He says that a good father should "take kids on picnics once in a while so that they don't act up so much at home, so that they don't feel cramped." Bill feels cramped—physically and emotionally.

One aspect of his view of the children's place in the family is indicated by his response to TAT Card B. After a long pause, the interviewer asks:

How do the people feel?

BILL: They're pretty mad, and I think they're mad at a kid because of the playthings on the floor in the next room.

INTERVIEWER: What do you think they're thinking?

BILL: If they're mad at a child, they're probably thinking of some punishment, and they're probably thinking of what made them get mad. . . .

INTERVIEWER: What is going to happen?

BILL: I don't know.

Bill, more than Susan or Nancy, dwells in the interview on events describing misbehavior and punishment. However, his comments about his parents describe them as helpful, interested in children, and strict. He refers very little to Susan in the interview but seems to prize her friendship: "The thing I like best about Susan is that she is quite a tomboy and likes to play boys' games. So I always have someone to play with when she's around." Nancy is visible as a member of the group, but she and Bill appear to have very little more than a casual family acquaintance. The "thing I like most" about Nancy, according to Bill, is that "she's always so happy."

Nancy might be described as a leftover child. Alert, talkative, and charming, she is working almost desperately to make space for herself at the family table. She, like the others, is very aware of the importance of companionship in the family psychic scheme, and in her report of the daily routine she talks more of what the family or the children do together than does either Susan or Bill. Nancy, like her father, is conscious of the daily schedules of the other family members and has an impression of what each member is doing most of the day. Her view of the family's close interaction appears in this description of a typical Saturday afternoon:

. . . then it's lunch time. At lunch time we all eat together. After lunch we go out, and the men work and the ladies sew. Some Saturdays we have visitors come in. Last Saturday we had so many visitors. We had ten. We showed them cubbyholes in the attic. When it's night, we have waffles or something for dinner. We make them. We have baths, the three of us. My mother and father have a bath. We don't get in bed at the regular time.

Nancy is aware of Susan's and Bill's feelings about her. It is apparent from her comments that the rift between the children is an openly acknowledged situation.

With my brother and sister and father I like to learn how to play ball. I don't like to play with Susan and Bill because they pick on me. I don't like it. They call me names.

INTERVIEWER: *What do you do?*
NANCY: *I call them names.*

However, there are occasions and activities that unite Nancy and the two other children temporarily, though this appears to occur in pairs rather than as a compatible trio.

NANCY: *I like my brother because sometimes he's nice. Sometimes he isn't. But sometimes he's really, really nice. I like my sister because she likes to play with me—dress up—that is what I like.*

She claims a clear preference for her father. Asked whether he ever gets very angry and loses his temper, she replies:

Oh, does he! He gets madder than my mother sometimes, but I like him better. . . .
INTERVIEWER: *In what ways would you like to be or not like to be like your mother?*
NANCY: *I want to learn how to make clothes for people. When I grow up and have a girl my age, I want to be more nice than my mother.*
INTERVIEWER: *How do you think she could be a better mother?*
NANCY: *I don't know. When I have a baby I'd take her along with me instead of baby sitters.*

Mrs. Steele is apparently unaware of Nancy's claim of preference for Mr. Steele. She recalls that Nancy, as a baby:

. . . was more a mother's child than the others. They—Susan and Bill—would go with anybody. From the time Nancy was a tiny infant she didn't want to be taken care of by anybody else. When she was a year and a half old, I used to take her to my friend's house for a half-hour while I went shopping. It was not too long before she realized that I would come back.

Mr. Steele also reports that Nancy is her mother's girl and that she tends to go to Mrs. Steele with her personal problems.

The central theme of the Steele family—companionability—serves different functions for the several family members and has different impacts upon them. The spirit of group unity which Mr. and Mrs. Steele have tried to foster has not been sufficient to prevent severe alignments within the family. The image of companionability is carried out in overt behavior and in the use and organization of space and time in the family's routine, but there are complications at the covert level that Mr. and Mrs. Steele scarcely recognize. The operation of the system appears to suit Mr. Steele's purpose best. It gives him access to the family on frequent occasions in what must seem to him an intimate exchange; it provides a substitute for social exchange with peers outside the family and offers a rationalization to deal with the potential discomfort over his own lack of social ability; it is congruent with his image of what a family should be and gives him a sense of achievement and satisfaction in his paternal and husband roles. The only serious problem that he sees is in Bill's emotional stability and reliability. However, he sees this as an individual problem rather than a reflection upon the co-operative unity of the group. He resents Bill's poor emotional control and at times seems to deal with it as if Bill were deliberately attempting to sabotage the family image. Thus in the crucial, most sensitive family issue Mr. Steele is unable to empathize with his son or to grasp to any significant degree the gravity or magnitude of the problem that Bill faces. A man of considerable strength himself, he is firm in his opinion that exercise of character and determination, together with a little conformity, would resolve the issue to the satisfaction of Bill and the group.

As the pursuit of companionability serves Mr. Steele's purposes well, it achieves, for Bill, the opposite effect. He feels bound by a family ideology which he can neither serve nor evade. The etiology of his present dilemma is not clear from our data, but there are circumstances which must have aggravated, if not initiated, his problems. To a degree, Mr. Steele rejected his son in infancy by taking Susan as his open favorite and assigning Bill to his mother. Even now, Mr. Steele's positive affect is more clearly directed toward his girls than toward Bill. The demands made upon Bill seem to him to be out of proportion with the warmth extended by the family group; conformity is insufficiently rewarded. In fact, there are occasions when he seems to be deliberately provoking his father and knowingly increasing his burden of punishment. Although he knows that he will be punished, he insists upon dawdling over his weekly task of cleaning his room. His inner feeling of exclusion from the family group is illustrated in part by his response to TAT Card 14. There is a long pause; then the interviewer asks,

What is happening?

BILL: *It looks like a boy is sitting on the window sill looking at something inside the house. . . .*

INTERVIEWER: *How does he feel?*

BILL: *I can't tell because you can't see any features on his face.*

For Bill, the image of what a family should be and what the family means to him are painfully disconsonant. His belief that other members find the family a source of satisfaction is little aid to him.

Mrs. Steele subscribes to the family image and gains considerable gratification from what she believes to be a significant congruence between the image and family behavior. She believes that her children have been provided with family cohesion to a degree that she did not know in her own childhood. Although she has some ambivalence over her own role in maintaining the family behaviors needed to meet the image, she manages to conceal these dissatisfactions most of the time. Like Bill, she feels some resentment over the pre-emptive manner in which Mr. Steele dictates the parent-child alignments with Susan and Bill. Possibly because of this, she did not give Bill as much emotional warmth as she might have under other circumstances. She feels that the family demands for close interaction are unreasonably pressing upon her. However, she is afforded partial relief by that part of the image which specifically places her and her husband at the center of the family and the children in a secondary position.

Susan is beginning to feel that the group's closeness has served its purpose for her, and she is initiating attempts to move away from the demands of the family toward more autonomous behavior. Recently she began attending Sunday evening church sessions by herself, and there are other indications that she is looking forward to adolescence with some eagerness. In her case, it is difficult to determine whether this is more than a developmental phase.

Nancy's position is in some respects opposite to Susan's. Nancy is attempting to involve herself more securely in the family network and to establish more clearly a place in the emotional circle. Her most open problem is the alignment between Susan and Bill that effectively excludes her from a great deal of interaction.

The family theme thus works itself out in different ways for the separate family members. All of them must relate to it; all of them are affected by it and by the responses of the other members. The satisfactions it provides are most readily available to the parents; the discontents most apparent in their children.

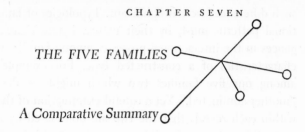

CHAPTER SEVEN

THE FIVE FAMILIES

A Comparative Summary

The families that we have described—the Clarks, Lansons, Littletons, Newbolds, and Steeles—are in a sense "typical" American families. They are typical in that the major social, cultural,
and psychological circumstances which influence their family interaction and activities are shared by many American families.
Our five families have worked out their own adaptations to the
gratifications and stresses of family life in a fashion that is generally acceptable to the communities in which they live. While
they are unique in the sense that all families develop unique interactional patterns, they are not deviant or, we believe, statistically unusual. They have been presented to illustrate something
of the complexity and variety of the solutions that nuclear family groups develop in their attack upon several central issues of
family living.

In summary we want to look across these five families in terms
of some of the issues and concepts we regard as salient in analyzing and understanding family interaction. Our purpose here ex-
pands the objectives stated in the opening chapter: to explore
the complexity of the family's emotional life and to introduce
and apply concepts for the understanding and study of everyday,
non-pathological American urban families.

Case studies oriented toward detailed analysis of intricate
psychological and social processes embody their own defects.
Five families cannot, of course, justify generalization to American families. On the contrary, the differences apparent among

these five families illustrate the hazards of treating them as if such differences were insignificant. Typologies of family interactional patterns must, by their nature, ignore significant divergences in the interactional processes among families sharing the characteristics of a constructed type. For example, we have among our five families two which might be designated as "mother-dominated." Yet a careful examination of the processes within each reveals that the two are dominated by mothers in quite different ways, for differing motives, and by quite different techniques. Moreover, the effects upon the children are vastly dissimilar, and the resulting family interaction indicates that domination of a family by the adult female can have greatly different outcomes.

We have chosen to emphasize the differences among our families rather than the communalities. In making this choice we had to forego, at least temporarily, the methodological advantages that attach to the use of typologies. However, it is possible, perhaps probable, that the dimensions of analysis we have tried to follow will facilitate, through empirical examination, the emergence of types of family interactional processes that will both discriminate among families and permit grouping of family units. This is a step that is clearly desirable if we are to examine the association among interactional processes and between these processes and other variables, particularly those concerned with the personality development of children.

Comparison across the five families serves both to reveal the usefulness of selected concepts for distinguishing among normal families and to hint at some of the possibilities of grouping families along these dimensions. Our summary will compare the five families across these dimensions, all of which were discussed to some extent in the introductory chapter.

FAMILY IMAGE AND THE NATURE OF MUTUAL REGULATION

The ways in which family members regulate themselves toward others and toward the group and their attempts to elicit and alter each other's responses are part of the expression of the effort to achieve congruent images among family members. Perhaps the most apparent illustration of this process is the parent's disciplining of a child. Here the parent tries to implement his image of the child by direct persuasive or coercive action. These experiences presumably teach the child something about the character of the image the parent has in mind; the child's internalization of this image is one measure of the effectiveness of parental discipline and teaching.

The model of a parent acting upon a child in the effort to produce a desired result in behavior is a familiar model of control and discipline within the family. From this basis, questions of dominance-submission, of democratic-autocratic types of family authority and their effects, naturally arise. We find these concepts insufficient in the discussion of the complexity of mutual influence and regulation. The question of how authority has been distributed among the family members is one useful point of reference, particularly since it reflects the parents' position toward the authority that is theirs by nature of their biosocial status in the family. It is also of interest to determine whether the stance they have assumed represents an implementation of a family image or a pattern of actions and attitudes into which they have been pressed by internal or marital conflict. However, we must move beyond the question of authority distribution and expression to understand the less obvious expressions of control, some of which are intended to limit the authority of the parents by the children and some to achieve specific objectives in interpersonal exchange within the family.

Mutual regulation of behavior is an outcome of several types of motivation or influence which the members of the family bring to bear upon each other and upon themselves. It is not necessarily intended to settle or demonstrate the issue of superiority in power of husband over wife or wife over husband. This may be an issue in some families, but in others—"wife-dominated" and "husband-dominated"—it is not a relevant question to present, since husband and wife have co-operatively worked out, to the satisfaction of each, the particular power or authority relationship that exists between them. They have evolved mutually satisfactory responses which, in a general fashion, give them what they want. Whether this pattern conveniently fits the cultural stereotype (or whether they care) is another matter.

In our analytic portraits of these five families we have sought to show not only the lines of influence within the family group but the techniques and motivations which the group as well as the individual family member uses to implement influence and achieve a particular behavioral result.

Some of the processes of regulation can be understood by examining the room for negotiation which the parent extends to the child—the extent of publicly recognized influence the child is permitted to exert upon the parent. This is, in part, a matter of how the parent construes and handles the generational difference between himself and his child. He may deny it, claiming that his family is a democratic one in which every member has an equal voice; he may hold that his generational advantage is a natural right and gives him the ability and responsibility to exercise the authoritarian control over his children in the service of socialization. Or he may abdicate his authority, neither sharing it nor exercising it, letting it lie dormant for want of initiative or purpose. In the extreme case, he may use his advantage as an opportunity for expressing hostility and non-disciplinary aggression toward his child.

These modes and techniques vary from person to person, though there seems to be some similarity among family members in the sense that attempts to persuade often cluster about family themes and issues. For the Lansons, the threat of disrupting family harmony and serenity is a psychological weapon used by all members of the family; in the Littleton family, attempts to increase or play upon feelings of guilt are the manipulative avenues to a desired objective. The Newbolds employ a direct, forceful approach intended to subdue or overpower the opponent. These characteristic modes emphasize the organizing role of the family theme and family image in shaping the group's behavior. Thus many of the encounters between two members of a family are not just the meetings of two persons; they are couched in terms of family issues and family concerns, providing opportunity or responsibility for influencing the other or testifying to one's own possession of family values.

The process of regulation is affected by the position the parent takes on the question of the origin of demands and expectations and the authority by which they are imposed. The Clarks, for example, see the church as providing the code for behavior. The parents stand as administrators of a higher authority. Through the parents, the children are accountable to God. As administrators, however, the parents need not examine or justify many of the behavioral demands—they need only enforce them. The children are thus at a disadvantage: there is virtually no room for negotiation with their parents. In a family of this type, the enforcement of behavioral standards is simplified once the child internalizes the moral standards and accepts the principle of divine imperatives as the origin of a behavioral code. Lucy and Jim Clark see deity as the ultimate source of authority; on many points, questioning their parents would be, for them, questioning divine imperatives. The Newbold family has worked out a system of control based primarily on parental authority and family tradition—the parents see themselves and family values as the origin of overt demands; justification of demands is phrased in terms of parental preference and continuity of family values.

Attempts to influence behavior occasionally take the form of adopting a preferred pattern of activities and attitudes in the expectation that other family members will respond appropriately. Thus Mr. Littleton refuses to take the initiative in seeking new business arrangements or in expressing preferences for the education and careers of his children. His inactivity arouses in his wife the feeling that she must take command and must provide the family with direction and action. Not all women would react in this manner, a fact that we assume Mr. Littleton also realizes. He has partly dictated her behavior by his own, limiting her freedom and range of response. On her part, she met Joe

Littleton when she was suspicious of friendships and wary of emotional commitments for fear that they would not last. She needed a man sufficiently dependent upon the support of a woman to reduce her fear of desertion. We may reasonably assume that her actions early in the marriage were, as they are now, intended to limit his course of action, to convince him of his need for her, and to impress upon him the significance of his own weaknesses and lack of accomplishment. While she criticizes him for not behaving more like a man, she could not accept a man strong enough to leave her. In effect, the Littletons need each other's weaknesses and each other's strengths. The interplay between Bobby Littleton and his mother illustrates the indirection with which attempts are made to influence responses and responsiveness in others. In general, within a stable family emotional matrix it seems almost necessary that such reciprocal interaction meet, in part, the needs of the members involved.

The subtleties of mutual regulation are seen in the Newbold family's response to Curt. He commands from them an adaptation to his variation from the family ideal. Both Mrs. and Mr. Newbold are willing to alter their customary pattern of activities in order to satisfy the demands that Curt makes by virtue of his differences from his brother and his wish to take off at a tangent from the family line. Here again is an example of the mutuality of regulation: Curt, who has the least status in the family as a Newbold, is able to influence and help regulate the behavior of the group. In turn, his feeling for them and his behavior are altered by their willingness to try to meet his unspoken demands.

The mutual fitting together of emotional patterns in the effort to achieve and maintain the desired family image is not always equally satisfactory to all members concerned. Adapting oneself to group demands or to expectations from husband or wife may occasion resentments which are repressed much of the time but which may find expression in indirect ways and be displaced upon other objects. Mrs. Steele is an example of this situation. She joins her husband in praising the benefits of the companionable family atmosphere they have created together. She, too, wants the children to be part of the tight family circle. But the family theme does less for her than it does for her husband. She resents the trips to the park and longs to get away from the children for a time alone with Mr. Steele. The children's needs and demands press upon her more insistently and more constantly than they do upon her husband. Her resentment of the ever present tight-little-family theme may be partially responsible for the irritation she shows with the children and their demands, both disciplinary and affectional, to which she must respond.

The direction of family activities is simplified in those families that have developed a family ideology or desired family image to which they relate activities and by which they evaluate themselves and each other. In a sense, the family image presents a persistent question or questions to each family member by which to judge his actions. In the Lanson family this question is, Does it promote family harmony and happiness? Of the five families, the Littleton family has defined less clearly than the others the questions that family members may use to evaluate themselves and to mark the areas in which achievement may be assured of a reward. This lack of a family ideology is related to the unevenness of discipline within the family and the uncertainty the children feel in attempting to demonstrate their worth within the family.

It is possible and useful to evaluate families in terms of what circumstances or factors play the most significant part in the regulation of family activities and emotional exchange. These factors vary from family to family. For the Newbolds, the two most central influences are the high value placed upon conformity to a family ideology and the father's authoritarian strength in implementing the family image. For the Lansons, the intensity of early socialization, which paved the way for a harmonious, superficially "democratic" family system, and the adherence to a firm concept of a family image provide the central regulating pressures. The Clarks lean heavily upon the code of behavior elaborated by the church. To this they add the impression of the mother as the dominating and giving force in the family, providing her with an unusually effective disciplinary position. In the Littleton family the most significant feature is the mother's attempt to reconstruct her own life through her children or, rather, to be certain that her children avoid some of the trage- dies of her own life and some of the faults of her husband. For the Steeles, the central pressures are the tightness of the family group, the deep wish to avoid weakness and ineptitude, the fear of isolation from the family, and the inevitability of punishment in response to violation of the family code.

The regulation of family interaction can thus be analyzed for our five families along seven dimensions: the effort to achieve desired individual and family images; the distribution of author- ity, in the formal sense, between husband and wife; the position taken on the power advantage inherent in the generational dif- ference and how this is to be used; the room for negotiation given the children and the basis on which it may be used; the clarity of a family set of behavioral rules, whether family ideology or other type of code, to which the family is expected to con- form; the emotional manipulation among family members, in- cluding the family members' ability to evoke desired emotional response from others; and the family's ability to defend itself against the threat of disruptive hostility.

FAMILY THEMES

The family theme or themes represent the critical issues— the central concerns—of family interaction as defined by the group itself. Identifying a family theme thus requires an under- standing of the family's view of the world and of itself. The theme partakes of the dominant inner concerns of family mem- bers as individuals. The extension of these concerns into the interaction of the group introduces the theme, which is then elaborated by the members' responses to one another.

The Clarks illustrate most clearly the manner in which per- sonal issues of the parents are developed as themes in the fam- ily's life. Both parents felt keenly the lack of stability and pre- dictable emotional gratification in their own childhood family experiences. Both determined to provide for their own children the economic and emotional security which they did not have. However, the loss they suffered cannot be completely forgotten or ignored; their efforts in behalf of their children are also efforts in behalf of themselves. The theme of their family life together is the avoidance of emotional and economic catastrophe, and this theme is seen in a different light by each family member. To Mr. Clark it means the effort to provide economically for the family and to secure for himself and the children the support and care of a strong maternal figure. His relationship to Mrs. Clark and to the children is an expression of this theme. It is illustrated by Jimmy's complaint that he and his father spend time together looking at the catalogue to select gifts for Mrs. Clark. The theme of avoiding emotional catastrophe is thus translated into attitudes toward females in general and toward Mrs. Clark as a person. Mr. Clark's concern, as well as his definition of women, is transmitted to his son directly by example and indirectly by defining emotional gratification as a sensitive and anxiety-arousing area.

Mrs. Clark joins the theme by defining herself as the center of the household—competent, providing, available when the children need her. She feels, however, that the demands upon her are excessive and that while her life has been satisfying in some respects, she has missed many of its pleasures. Her inner resentment taps her emotional resources. The fear of emotional and economic disaster has never completely left her. Her children have an awareness of this apprehension, but they cannot see its justification in events about them. In a vague sense they share her fear. Their anxiety is allayed in part by conformity to a religious code which is somewhat more explicit, but even this effort is sometimes experienced as a vague concern about "being good" and a sense of the presence of evil. The theme of avoidance and its related themes of conformity and the search for protection have helped the Clarks to order their daily life and to achieve stability and a degree of security.

The Clarks' theme is largely inarticulate and unconscious.

While they deliberately and consciously strive to improve their position in relation to the circumstances of their families of origin, they are not aware of the extensive consequences of the theme for the family's life. The Newbolds, however, have articulated the theme of their family group, and they keep it in constant awareness. The theme of active mastery is visible to the family, and its application to the behavior of individual members is a matter for open discussion. Some of the competitive elements are extensions of individual family members' repressed aggressive impulses, and this is one way the group theme is related to individual psychodynamics. But these competitive components are most directly exercised in encounters with persons outside the family. The members not only prevent open hostility within the family circle but actually contribute to a feeling of achievement of the family image and maintenance of its ideology. The feeling of satisfaction and accomplishment that the boys, especially Ted, get directly from their own conquests and vicariously from those of other members of the family accentuates their participation in the family theme and its role in their personal development. As with the Clarks, the theme is transmitted to the children. It is likely that a version of this theme will be found in the families which they establish for themselves as adults.

The importance of the family theme to the group is apparent in the concern it reveals about Curt. The positive features of the theme are used as a criterion for evaluating his behavior. By the standards of some families he would be regarded as a source of pride; in this family his lack of enthusiasm for active mastery makes the other members qualify their pride and praise of his abilities. Ironically, it is the strength of the competitive family spirit itself which places Curt at such a psychological disadvantage in comparison to his brother, whom he cannot outdo, and which compels him to retreat.

One element of the theme is preparedness for competition. Ted expresses this in his comment that one should not attempt a task until he is ready to do it well. Curt's behavior is thus not refusal to accept the family emphasis on active mastery and eagerness of challenge; it reflects, instead, an acceptance of the family's aims. His withdrawal is an effort to evade the implications of his immaturity and lack of ability in comparison to his older brother. The family theme is, for Curt, a critical issue to which he responds and which affects his life outside the family as well as within. Other family members deal more directly with the issue, each of them solving it to his own satisfaction. The Newbold family illustrates the point that a family member need not represent the dominant form of the family theme in order to become deeply involved in it.

Among our five families, and perhaps more generally, the family theme represents an unresolved psychological issue in the group. It is also an unresolved personal issue for at least one of the parents and is likely to be a prominent area of concern for the children. Often its heaviest impact will fall upon one child, as if his parents used him as the instrument for trying to come to grips with the problem, leaving other children less involved or involved in a less intense fashion. The Steeles illustrate a type of family in which the theme compiles more stress for one family member than for others. The Steele family has twin themes: the desire to ward off feelings of incompetence and the desire for companionability and co-operation in family interaction. These are related, as we have seen, in John Steele's background. It was he who brought to the family both themes. They are involved in the family daily and weekly group activities; they are the basis for most effective disciplinary techniques developed by the parents; and they define the relationship of the family to the outer community.

The Steeles' underlying psychological position is that support and strength are found in the family group. This support is necessary to help the individual member overcome his weaknesses. Mutual helpfulness and co-operation are affirmed and illustrated by the family's constant companionship. This statement of the family's definition of its place in the world and of the group's dominant psychological concerns takes into account the partially conscious issues—the fear of loneliness or social isolation generated by a mistrust of human relationships and the fear of incompetence and inadequacy. These concerns stimulate attempts to deal with them by family companionability and the need for individual and group strength.

The positive features of the Lansons' theme, which are more apparent than its limiting effects upon the individual family members, portray the family as a group earnestly striving for outward tranquillity and harmony. Life has no major external problems. Issues of social mobility, of income, or of recognition in the community and life have been met and mastered. The family's prize is harmony with each other and with the social surroundings, both community and class. Constriction of emotional expressivity and spontaneity is one of the costs, but they do not know how to avoid paying it. Harmony and serenity are the coin of interactive exchange; not only is intense emotional interaction unnecessary, it would be jarring.

The Lansons' theme, like the Steeles', expresses a specific quality of interaction among family members in which physical presence is essential. Whereas the drive for mastery over self and others that is apparent in the Newbolds is a theme which can be pursued individually, the Lansons' theme requires interactional situations involving at least two and preferably all members of the group. Mrs. Lanson's comment about enjoying holidays because the girls worked alongside her so well is one illustration of the interactive nature of this family's dominant psychological concern.

The Littletons' family theme is the most complicated and the least easily discernible of the five families we have described. The family sees its position in the world as essentially unsatisfactory and unsatisfying. The past is heavy with unfulfilment and neglected opportunities. The members cannot turn to one another, for none has sufficient warmth to serve the group. Their disappointment with each other is also a frustration, and they avoid close and frequent contact in order to maintain the general form of the family and assure themselves that the family will not dissolve. The family members weave back and forth between the frustration of attempted emotional gratification and the fear of isolation. The constant efforts expressed by this theme appear in the family's daily interaction, in the alignment and opposition to it among members, in the utilization of time that might be made available for exchange among family members.

CONNECTEDNESS AND SEPARATENESS

How to secure a satisfying degree of connectedness is interwoven with the problem of autonomy or separateness. They may be viewed as constituting together a single central family concern; as the family alters its position on one, it necessarily affects the achievement of the other. The individual member is only partially at liberty to determine his resolution of this dilemma for himself—he may be forced into closer contact or into isolation in contradiction to his preferences. The family may bind this issue into the family theme or the image they hold of themselves, giving it emphasis and constant attention. The meanings of connectedness and separateness are, of course, a subjective matter; in some cases the family may attempt to deal with them by erecting an overt structure of activities which symbolize the family's stand on the issue. Some families find it difficult to move beyond the overt signs and observable representations. Connectedness is a matter of what they, as a family, do together, not how they feel. Separateness, too, as a subjective experience may deny the demonstrations of the group's activities together; the inner feeling does not necessarily coincide with the public announcements.

Just as there is a fear or apprehension about the pain of separateness, there is a mistrust and fear of connectedness. It is customary to emphasize the binding and constraining dangers of family closeness, but more is involved than a threat to autonomy. Some members of our families mistrust the vulnerability of closeness; emotional interaction poses a threat to their self-image. Mr. Newbold presents himself as "not the billing and cooing kind" and in other ways avoids the kind of affectionate, tender exchange that often is expected in family interaction. Here, in part, is the definition of masculinity in this culture—a definition that is frequently interpreted as requiring the inhibition of expression of tender feelings to all except sweethearts, brides, and babies; and even baby boys grow out of this category in a year or two.

Mr. Newbold's behavior toward Curt is in partial contradiction of his attitude of reserve: an unspoken intimacy exists between them, an interaction which touches only part of Mr. Newbold. Between Mrs. Newbold and Curt is also a greater warmth than is apparent between her and Ted. In a curious fashion, it is Curt who is less congruent with the family's highest values and image, yet it is he who most nearly approaches a close emotional connectedness with his parents. Ted's ties with the family are concentrated in the areas of image and ideology— he is in close harmony with the ideology; Curt is in closer contact with the people. Thus connectedness and separateness may be expressed in terms of personal contact or in terms of adherence to a family image, a constantly repeated validation of integration with the family and its ideals. The Newbold family dinner as an occasion for group spirit based upon exchanging reports of extra-family conformity to the family ideals provides an example of connectedness founded on allegiance to a common image.

Whereas the Newbolds stress family cohesion grounded upon approximation to the group ideology, the Steeles define family closeness more nearly as physical proximity and joint activity. The restraints exercised upon family members to maintain group contacts are readily apparent in the family comments. Mrs. Steele goes to the park with the family even though she gets less satisfaction than they from the excursion itself. To this family, it is her physical presence that represents family harmony and cohesion. The Steeles have incorporated the notion of family intimacy into their family image; it is also one of their central interactional themes. The emphasis they place upon it reveals its prominence in their psychological economy. To the children and Mrs. Steele, the issue is unbalanced on the side of group closeness; they would prefer more autonomy, more separateness. For them, the tight family interactional system is a burden as well as a support. For Mr. Steele, close family interaction is a partial resolution of a personal need. He has elaborated this need into a family theme and a significant component of family self-regard and pride. As such, it has become an important condition of personal worth for each family member.

The Lansons have dealt with this issue by making interpersonal harmony the symbol of family togetherness. Unity is demonstrated by consensus; separateness and autonomy are viewed as hazardous violations of the family image. For them, disagreement with the group or with other family members is an expression of the wish to withdraw—a sign of rejection. Once family consensus has been accepted as a desirable goal and has been achieved in overt behavior, it takes on the compelling force of an emotional contract, agreed to and followed by all members. The merits of autonomy thus become vague and unfamiliar and are regarded not in terms of their value to the individual member but in the light of a breach of faith with the group. This family de-emphasizes or denies the positive aspects of autonomy and the negative consequences of constant consensus. Their view of the total issue is one-sided, concentrating upon the solution that seems to them to produce least interpersonal friction. They meet the possibility of family conflict by stamping as unacceptable those behaviors that create interpersonal stress and group disagreement. Autonomy is necessarily taboo; it implies self- rather than group determination, and it opens the path to group disagreement, disturbingly intense emotions, and individual experience. In this group, the evidence of unity is verbal agreement, shared experience, and equanimity.

The search for a solution to the issue of connectedness and separateness may appear in alignments among family members. The close friendship between Susan and Bill Steele not only offers each of them the opportunity for sharing experience, it allows them both to move out from the confining family circle. Mrs. Steele tells us that they wander over the neighborhood together and that she approves their explorations into the community. For them, an intimate bond is a route to a limited separation from the group. In other instances, a family alignment may have intimacy as its primary objective. This appears most obviously in the Littletons, where each parent has chosen one of the children as a favorite. Each chose a child of the opposite sex, and both of these pairs have a more affectionate tone than does the relationship between Mr. and Mrs. Littleton. Mrs. Littleton describes Bobby as more demonstrative and affectionate than her husband; Mr. Littleton is more affectionate to Sally than he customarily is to his wife. The tie between Mr. Littleton and Sally is a threat both to Betty and to Mrs. Littleton. Intimacy within a family may act to isolate family members if it is not distributed in a fashion intended to satisfy the demands of the entire group.

In the Littleton family, isolation and separateness, rather than connectedness, are the dominant tones of interpersonal and family interaction. Separateness helps keep this group together. The intensity of each member's personal needs is great; no family member is able to fulfil the emotional demands made upon him. The closer interaction and personal contact become, the more aggravated is the frustration of unmet needs. Family members avoid one another in order to keep irritation and hostility within bounds. The tenuous quality of interaction is illustrated by Bobby's comment, quoted earlier, about his father.

I think he likes me the best. I never bother him. That's why.
INTERVIEWER: *What bothers him?*
BOBBY: *They always sit on his lap when he doesn't want them.*

Here is separateness seen as a condition for approval and approachability. The demands of intimacy cannot be met; in its place approval is extended at arm's length.

These families illustrate versions of the attempt to shape some form of connection and yet deal with the need for separateness.

This issue is met with varying degrees of concern, and its relation to other family problems depends upon the intensity of this concern. Different members of the same family find the group stance toward this issue differentially satisfying. The overt acts intended to promote and demonstrate family unity are not necessarily matched by the subjective experience of the individual members. Cohesion may be confining or comforting; perhaps more frequently, it is both.

FAMILY BOUNDARIES AND THE ARENA OF VALIDATION

For all the research group, the boundaries of the family are established by the families themselves, with virtually no restrictive or coercive pressure from sources external to the family.[1] The family life space was "staked out" by family preference or, on the other hand, was left relatively uncharted and undefined through lack of a clear design for family life.

The family world has boundaries which are, in a sense, geographical. It is defined physically to the extent that the family is aware of its physical surroundings and uses them in pursuit of family goals. The Steeles draw close boundaries, in a geographical sense, about the family world. Significant family interaction and activity take place primarily in the house or yard; the children are encouraged to spend time playing at home; on Sunday, friends of the children are not permitted to come and play. The group has never been on a vacation, although Mr. and Mrs. Steele had one vacation together years ago. The family excursions to park and forest preserve provide another place for the family to be alone together. The members move in toward each other, away from experience with the outside world.

The Newbolds, however, see the outside world as their oyster.

[1] The family's world may, of course, be limited drastically by formal and informal social influence and sanction, by law, and by other circumstances which forcibly inhibit freedom of movement or social exchange with other members of the society. Within rather broad limits, the families described here were at liberty to shape their own worlds, unencumbered by external restraints.

Space is to be exploited. Vacation trips across the country, visits to historical sites, excursions to relatively unknown places in Chicago, and plans for a trip around the world all indicate their view of family boundaries which are widespread and flexible. Both these sets of parents prefer to rear their families in a house, rather than an apartment. They both believe that houses are the most appropriate locale for families, and they have chosen the physical context that they believe suitable to their view of the family. The Littleton family is less definite in its conception of what physical boundaries and equipment should surround the family. They want more space rather than a house. Vacations are rare for them. Characteristically, Mr. Littleton is separated from his family on his vacation. Space, for the Littleton family, means opportunity to avoid the discomforts of proximity and interaction. They use space to move away from each other; the Steeles use it to push the family into even closer interaction.

The world of the Clarks, on the other hand, utilizes physical boundaries very little in defining the family. An occasional vacation trip, frequent jaunts to the museum or zoo, and infrequent visits to relatives are the pattern of this family. The children interact freely with other children in the neighborhood. Geography presents very little challenge, excitement, or relief from the routine of every day. The Lansons' world has relatively narrow physical boundaries, but they use vacations and other extensions of experience as cautious experiments with new stimulation and as an exercise in family harmony in an unfamiliar setting.

The family's world is also defined by the intensity of experience it encourages and permits among its members. The depth of feeling and the areas of feeling that are emphasized and returned to again and again form a crude map of another dimension of the family's universe. The Lansons illustrate one extreme among our five families in their modulation of emotion, their taboos against intense feelings and the expression of impulse. In this dimension their family world is even but thin; spontaneity is a characteristic that has not been encouraged. The lines that are drawn to define appropriate intensity of experience emphasize moderation and homogeneity.

The Littleton family stands in sharp contrast to the Lansons on this dimension. They permit and encourage strong and even violent emotions. Their comments of screaming, fighting, and unhappiness suggest the wide range of emotional experience and display permitted in their family. Although the more excessive demonstrations are verbally discouraged, they are actually allowed as a legitimate part of personal experience and interpersonal exchange. Mrs. Littleton's comment about her own anger with the children shows, in part, how intense feelings and their expression are incorporated into acceptable family behavior: "When I get angry, I explain if I didn't care about them [the children] I wouldn't be angry." Expression of affection is also encouraged, particularly in Bobby.

The Newbolds prefer a range of intensity characterized by self-control and restraint, but they allow an intensity of feeling when its display is carefully controlled. In fact, there seems to be some tendency to see themselves as needing more intensity of feeling in some areas. Mrs. Newbold speaks of wanting to give her children warmth which she felt her own mother never gave; Mr. Newbold takes Curt to see a morning storm but, in the interview, plays down his own emotional feelings. In addition, experience must be varied and stimulating. A vacation on a quiet, small lake would "kill Mr. Newbold and Ted," according to Mrs. Newbold. This family, with all its concern about self-control, wants excitement and stimulation—the family boundaries must be expanded to include them.

The Clarks wish to avoid excitement and contrast, but they permit an intensity of experience that ranges from devotion to anger. Excitement is provided by visual stimulation—the museum, zoo, and TV. In this regard, they resemble the Littleton family. They are more attentive to subjective feelings than are the Newbolds, more willing to explore their own emotions—particularly in religious experience. While they permit some expression of impulses and religious affect, the general emotional tone of the family lacks depth. Intensity of experience is restricted to a relatively few areas, but within these limits it may show considerable range.

The family's universe is also bounded by the evaluation that is placed upon behavior. Actions are defined initially by parents, later by siblings, as within or outside the acceptable range of proper or appropriate experience. Evaluation is an attempt to set limits on experience, to shape it and translate it into acceptable forms. Families differ in two ways on this dimension: in the extent to which evaluation is applied to behavior or experience and in the nature of the evaluation that is applied. The terms of evaluation may be strongly religious or couched in phrases suggesting rationality. Thus the Clarks speak of behaviors as being good or bad; the Newbolds evaluate behavior by its congruence with their family image of self-control and reasonableness; the Steeles view children's behavior in terms of its contribution to the individual member's ability to handle himself and his environment adequately; the Lansons judge their behavior through the prism of family harmony and agreement. All the families have standards for distinguishing between acceptable behavior and actions which must be rejected or corrected, but the specific acts which fall into these categories vary from family to family as the criterion of evaluation is applied in the attempt to achieve that particular image which the family holds for itself.

The range of behavior over which evaluation is exercised is also in part a function of the nature of the evaluating criteria. Curt Newbold stimulates some concern in his parents because he is not prompt in volunteering for action; in the Clark family this reluctance would have received no concern or comment, except that it might be rewarded as a sign of modesty or courtesy. In some families of our study parents allowed their children to "talk back," disagree, and argue, on the rationale that children have a right to express their opinions even as parents do. On the other hand, Mrs. Littleton says about her children: "They can think anything they want. They can think I'm crazy, but they have to keep it to themselves." Here silence becomes a way of defining the boundaries of an individual family member and sets limits, presumably, upon the nature of interpersonal exchange. In some families the evaluation of behavior extends to censoring or at least to an attempt at interpreting television shows, popular songs, and other expressions of popular culture. Stimuli from outside the family are screened and colored by the parents' perspective and the kind of experience they prefer their children to have. Evaluating may be a deliberate attempt to encourage or discourage discrimination, or it may be a subtle inadvertent extension of the parent's opinion and bias.

Evaluation is placed upon acts in a selective fashion. The issues of the family—its themes and images—determine the range and selectivity of objects for evaluation. The family's ideology determines the nature of the criteria and the degree to which the judgments made are moral ones. These elements also help to determine the kind of punishment to be expected if standards are not met and, in consequence, the kind of motivation which prompts the child to align his behavior with the family code.

The family's universe has internal boundaries—lines that draw distinctions between sexes, between generations, and among individual family members. This is in part a question of the tolerance of individual differences within the family. To what extent is the single member permitted to develop in areas which have little of the family communality? What differences in preference, temperament, and overt behavior are tolerated? In the Littleton family, differences among the children are permitted, even encouraged. The children are seen and accepted as quite different from each other and, to a degree, from their mother's preferences. The Clarks, however, demand a large area of communality between the behavior and personality of the children and the values of the church. Differentiation is not a thing to be encouraged, prized, or permitted except within rather narrow limits. The Newbolds and Lansons also permit less room for differentiation than they like to believe. This is the result, and the problem, of a strong family ideology and an effective disciplinary technique.

Family boundaries are an expression of the family's concerns and the family's aspirations. They are consistent with the family's image of itself—an evidence of the family's sense of identity. The dimensions, both external and internal, are designed to serve family purposes. In doing so, they necessarily affect the perception that the child develops of the physical, emotional, social, and cultural world in which he lives.

GENERATIONAL CONTINUITY AND FAMILY IDENTITY

The structure of the nuclear family creates psychological issues on which the parents are obliged to take a stand. These issues, which are inherent in family life, provide dimensions of family behavior upon which families must of necessity distribute themselves. They involve decisions for action forced upon the parents—decisions which affect the basic interactional patterns of the group. The position that the parents, deliberately or not, take on these issues is in part a function of the image the parents themselves hold of their family and what they wish it to become.

One of the issues of this nature is the question of the continuity of tradition, ideology, and overt behavior from generation to generation. In effect, the parents must decide the question of what characteristics of themselves and of their families of orientation they wish to transmit to their children. Do they see themselves as part of a continuing, unchanged family tradition and behavior, or do they see themselves as altering the generational trend, either in their own behavior or in that of their children? Parents draw upon various resources for the patterns of behavior that they emphasize in the socialization process. The tendency of parents in our society to call upon or listen to child experts for advice about child-rearing techniques and evaluation of children's behavior suggests a strain of uncertainty about their proper role and stance in the transmission process. This very uncertainty indicates dissatisfaction with their families of origin and with themselves as products of it. In our research group it was unusual for a parent to profess to be satisfied with his own behavior and willing to attempt to pass it along to his children without considerable modification. These expressed attitudes were reinforced by the evidence available to us on the socializing behavior of the parents. A curious result of their dissatisfaction with themselves and the families from which they came is the inclination of many parents to deal most severely with behavior in their children which repeats the parents' own faults. The children are expected to amend the personality and behavioral flaws of the parents; the parents are often puzzled when this is not achieved. They feel that since they now realize the mistakes of their own childhood and have warned their children against them, it is a sign of obstinacy if the child, against the counsel of his wiser parents, duplicates their errors. The function of the parent for those who would transform their children is thus to produce a better product. Aware of their own faults, they turn to experts for help in producing children which are unlike themselves.

Several characteristics differentiate parents' positions on the issue of generational continuity. Perhaps the most significant is the image the parent holds of his family of origin and his place in it. The parents in our five families cover a wide range of attitudes in their evaluation of their own parents. Mr. Newbold speaks of both his father and mother with pride. His statement on the SCT ("My father / is the best man I've ever known") is matched by his adopting the same profession and general style of life. Mrs. Newbold speaks of her husband and his father as being very similar and praises both of them highly. Mr. Newbold is also satisfied with himself as a father and wants his sons to pattern themselves after his model: "I'm satisfied [with myself as a father]. If I felt there was something I ought to change, I would." Here is deliberate, direct, unashamed effort at transmission by duplication. However, admiration for one's parents and satisfaction with one's place as a child in the family does not necessarily lead to attempts at continuity. Mr. Littleton speaks also of his father as "one of the finest men I [have] ever known" and says that he had the respect of his children. However, he sees his own childhood as lacking in freedom and range of activities. In spite of this report of his recollection of his own family, he takes an opposite position from that of Mr. Newbold. Joe Littleton would prefer, he says, that his children not use him as a model; he denies that he has qualities, except honesty, that he feels they should have. He believes that he and his family have little to offer and prefers to think of his children as receiving from their mother characteristics that will prepare them for a more satisfying way of life than he has himself experienced.

The discontent that a parent may feel with his parents may be in the nature of criticism of personal deficiencies of the parent or of more impersonal circumstances that affected the parent-child interaction. Mrs. Steele, for example, criticizes her parents openly. She feels that they neglected her, were too distant, and finally deserted her. Mrs. Newbold, also, speaks of the lack of emotional warmth in her mother. The most intense dissatisfaction with one's parents is shown by Mrs. Littleton, who believes that both her parents deserted her. Mr. Clark, on the other hand, while he sees his own home life as unsatisfactory, is inclined to see the deficiency as an economic problem. He is less concerned about being the right kind of person than he is about establishing a family situation that provides security for all.

The handling of the issue of generational continuity is also a function of the image the parent has of his place in the three generation stages—parent, self, child. One stance that may be assumed is that of having made good despite the parents and family conditions but being determined that the children shall do even better. In some ways this is the attitude of Mrs. Littleton, of the Clarks, and of Mrs. Steele. In these cases, the parent feels that he has something to pass along to the child—not as much as he would like but a long step toward the better life. One of the fathers of the research group in effect said, "I'm a better father than my father was; my boy will be a better father than I am, especially if he has some of my characteristics and some of his mother's." They see themselves as providing many of the resources that they feel the children need. Mr. Littleton and, to a degree, Mr. Clark experience feelings of despair and unworthiness and claim that they have little to offer.

The alternatives chosen by the parent who wishes to avoid duplication offer other criteria for differentiating themes in which the problem of continuity is handled. Mr. Littleton withdraws in favor of his wife; Mr. Clark abdicates his position in the transmission line in favor of his wife and supports her position in the family and her socialization techniques. They have, at least, agreed upon the values which the children should assume and the general style of life they should adopt. The Steeles, Lansons, and Newbolds see the transmission problems as undertaken jointly, with parental agreement and participation; each feels that both parents have significant charcteristics to pass along.

The problem of continuity may be approached from an essentially negative angle—the desire to avoid or reject behavior in the children that the parents themselves have not been able to handle in their own personalities. Thus the parent in such a case is inclined to make an issue of the behavior in question, to sensitize the child to the importance he places upon it, and, not infrequently, to create a similar problem for the child. Mr. Steele's fight over his own shyness and his desire that his boy should overcome his emotional instability and timidity illustrate the transmission of problem areas from parent to child.

The family's sense of identity is profoundly affected by its stance on the continuity issue. A sense of pride and accomplishment may be gained by maintaining a tradition; it may also be gained by successful transformation of a family unit. Identity, however, is an accumulative, subjective, and reputational state, and the recently arrived is always at a disadvantage.

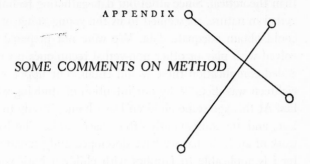

SOME COMMENTS ON METHOD

Much of the way in which this study was done is implicit in what we have written in this volume. In these appended pages we wish to spell out in some detail the research methods, giving consideration to the procedures and reasoning that were used in selecting the families, in obtaining data from them, and in analyzing the data.

BACKGROUND

The central aim of the research was to study families as groups of persons. This objective led us to formulate specific criteria for selecting families. The comments that follow refer not only to the five families presented in this book but also to the total group of thirty-three from which data were collected and from which these were chosen. These are the defining characteristics of the families studied:

1. The unit of study is the nuclear family—parents living with their biological children. Families with adopted children were excluded, since our concern was with ordinary, intact families. Since, further, our interest lay primarily in understanding the interior organization of the unit made up of husband, wife, and children, we did not study the extended family—the unit that includes uncles and aunts, cousins and grandparents, as well as the nuclear family.

2. The children in these families are between the ages of six and eighteen. This criterion is based more on practical grounds

than theoretical. Since all of our data-gathering techniques were verbal in nature, six seemed to us the youngest age at which we could obtain adequate data. We were not prepared to get involved with play or other non-verbal techniques because of the added complication these would entail. The upper age limit of eighteen was dictated by our intention of studying whole families. At this age some children leave home, if only to go to college, and are consequently often inaccessible. The basic framework of analysis that we have developed and presented in chapter i is applicable to families with children both younger and older than those of the present study, but its application would almost certainly require modifications in the data-gathering procedures.

The age range adopted is a wide one. The terms of our analytic framework are cast at a level of generality that does not tie them to particular age levels or forms of sibship. For our purposes, it sufficed to have some families with boys, some with girls, and some with boys and girls. The age span adopted had the distinct advantage of enabling us to develop a framework that was general and not age-restricted.

3. The families are northwest European in ancestry. This defining characteristic follows from our aim of studying a group of families relatively homogeneous in ethnic background and of minimal ethnic visibility in American society. Our interest was in understanding something of the differences that exist in that broad band of families who make up the core culture of the United States and who have no sense of tie to or inner conflict over minority group membership and tradition. The families selected are, in a broad sociological sense, not "special" in any way.

One may quarrel with the degree of homogeneity actually represented by the term "northwest European," if one wishes to press the point that only those of English ancestry have no "minority group" characteristics in this society. The objection hardly seems a serious one. There has probably been, in this country, more intermarriage within the northwest European group than between it and central or south Europeans. In addition, persons of Dutch or German or Scandinavian ancestry have on the whole lost their ethnic visibility much more rapidly than persons of, say, Slavic or Mediterranean ancestry.

4. The families are all resident in metropolitan areas, though in some instances the parents were born and spent their early years in small towns.

5. The families range, along the dimension of social class, from upper lower to upper middle. This variation was deliberate, since we expected that important differences in family life would exist along this dimension. Variation in social class membership was intended to assure a range of differences that might be expected to influence family life. Social class has been a background concept, rather than a focal point, of our analysis. At the same time, this breadth served us in the same way as did that of the children's age span: it facilitated developing concepts for family analysis that are not class-bound, just as they are not age-bound. A wide range of occupations was included, a range generally represented by the families discussed in this book.

6. The families are selected from the community at large and not from a clinic population. The significance of this criterion again derives from our basic objectives. We wished to study the "psychosocial interior" of families, an area that has largely been the province of psychiatrists, psychologists, and social workers treating persons with psycho-clinical disorders. Our study was directed to understanding psychosocial ties in ordinary families.

These, then, are the specifications for the families we set out to study. In the period allotted for field work, we succeeded in collecting data from thirty-three families. In the course of obtaining these, approximately twenty-five families who met our selection criteria and who were approached declined to participate in the study. In addition, one family that had agreed to be studied refused to continue, after half the data had been collected. This was the only dropout.

The names of potential families for study were obtained in two ways. Various people in the community who might be able to furnish names of families were approached. Our aims were explained to them in the same terms as they later were to the families themselves: "Everyone knows the saying 'like father like son,' and we also know that it isn't always true. We would like to know more exactly just how children are like their fathers and mothers, or if they are not, why not. We are interested in studying normal, typical American families. Much research has been done on unusual or abnormal families, but relatively little on the great number of normal families that make up a community. We hope that our work will contribute more information about the important matter of bringing up our children." Preservation of the anonymity of the families to be studied was, of course, stressed. We also indicated something of the range of topics our interviewing would cover and stated that we would not be probing into the most intimately personal aspects of family life but that our interviewing would deal with the ordinary events of daily living.

The great majority of families contacted were obtained from those people in the community who were in a position to refer us to several. The second source of family names was the families actually studied. In response to our request, some referred us to families of their acquaintance. Of the total group of thirty-three, six were referrals from participating families.

The objectives of the study were explained to the husband or wife, or both, of each family contacted. It was also explained that the interviewer would want to talk with each member of the family privately and that what one member of the family said would in no instance be repeated to any other member of the family. The parents were told that all the procedures would require approximately fifteen to twenty hours of the family's time—no more than three or four hours with any one person.

In most instances the explanation of the objectives and time demands of the study were sufficient. In a few cases, families wanted to know what direct benefit they would derive from the study. For some of these, the question meant whether they would receive assistance with their own family problems. For others, the question was vaguer in intent. We explained that we could not offer counseling on family problems and that we would not in any way interpret the family to itself. To have done so would not have been consonant with the principal research condition we established—that each family member would talk about himself and his family in privacy with the interviewer and with assured confidentiality.

We explained that the only reward the family could expect was the satisfaction that, by their participation, they were contributing to scientific knowledge about family life and that, we hoped, this would ultimately be of benefit to other parents in bringing up their children.

The motives for participating in the study were not explicitly or systematically explored. Some of the parents, particularly but not exclusively the less sophisticated ones, voluntarily said that they were pleased and even flattered that they could make a contribution to scientific knowledge in this fashion. Some appeared to use the research as an occasion to express their satisfaction with what they had achieved in family living. Others seemed curious about what such a project could be like or simply welcomed this novel addition to their lives. A few perhaps still hoped, despite our explanation, that they would receive some direct assistance with their immediate problems. We received only one such explicit request from a parent concerning a child; though declining to counsel directly, we did refer the parent to an appropriate agency.

In a few instances a parent attempted to find out how a child had conducted himself with or what he had said to the interviewer. Such probing was quickly discouraged by the interviewer, who made it plain that she would not violate the confidentiality that had been promised all the members of the family. Attempts to find out what a spouse had told the interviewer were even fewer in number and were handled according to the same principle.

After the family had agreed to participate in the study, the interviewing began with the obtaining of background information on the family. This initial session was most often held with both spouses present, but occasionally only with the wife. The former method was the one we preferred, but it was not always feasible because of the family's schedule. When this was the case, supplementary material was later obtained from the husband. This opening interview, in addition to serving as a warmup and allowing the parents to begin to feel at home with the interviewer, covered two main areas:

A. Face-sheet data
   1. Ages of all family members
   2. Birthplaces of each member
   3. Family's residence history
   4. Education of husband and wife
   5. Current and previous occupations of husband and wife
   6. Nationality ancestry
   7. Religious affiliation
B. Data on early life of husband and wife
   1. What kind of people their parents were
   2. Information about brothers and sisters
   3. A characterization of what their home life was like

In retrospect, it seems that a fuller investigation of the early home life of the parents would have been helpful in further illuminating their contemporary motives in the family.

Several types of data were obtained from each family member: an interview, obtained sometimes in one session but often in two and occasionally in three; a TAT; a Sentence Completion; a brief essay from each child on "The Person I Would Like To Be Like"[1] and an essay from each parent on "The Kind of Person I Would Like My Child To Be." The data gathering—all of which was conducted in the family's residence—was concluded with the administration of a set of five TAT-type pictures to the

---

[1] This technique is described in R. J. Havighurst, M. Z. Robinson, and M. Dorr, "The Development of the Ideal Self in Childhood and Adolescence," *Journal of Educational Research*, Vol. XL, No. 4 (December, 1946).

family as a group. These pictures were especially designed for this study. To each picture the family was asked to discuss and develop among themselves an agreed-upon story. The discussions as well as the story were recorded.

Each person was interviewed in privacy for periods of an hour to an hour and a half for children and for two and a half to three hours for parents. The number of sessions devoted to interviewing any one person depended upon individual circumstances. Each member was interviewed on substantially the same topics. The questions were open-ended, designed to encourage the person to comment freely on general topics raised for discussion. Initial responses were followed by more specific probes where indicated. The interview guide covered these areas:

1. Each member's view of his family—what it is like, what the important things about it are.

2. The family's daily life—what they do and how they feel about it. The extent and variety of their activity, inside and outside the home. How the weekends differ from weekdays. The concrete happenings that occur and the kind of interaction among family members that is woven through them.

3. The work and responsibility roles of each member, including not only the earning role of the husband-father and others' feelings about it but also the assignment or assumption of household management responsibilities. Also extra-familial responsibilities in school, church, civic organizations.

4. The course of the family's development, beginning with the parents' own families of origin. What their parents and childhood homes were like. How the parents now see themselves in relation to their backgrounds—what their aims are for themselves and what they want for their children. Their goals, aspirations, regrets, and disappointments.

5. Related to the foregoing, the socialization of the children. Generally, how the parents deal with their children, how they construe the parent-child relationship. What behaviors they consider to be offenses and how these are handled.

6. How the family members perceive and feel about one another. In what ways they feel they resemble or differ from each other.

7. What problems each member feels he has in relation to himself or in relation to other family members. What he particularly likes

about each other member. What changes he would like to see in himself and in the others.

The progress of the interview generally followed this order of topics, though the procedure was a flexible one and was adapted to fit individual circumstance.

TAT stories to at least ten pictures were obtained from each person. Two of the pictures were from the specially drawn set mentioned above. The remainder were selected from the Harvard TAT. Parents and children were shown the same pictures. However, some of the pictures used with the first families studied were later dropped as not yielding material sufficiently useful to warrant inclusion. A list of the pictures used is given at the end of this Appendix. The pictures selected were those that seemed to promise useful material for family analysis. Some which we did not include—12BG, for example—might also have proved quite profitable.[2]

Two forms of the Sentence Completion were devised, one for use with younger children, the other administered to older children and parents. These forms are also given at the end of this Appendix.

With the group TAT procedure mentioned above, we sought to obtain concurrent projective and interaction data. We have not yet devised a satisfactory method of analyzing this material, though several have been tried. In the present volume, we have occasionally drawn on the protocols for illustration. In none of the cases here does an interpretation rest primarily on this material.

Supplementing the data obtained directly from the family members is the interviewer's record. The interviewer described the family's residence and each member of the family. She also described their demeanor during the interview and testing sessions.

[2] For a systematic account of the nature of TAT data, see William E. Henry, *The Analysis of Fantasy: The Thematic Apperception Technique in the Study of Personality* (New York: John Wiley & Sons, 1956).

The various techniques employed to gather the data for this study are all relatively unstructured. This research strategy was deliberate and was designed to maximize freedom in two directions. It was designed to allow our informants to express themselves as freely as possible about their families and themselves, and it was also intended to allow the investigators a wide area of interpretive freedom. Our aim was clear: to find a way to describe and understand families as units while concomitantly relating the personalities of component members to the unit. This meant that we had to be prepared to work with concepts derived from psychology, anthropology, sociology, and social psychology —but in what combination we did not know in advance. Our task has been one of analysis and interpretation, as it is in any research. In carrying out this task, we have made three fundamental assumptions: (1) The data do not speak for themselves but gain coherence only as they are brought into relation with useful ideas about them. (2) The responses each informant gives us potentially convey much more than his words at face value indicate. He is also informing us about the implicit principles that guide his life and about how he organizes reality. He indicates something of his scope, his energy, his conventionality. Conclusions about such characteristics can be reached by attending not only to what is said but to how it is said. They can confidently be reached only from attending to a great deal of what a person has said, considered together. (3) What each family member says takes part of its meaning from what the other family members say.

These assumptions have guided the way we have handled the data. The essential research procedure can be described as "movement"—of which there are three kinds. We have moved freely back and forth from one type of data to another, evaluating what each person has said on each instrument, utilizing it with whatever skill and understanding we could bring to bear.

It was not part of our purpose to compare the various types of data.

We have moved back and forth from one family member's material to another's, looking for meanings in both that connect them to each other. Each member in succession was taken as a point of reference; examining every other member's view of him—as well as his view of himself—we then attempted to follow out the consequences of these congruences and incongruences of image. From any particular congruence, for example, we tried to describe how members were brought together or driven apart; what kinds of overt familial behavior were fostered and what kinds of feeling were discouraged; how each member defined his place in the family and how he was assigned a place by others. In reading across all the material from a family, we asked such questions as these: Is there a clear family image, or is it diffuse? How does the family set its boundaries? To what sources does it turn for stimulation? What experiences and feelings are urged upon the members and which are shunned? How does the family regulate behavior? What opposition is there between implicit and explicit tendencies? How are the distinctions of age, sex, and birth order being treated in this family?

Finally, we moved back and forth from one family to another, considering each as a unit and asking, What distinguishes this family from others? In this procedure, the family as a group is placed in sharper focus, and the characteristics of particular individuals are assimilated to this more inclusive view. At this level of discourse, the various personalities and relationships within the family are expressed in the form of some group tendency. It is then possible to make such statements as: The Lansons provide no overt channels for intensity, which must then be contained in fantasy. The Newbolds demand intensity and assertion, and they react against evidence of its lack. Conclusions such as these are possible only if all the members of the family are studied and only if one family is compared with another.

In setting down the principles according to which the work proceeded, we are nonetheless obliged to say that their utilization cannot be made a matter of precise prescription. On two counts, the application of these principles remains at present beyond the reach of exact method and measurement. First, there is the issue of what the investigator is willing and able to conclude from his data. What he brings to bear and how far he is ready to carry his inference will determine the nature of his conclusions. Second, it is not possible to specify exactly where to look in the data for the answer to any particular question. Scrutiny of our data has taught us that we cannot predict where a person will most clearly and significantly declare himself. Presumably everything that one person says is of a piece, if we knew how to find its shape. In some cases this is easier than in others. But in any case, there is no substitute for sifting and analyzing until the investigator reaches a descriptive interpretation congruent with the data at his disposal.

TAT CARDS

The following cards from the Thematic Apperception Test were employed in the research program. Descriptions of the pictures are taken from the TAT Manual by Murray.[3]

1. A young boy is contemplating a violin which rests on a table in front of him.

2. Country scene: in the foreground is a young woman with books in her hand; in the background a man is working in the fields and an older woman is looking on.

3BM. On the floor against a couch is the huddled form of a boy with his head bowed on his right arm. Beside him on the floor is a revolver.

4. A woman is clutching the shoulders of a man whose face and body are averted as if he were trying to pull away from her.

6BM. A short elderly woman stands with her back turned to a tall young man. He is looking downward with a perplexed expression.

7BM. A gray-haired man is looking at a younger man who is sullenly staring into space.

7GF. An older woman is sitting on a sofa close beside a girl, speaking or reading to her. The girl, who holds a doll in her lap, is looking away.

[3] Henry A. Murray, Thematic Apperception Test (Cambridge: Harvard University Press, 1943). Reprinted by permission of the publishers.

8BM. An adolescent boy looks straight out of the picture. The barrel of a rifle is visible at one side, and in the background is the dim scene of a surgical operation, like a reverie-image.

9GF. A young woman with a magazine and purse in her hand looks from behind a tree at another young woman in a party dress running along a beach.

11. A road skirting a deep chasm between high cliffs. On the road in the distance are obscure figures. Protruding from the rocky wall on one side is the long head and neck of a dragon.

12M. A young man is lying on a couch with his eyes closed. Leaning over him is the gaunt form of an elderly man, his hand stretched out above the face of the reclining figure.

14. The silhouette of a man (or woman) against a bright window. The rest of the picture is totally black.

18GF. A woman has her hands squeezed around the throat of another woman whom she appears to be pushing backwards across the banister of a stairway.

19. A weird picture of cloud formations overhanging a snow-covered cabin in the country.

Two cards were added from a set drawn for use as a family group projective picture technique. These may be described as follows:

B. In the foreground stand a man and a woman, apparently under emotional stress. Behind them, through a doorway to an adjoining room, a wagon and a doll are seen on the floor.

C. In the left foreground a woman is seated in an easy chair. In the background on a sofa are seated a young girl with something in her lap and a man holding a newspaper. He appears to be looking up from the paper. A young boy is stretched prone on the floor, center foreground, and an older boy is standing at the far right.

INCOMPETE SENTENCES (ADULT)

Complete all of these sentences as fast as you can. Write the first idea that comes to your mind!
1. There are times when I
2. What people like most about me is
3. It's fun to daydream about
4. People think I am
5. My father
6. When things go wrong, mother
7. One thing I can't stand is
8. To get along with people, I
9. My mother

10. My greatest fear is
11. If I only hadn't
12. I want my children to
13. The weakest part of me
14. The fact that I failed
15. Children
16. Secretly I
17. Other people
18. I often think of myself as
19. If only my father had
20. I think my friends
21. Most women
22. Fathers sometimes
23. Being sick
24. I cannot understand what makes me
25. I despise
26. I don't like the sort of person who
27. When somebody makes fun of me
28. A good mother always
29. I don't like the sort of kids who
30. No one can make me
31. Mothers sometimes
32. If I had my way
33. Compared to women, men are
34. When father comes home
35. Sometimes I feel like
36. Compared to men, women are
37. When told to keep my place, I
38. When they avoided me,
39. Around here, too many people
40. When the family is together
41. Bosses can
42. Most men
43. People under me are
44. When I'm put under pressure, I
45. Nothing makes me madder than
46. When others do better
47. Brothers and sisters
48. Our family
49. If they tell me its dangerous, I
50. Most people don't know that I
51. I get down in the dumps when

52. Children would be better off if their parents
53. The strongest part of me
54. Even the best person will
55. What gets me into trouble is

INCOMPLETE SENTENCES (CHILD)

Complete all of these sentences as fast as you can. Write the *first idea* that comes to your mind.
1. My mother and I
2. When the family is together
3. My father and I
4. When things go wrong, mother
5. I am most scared of
6. When I do something wrong, father
7. When the kids don't play with me
8. People think I am
9. My father
10. My mother
11. I am sorry when I
12. I want my children to
13. What gets me into trouble is
14. Children
15. If my father would only
16. Mothers sometimes
17. Secretly I
18. Fathers sometimes
19. I hate
20. When father comes home
21. I don't like the sort of kids who
22. If I had my way
23. The thing that really makes me mad is
24. What people like most about me is
25. Brothers and sisters
26. Our family
27. If they tell me I shouldn't, I
28. One thing I can't stand is
29. To make people like me
30. Other kids
31. Teachers are
32. I think my friends
33. Most girls

34. Being sick
35. I don't like the sort of person who
36. When somebody makes fun of me
37. No one can make me
38. Sometimes I feel like
39. Most boys
40. When I take care of younger kids
41. When younger kids hang around
42. It's fun to daydream about
43. I feel sad when
44. Children would be better off if their parents

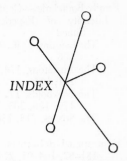

INDEX

PRINTED IN U.S.A.